# How Ea...

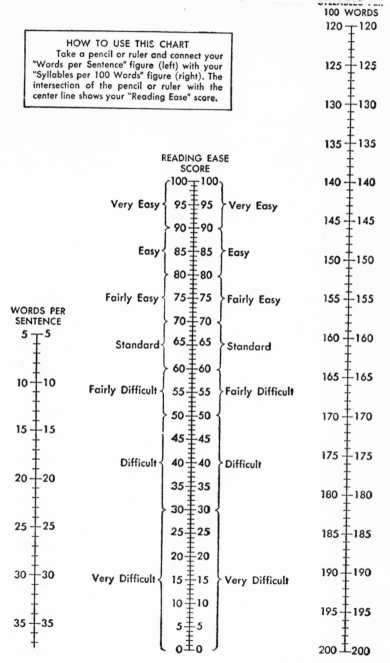

HOW TO USE THIS CHART
Take a pencil or ruler and connect your "Words per Sentence" figure (left) with your "Syllables per 100 Words" figure (right). The intersection of the pencil or ruler with the center line shows your "Reading Ease" score.

SYLLABLES PER
100 WORDS

READING EASE
SCORE

WORDS PER
SENTENCE

Very Easy
Easy
Fairly Easy
Standard
Fairly Difficult
Difficult
Very Difficult

© 1949 by Rudolf Flesch

*The Art of*
*Readable Writing*

# The Art of
# Readable Writing

RUDOLF FLESCH

*25th Anniversary Edition*
Revised and Enlarged

WITH THE FLESCH READABILITY FORMULA

HARPER & ROW, PUBLISHERS
New York, Evanston, San Francisco, London

Library of Congress Cataloging in Publication Data
Flesch, Rudolf Franz, 1911-
    The art of readable writing.
    1. English language—Rhetoric. I. Title.
PE1408.F4773        1974        808        73-14260
ISBN 0-06-011293-X

*To my six children*
Anne, Hugo, Jill, Kate, Abby and Janet

# CONTENTS

# PREFACE TO THE
## 25TH ANNIVERSARY EDITION

When I wrote this book 25 years ago, I filled it to the brim with examples of good and bad writing.

Now a quarter century has passed, and though the approach of the book and the readability formula are still as valid as they were originally, all the examples are dated—some of them may have historical interest, some are merely quaint.

I could have replaced the illustrations with corresponding ones from the early '70's, but that would have meant taking the book apart and rebuilding it again from scratch. I didn't see much point in doing that, and so I left the original text much as it was—with a few minor changes—and added postscripts to those chapters that needed updating. The postscripts deal with what I consider progress in the art of writing and try to make the book more helpful to beginners and students. I suppose when I wrote it I thought the facts would more or less speak for themselves. After 25 years in classrooms and training seminars I know better. So I spelled out what was only suggested or implied.

I hope the second generation of readers will find this book as useful as the first.

R. F.

*Dobbs Ferry, N. Y.*
*September, 1973*

# PREFACE TO THE ORIGINAL EDITION

Three years ago I wrote a book called *The Art of Plain Talk*, in which I tried to popularize the concept of readability. The idea apparently struck a responsive chord and the book was a success.

Even before I wrote *The Art of Plain Talk* I realized that the plan of the book covered only a narrow field and that there was a place for a more general work on what might be called scientific rhetoric. (Later a friend remarked that *The Art of Plain Talk* actually was not about writing but about rewriting.) I confess that originally I had the ambition of seeing my name on the title page of a comprehensive scholarly work; but somehow the subject resisted such a treatment and what I came up with was another book for laymen with some bibliographical notes. *The Art of Readable Writing*, then, is neither a rehash of *The Art of Plain Talk* nor a sequel to it; rather, the two books complement each other. Those who have read the earlier book will find that there is hardly any overlapping; and those who haven't won't feel, I hope, that they have missed the first half of the show.

The new readability formula wasn't part of the original plan either. After a few years of experience with the formula that appeared in *The Art of Plain Talk*, a revision seemed worthwhile; and once I had worked out a new formula, I naturally decided to put it in my new book. Users of the old formula will want to know the whys and wherefores of the changes; these are explained in the notes to Chapter 14. Otherwise, I can only repeat what I said in the preface to *The Art of Plain Talk*: "Some readers, I am afraid, will expect a magic formula for good writing and will be disappointed with my simple yardstick. Others, with a passion for accuracy, will wallow in the little rules and computations but lose sight of the principles of plain English. What I hope for are readers who won't take the formula too seriously and won't expect from it more than a rough estimate."

Scholarly-minded readers will probably find the bibliographical references sketchy and feel that the book isn't well enough documented. I can only plead that the subject of scientific rhetoric is in its infancy and that experimental evidence is scattered and ill-assorted. (Until 1948 *Psychological Abstracts* didn't even have a special section on language and communication.) Doubtless there are many pertinent studies that I have missed; and many more are going to appear.

Readers of *The Art of Plain Talk* have been extraordinarily generous. They—as well as my students and friends—have helped me tremendously with references, suggestions, and comments. Many thanks to all of them.

R. F.

*Dobbs Ferry, N. Y.*
*July, 1948*

[ xii ]

# ACKNOWLEDGMENTS

Most of the material in this book, including my own readability formula, is based on accumulated research findings in many different fields of science. Directly or indirectly, I am therefore indebted to the work of hundreds of researchers; some of them are mentioned in the bibliography, but most of them are not. My own work goes back to the experience I gained in the now defunct Readability Laboratory of the American Association of Adult Education at Columbia University. I owe a large debt of gratitude to its director, Dr. Lyman Bryson.

I also owe thanks to the following persons and organizations for their gracious permission to quote copyrighted material:

Mr. Don Herold for the excerpt from the folder he prepared for the Chase National Bank; Mr. Hal Boyle for his column on the freckle; *The Saturday Review of Literature* for the excerpt from "Duet on a Bus" by Douglas Moore; *The New Yorker* for the excerpts from the Profile of Beardsley Ruml by Alva Johnston, the Profile of Dr. Emery A. Rovenstine by Mark Murphy, and the article "Soapland" by James Thurber; *The Saturday Evening Post* for the excerpts from "The Two-Fisted Wisdom of Ching" by Beverly Smith and "You're Not as Smart as You Could Be" by David G. Wittels; *The New York Post* for the article "Fate and Vivian" by Jay Nelson Tuck and part of Jimmy Cannon's column of September 19, 1947; *Time* for the story "A House With a Yard" (May 17, 1948); Mr. James Marlow for part of his column on reciprocal trade agreements; The Viking Press, Inc., for the excerpt from Irwin Edman's *Philosopher's Quest*; Prentice-Hall, Inc., for the excerpt from the Christmas letter quoted in *Smooth Sailing Letters* by L. E. Frailey; Dr. Harry Dingman for the quotation from his book *Risk Appraisal* and the letter he wrote me; Mr. Fred Reinfeld for the quotations from his two chess books; The *New York Herald Tribune* for the editorial "No, No, No, No, No, No" (March 3, 1948); *Life* for the article "Pain Control Clinic" (October 27, 1947); Mr. Howard Whitman and *The Reader's Digest* for the article "Let's Help Them Marry Young"; Mr. Albert Deutsch and *The Reader's Digest* for the excerpt from the article "Unnecessary Operations"; Mr. Ray Bethers and *This Week* for the column "What's Happening to Where You Live"; and Oxford University Press for the extracts from the original and abridged versions of Arnold J. Toynbee's *Study of History*.

For permission to reprint material in the revised edition I owe thanks to the *New York Times* for "The Road to a Bank Robbery Charge—at 13" by George Goodman, Jr. (February 21, 1973, p. 86); "Granddaughter Seized in Killing" (March 3, 1973, p. 15); and "Corsicans of France Are Feeling the Sting of Publicity Given to Criminals" (January 7, 1973, p. 13).

# CHAPTER 1

## YOU AND ARISTOTLE

---

*Simple English is no one's mother
tongue. It has to be worked for.*

JACQUES BARZUN

---

To COME right out with it, this is a book on rhetoric. Its purpose is to help you in your writing.

Chances are, you learned how to write—indirectly—from Aristotle. Look up the history of English grammar, composition, and rhetoric teaching; you'll find that it all started a couple of centuries ago when people first hit upon the idea of teaching English-speaking boys and girls not only Greek and Latin, but English too. Courses and textbooks came into being; naturally, what was taught was simply Greek and Latin grammar and rhetoric, applied to English. Now since all Greek and Latin grammar and rhetoric go straight back to Aristotle (as any encyclopedia will tell you) and since the principles of English teaching are still much the same as they were two hundred years ago, what you were taught in school really comes down from Aristotle.

Take two rather striking examples, one from composition and one from grammar. In composition, probably the most important rule you were taught is the rule of unity. It is pure Aristotle—based on his famous principle that everything must have "a beginning, a middle, and an end." And in grammar the first thing you were taught was the parts of speech. Who first thought of parts of speech? Aristotle again. So whether you like it or not, you are an umptieth-generation Aristotelian.

[ 1 ]

There are several things wrong with using Aristotle as an English teacher today.

In the first place, Aristotle was using ancient Greek; we are using modern English. And though these two languages are distant cousins, they're as different as can be. Besides, Aristotle was living two and a half thousand years ago. Quite a few things have happened since. As to speaking and writing, things have changed considerably—what with paper and printing, books, newspapers, the telegraph and telephone, the movies, radio and television, compulsory education, and advertising.

Nowadays you—like everybody else—need writing skill for business letters, luncheon speeches, advertising copy, promotional literature, press releases, and a thousand other practical purposes. In Aristotle's time, according to his *Rhetoric*, all nonfiction consisted of three kinds of speeches—"deliberative, forensic, and epideictic." In other words, his rules were meant for political speeches, pleadings in court, and funeral orations. You'll have rather few occasions for these three types of writing but plenty for all sorts of other writing chores that come up every day.

These are a few of the reasons why it's time to free yourself from Aristotle.

Another reason is not so obvious. Let me explain with something I read recently in an educational journal. It was a paper written by some young speech teacher somewhere in the Middle West, about the arrangement of arguments in a speech. Aristotle had taught that you should build up your arguments and wind up with the most impressive one as climax. But the young American instructor started his paper by saying that Aristotle—and a host of other famous rhetoric teachers—were wrong in this. He said you should start with your best argument and let the others trail behind.

How can some English teacher have the effrontery to dispute the teachings of Aristotle? you'll ask. Here's the answer: he took a speech that was arranged in conventional Aristotelian fashion and put it on phonograph records. Then he rearranged the same speech in anticlimax order and put *that* on phonograph records. Next he assembled two groups of carefully matched students and had them listen to the records. When they were through, he asked each of them what he remembered and whether the speech had changed his mind on the subject. Then, after some time had passed, he bombarded them with another set of questions about the speech. Finally he settled down and started working with statistics. And after he had collected a bagful of standard deviations and correlation coefficients, he announced to the world that Aristotle was wrong.

In other words, our young American arrived at his conclusion by using scientific methods. I don't mean to say that Aristotle did *not* approach his subject scientifically—he did—but he did not carry on any experiments; and if he had, they would prove something about ancient Greek audiences rather than modern American readers and listeners. And that's the most important reason why you can't go by Aristotle any more in doing a writing job today.

The fact is, we have an enormous amount of scientific information about English grammar, usage, and composition. But it's hardly ever used for English teaching in schools. To be sure, there is a movement toward modern, scientific instruction among English teachers, but it's making headway only very slowly. Let me illustrate the present state of affairs with a story I heard some time ago: Professor C. C. Fries, one of our leading "liberal" English teachers, once told his students that there was no such rule as "Never use a preposition at the end of a sentence." (Actually, it is an old superstition based on the Latin derivation of the word *preposition*.) "Do you mean to say that the rule has been changed?" a student spoke up. "Changed? No," Professor Fries answered. "Who would have the authority to make or change such a rule?" "Why," the student stammered, "whoever deals with these things . . . the authorities . . . the experts . . .

the English Teachers Association . . ." "That would be the National Council of Teachers of English," said Professor Fries. "Well, if they issued any rules lately, I ought to know about it. I am president."

Teachers like Fries are still rare, and students and laymen who believe in "rules" are to be found everywhere. Unless you are different from most people, your knowledge of rhetoric probably consists of a handful of half-forgotten rules, overlaid by the vague notion that they apply to the writing of themes but hardly to anything a grownup person does between nine and five on a weekday.

If you look at some random samples of current writing, you will find precious little of Aristotle in them. Some of them are written as if the writer had made a special effort to forget every single rule that was drummed into him in school.

Here, for instance, is part of a Gimbels ad:

> When a teenager asks "How's the apple pie?" and she's told it's gone—does she order peach? No! She shrieks, "Give me a double hunk of that gone apple pie." "Gone" to her means good—tops—out of this world. "Real gone" means absolute tops. That's how Gimbels feels about Russel Wright dinnerware, Winter pianos, Bigelow broadlooms, antique paperweights. They're tops, the best—they're real gone.

Now this, of course, contains the slang word *gone*. But I'm not talking about that. I'm talking about the tone of the whole thing, which is slangy and against all the rules of how you should write for publication; I'm talking about the word Gimbels uses to *translate* the slang word *gone*—*tops*, another slang word that hasn't even made the dictionary yet.

But, you'll say, this is department store advertising and really something special. That sort of language isn't used for more serious purposes, say for advertising by banks; they write sober, conventional English, following all the standard rules. (Which

[ 4 ]

is probably why Miss FitzGibbon, Gimbels advertising director, recently called it "a lot of malarky.") But nowadays you can't even tell with banks. Consider this (by the master copy writer Don Herold):

> Most men think they have done swell by their families when they get their lives insured for a *round sum.*
>
> "It will be nice for Mary and the children to get $50,000," they say. (Or some other round sum.)
>
> The trouble with leaving a round sum is that the optimists immediately gather round. Mary's brother from Detroit appears with a grand scheme to double it. Friends come in with bright suggestions, and stock salesmen gallop up with glib tongues.
>
> Even you and I, smart as we are, have found it difficult, maybe, to keep round sums round in recent years. What can we expect of them, then, in the hands of a bewildered widow and inexperienced youngsters?
>
> No, a round sum of life insurance can never take the place of *you.*
>
> What you should do (I am just suggesting) is to make your life insurance act as nearly as possible as a *substitute for you* when you are gone.
>
> You wouldn't dump $50,000 or more into your family's lap in one chunk if you were alive—especially not these days; what would they do with it?
>
> No, you'd probably invest the lump sum safely and give them the income from it, with maybe little nicks off of the principal in certain emergencies.
>
> Well, a *Life Insurance Trust* can handle your life insurance in exactly that way.
>
> Have your policy proceeds made payable to a bank in trust for your family—perhaps the Chase National Bank. Let the Chase be *you* when you're gone.

[ 5 ]

To get the Chase National Bank more customers, this is doubtless superb. But give this piece of prose to some run-of-the-mill English teacher, and he (or she) won't like it a bit. In fact, he will immediately proceed to take it apart. He will start with marking the third sentence as a "sentence fragment"—to be touched only with a ten-foot pole—and will go down the page until he comes to *off of,* whereupon he will mark the whole thing F and give Mr. Herold a stern warning never to do that sort of thing again.

Want an example that is *not* advertising copy? How about some political reporting? Here is John Dos Passos, writing from England in *Life* magazine:

> . . . By the time we had finished tea the rain had stopped. We stepped out into the freshwashed afternoon and looked down the line of low stone farm buildings that shone brown as chocolate against the emerald hedges and the misty blue-green fields of oats that rolled down towards the ferny headland beyond the road where cropping sheep moved slowly against the leaden stretch of the North Sea. Our host was a grizzled blueeyed man with a fresh tanned skin. He had broad shoulders and a light footfall and he laughed a great deal. No, he said merrily, talking back over his shoulder, the controls didn't bother him too much. Of course he had trouble getting parts for his machinery. And nails. My word what a lot of forms you had to fill out to get nails . . .

*Freshwashed* and *blueeyed* and no commas after *of course* and *my word* would surely enrage most English teachers. But, after all, this is Dos Passos, the novelist, who may be expected to take some liberties even when he does straight reporting. How about some example from ordinary, day-by-day newspaper writing? Here is Hal Boyle, AP feature writer, doing a particularly charming column for his millions of readers:

> Where can you buy a freckle?
> I need one bad. I'm in a jam.

If I don't find one soon a little girl is going to be mad at me. She said I took it and haven't brought it back.

Other people's kids—they get me in more odd predicaments. But I don't have any children of my own, so I have to play with those that belong to other people.

Children do for me what music, books, movies, golf or gambling does for many grownups—that is, they lift me out of the world of worry and the high cost of living.

Critics who complain the modern world has lost the art of conversation must never talk to children. If you try to talk down to them, they quickly find you out and shut up. But if you can take the anchor off your adult imagination— what a wonderful realm you enter with them. Commonsense is nonsense, and nonsense is commonsense, and every sentence holds a surprise.

Someday it will be a penitentiary offense to put a rein on the fancies of children, who are born poets and die—well, something less than poets.

My games with children, however, usually put me in Dutch with their parents, who complain later:

"It took us two hours after you left to quiet Junior and get him to go to bed. You get him over-excited."

I am in bad standing now at one household which has a small boy who wants to become another Thomas Edison. This young mechanical genius asked me about heaven, and I did my best to explain to him all about this place where I hope some day to get my mail. I answered all his questions with the latest information I have.

But the other day his father reproached me bitterly:

"What ideas are you putting in my son's head anyway? He has informed his mother he never wants to go to heaven because it doesn't have an escalator. He says he would rather go to a department store."

The only deal with the younger generation I have come

out ahead in recently concerns the purchase of a dog by two children of some friends in Indianapolis. The kids earned the money themselves. But I made a small contribution to the fund, and another friend later put in some, too.

The kids bought a dachshund. It was so long they decided it needed two names. So they named the front end "Hal" for me—and generously named the back half "Charley" in honor of the last contributor.

Now, about that freckle. I playfully pretended to pluck it off the nose of this five-year-old girl after a visit a month ago.

Last week I called again, and she crept up behind me and whispered in my ear:

"Please, I want my freckle back. I think it is lonesome for me."

"I am taking awfully good care of it," I replied.

"Do you take it out for a walk every day on a leash?" she asked.

Somewhat flabbergasted at the mental picture of a freckle out for a stroll, I hemmed and hawed and she said very solemnly:

"I really do want my freckle back. Please mail it to me this week, and don't forget."

What happens now? The only thing I can think of is to tell her the freckle changed into a chocolate bar and mail her one.

But this could start a game that would put me in the poor-house. She has about 1,265,347 freckles now—and growing more every day the sun shines.

You like this? I do too. I think it's splendid writing. But where are the rules? You couldn't possibly detect the good old stand-bys "unity, coherence, and emphasis" in this piece. You can't even pin Hal Boyle down as to parts of speech. Right in his second sentence he uses *bad* instead of *badly*.

So what can you do to improve your writing and come a little closer to the skill of advertising wizards like Miss FitzGibbon or Don Herold, famous authors like Dos Passos, or Pulitzer-prize newspapermen like Hal Boyle? Obviously, just learning the rules won't do. In fact, if you remember too many of the rules from your school days, they will get in your way. What you really need is a good working knowledge of informal, everyday, *practical* English.

I am sure you realize by now that this book is not dealing with what usually goes by the names of grammar, usage, composition, or rhetoric. On the contrary. If you want to learn how to write, you need exact information about what kind of language will fit what kind of audience. And scientific data about the psychological effects of different styles. And handy, usable facts and figures about common types of words, sentences, and paragraphs. And knowledge of the results achieved by various writing techniques. In short, you need a modern scientific rhetoric that you can apply to your own writing.

That's what I tried to put into this book.

## PS

Rereading this chapter after 25 years, I find that it's still as true as it was when I wrote it. Sure, the examples are dated by now, but the basic truth still stands: people don't know how to write because they can't shake off the traditional rules they were taught in school.

Scientific progress is slow. It's fifty years now, at least, since scientific linguists declared war on traditional English teaching and so-called correct grammar; but the English-teaching fraternity has devised innumerable dodges and rearguard actions to defend their indefensible positions. Yes, they say, there's a difference in levels of usage; yes, informal or colloquial writing is all right for most practical purposes. But then, by innuendo and implication, they take it all back and tell students from grade school up through college that they'd better learn not to write "it's me"

[ 9 ]

and never split an infinitive or they'll be shunned by society in later life and never get a decent job.

So this book, even at this late day and age, still has a valid message: forget the rules of grammar and usage you learned in school. Learn to write the way you talk. Go out of your way to relearn informal, colloquial English and train yourself to put it on paper.

The greatest single element of progress in this field was the publication in 1961 of Webster's Third International Dictionary. Its predecessor, Webster's New International Dictionary, Second Edition, had been published 27 years before, in 1934. Its attitude was traditional and prescientific. Whenever its editors felt a word or phrase wasn't good enough for writing, they labeled it "*Colloq.*," trying to give everyone who used it in writing a feeling of guilt and shame.

By the time the Third Edition came out in 1961, the Merriam-Webster editors had decided they could no longer resist the unanimous views of modern scientists. The label "*Colloq.*" was abandoned; informal English words and expressions by the thousands were admitted as suitable for writing and printing; and hundreds of usages fought to the death by the traditionalists were labeled simply as "in reputable use though disapproved by some."

The traditionalists fought back ferociously; withering reviews appeared in learned and unlearned journals; new books on usage were published to furnish further ammunition to the enemies of science; and even a new dictionary, the *American Heritage Dictionary,* was produced at a cost of $4 million to counteract the evil influence of of those wicked Merriam-Webster people in Springfield, Mass. But the Unabridged Third Edition stayed in full command of the field, and millions of the desk-size abridgments, *Webster's Seventh New Collegiate Dictionary* and *Webster's New Collegiate Dictionary* (8th edition), are in daily use everywhere.

Let me show you what this means by tracing the dictionary entries of some of the words mentioned in this chapter.

First of all, let's take the slang word *gone*, in the sense of "great," as used in the Gimbels ad. There's no problem about this word. It's listed as slang in Webster's Third and today is no longer used and almost forgotten. A slang word, by definition, is a word suddenly taken up and later, just as suddenly, vanished from the scene.

Now let's go on to the word *swell*, used in the first line of the Chase National Bank ad. Is *swell* a slang word that shouldn't be used in writing? Most people would probably think so, and certainly most of my students shuddered at the thought of putting the word *swell* on paper. But what are the facts? Sure, Webster's Second, in 1934, branded the use of the word in the sense of "tiptop; first-rate; grand; excellent" as slang. But the scientifically compiled Webster's Third, in 1961, gives no hint of any such scruples. *Swell*, it says, means "excellent, great, wonderful" and to prove the fact that the word is in good English usage it gives three quotations: "Makes a swell impression and is hired" (W. H. Whyte); "she was a really swell girl" (W. F. Jenkins); and "it's a miracle . . . I feel perfectly swell" (Somerset Maugham).

Next, let's look at the word *bad*, used in the sentence "I need one bad" by Hal Boyle. Can *bad* be used as an adverb like that? The schoolteachers and textbook writers shudder at the thought. Webster's Second dismissed it as "*Colloq.*" But Webster's Third doesn't raise an eyebrow and again gives three quotations to prove that the word is now good English: "Want something bad enough to fight for it"; "the man was not doing so bad despite handicaps"; and "the Americans didn't know how bad off they were until daylight" (E. J. Kahn). Mr. Kahn, the author of the last sentence, is a staff writer with the *New Yorker* magazine, famous for its immaculate prose style.

Next: Hal Boyle wrote "Some little girl is going to be mad at me." Can you use *mad* in this way? Or do you have to use *angry* because, according to the dictionaries, *mad* really means *insane?* Miss Margaret Nicholson, in the widely used *Dictionary of American-English Usage*, says flatly, "The use of *mad* for *angry, annoyed*

[ 11 ]

is US slang." She's wrong. Even Webster's Second lists the meaning of *mad* "carried away by anger" as standard English and quotes, of all things, the Bible (Acts xxvi, 11): "And being exceedingly mad against them, I persecuted them even unto strange cities." Webster's Third naturally agrees and says simply that *mad* is a synonym of *angry*.

Then Hal Boyle several times uses the word *kids* in the sense of "children." Can you use the word *kids* in ordinary writing? The *American Heritage Dictionary* says no and marks the word as slang. Webster's Second disagrees and again says mildly "*Colloq.*" But Webster's Third shows not the slightest sign of disapproval. It says *kid* means "child, youngster" and gives three sample quotations to prove its point.

The prejudice against certain generally used words is so ingrained that examples can be found everywhere. The *New York Times* never uses the word *gas* in the sense of "gasoline" without apologetic quotation marks. " 'Gas' Stations Lead List of Complaints in Repairs of Cars," a headline said the other day. Is *gas* slang? Of course not. Again, Webster's Second marks it "*Colloq.*"; Webster's Third lists it as standard usage.

Or take this sentence from a TV review: "This new version of the Gershwin musical attempts to duplicate the 'feel' of a live theater production." Obviously the reviewer thought the word *feel* was slang and could only be used with quotation marks. Was he right? No. Not only is the word listed as standard English in Webster's Third, with no less than nine literary quotations, but even in Webster's Second it is given full approval, with a sample quotation from the famous novelist D. H. Lawrence, "The factory had a homely feel."

How about the word *fence* in the sense of "receiver of stolen goods"? Columnist Jack Anderson, reporting on a Congressional investigation, recently used telltale quotation marks every single time he used the word *fence*. And yet, both Webster dictionaries agree that the word *fence* is in perfectly good standing. Yes, it was originally a slang word used among thieves; but since this usage dates back to the year 1700, the Webster editors thought they could safely give it the nod.

Is the word *fire,* in the sense of "dismiss from a job," a slang word? Look it up in the *Dictionary of Contemporary American Usage* by Bergen and Cornelia Evans and you'll find that the authors call it "an American slang term." Again, Webster's Second marks it *"Colloq.";* Webster's Third lists it as standard usage.

How about the word *phony?* Mr. Theodore Bernstein, author of the widely used handbook *The Careful Writer,* calls it slang and warns against its use. Webster's Second also calls it slang. But Webster's Third has no objections to the word at all. It defines *phony* as "fake, sham" and gives two quotations: "This political issue—absenteeism—is a phony if there ever was one" (Thomas R. Ybarra) and "He who writes or composes without the true inner fire . . . will always be a phony" (Hendrik Willem Van Loon).

Or would you dare to use the word *lousy* in your writing? In Webster's Second it's listed as slang. But in Webster's Third *lousy,* meaning "miserably poor or inferior," appears as an irreproachable English word, used by Supreme Court Justice Oliver Wendell Holmes Jr. when he wrote "Forgive me for writing on this lousy paper."

I don't mean to say that from now on you should pepper your writing with words like *swell, phony* or *lousy,* regardless of whether they fit your purpose or not. But you should learn to forget the false rules of prissy or overformal English implanted in your nervous system by your teachers and textbooks ever since you entered first grade.

Here's an example. In the summer of 1972, during the Fischer vs. Spassky world championship chess match, the *New York Times Magazine* carried a long article about chess. It was written by Harold C. Schonberg, the *Times* music critic, who also happens to be a chess expert. The article covered a lot of ground, including chess played by computers as compared to chess played by the grand masters. "Computers," Mr. Schonberg wrote, "play lousy chess."

Would it have served Mr. Schonberg's purpose to write "Computers play poor chess"? Or perhaps "Computers play very poor chess"? Obviously not. He had to forget all prejudices against the word *lousy* to tell the readers of the *New York Times Magazine* exactly what he meant.

This book is a handbook of writing based on the scientific study of the English language as it is used today. If you want to write readable prose that'll be easily understood by those you're writing for, you must first *unlearn* the rules you were taught in school.

## CHAPTER 2

# OTHER PEOPLE'S MINDS

*Social study should begin with careful observation of the capacity
of groups to communicate effectively and intimately with each other.*

ELTON MAYO

ON FEBRUARY 21, 1945, the Allies for the first time bombed
Berchtesgaden. The news was such a sensation that correspondents asked the successful fliers for an interview. They were
in for a surprise. "Neither Major John L. Beck, the flight leader,"
the *New York Times* correspondent wrote, "nor presumably the
pilots with him knew that Berchtesgaden was where Adolf Hitler
had his principal home . . . Berchtesgaden was just another name
to Major Beck. Neither at the University of Idaho, nor at the
aircraft factory where he worked before he entered the Air Force,
nor in the Army itself had it ever come to his attention that
Hitler had built a fortress palace outside Berchtesgaden called
the Berghof and from there had directed most of his nefarious
international affairs for years."

The *New York Times* was so shocked by this that it ran an
editorial about Major Beck's astonishing ignorance. But it needn't
have been shocked. Major Beck, who "didn't know from nothing,"
was a typical American; his countrymen, polled around the same
time on various items of general information, answered like this:

Thirty-one percent thought that England was mainly an agricultural country; 60 percent thought that in Russia everybody
gets the same pay, no matter what his job; 86 percent didn't
know what side Russia was on at the time of Munich.

Nor did four years of global war teach Americans much. After
weeks and months of front-page news about the Bikini bomb
tests, 20 percent of the people had never heard of them. After

half a year of public debate, 52 percent of American farmers had never heard of the Marshall plan. And two-and-a-half years after the death of Franklin D. Roosevelt, 30 percent of the citizens of Cincinnati had never heard of the United Nations.

One reason for this may be that the average American's picture of the world is somewhat hazy: for instance, he can't properly locate more than half of the countries in Europe, or more than a third of those in Latin America.

Does this mean that the ordinary person knows more when it comes to domestic rather than foreign affairs? It does not. In 1946, only three out of five Americans had ever heard of the widely publicized Wagner-Murray-Dingell health bill; in 1944 only one in seven knew anything about the Little Steel Formula, which had been in the headlines for months.

There's a simple explanation for all this: people don't read enough to be well informed. According to library surveys, they hardly ever read any serious books; according to newspaper surveys, they pay more attention to the comics than to anything else in the paper. In studies of over a hundred newspapers, it was found that only one news story in twenty-five is read by even half the readers.

Some people say the trouble is that newspaper language is too highbrow. There's a lot in that. Consider that good old expression *free enterprise,* used in hundreds of editorials every day. When the Gallup poll asked people what it meant, only 30 percent had any clear idea. The others either couldn't define it or thought it meant freedom to put over a fast one in a business deal. Or consider a phrase like *Magna Charta.* They polled Canadians on that. (Americans would probably do worse.) The result? The phrase was known to 18 percent.

If you think you could do better than that, remember that Congressional debate when Representative Walter G. Andrews (Princeton, '13) flunked several items from the Army General Classification Test. Among other things, he couldn't define the words *ambient, torsion,* and *recondite.*

Well, you say, people do better on ordinary words. Depends on what you mean by "ordinary." Tests have shown, for instance, that a good many American farmers don't know the meaning of *essential, equivalent, specified,* or *sufficient.* And there's the true story of the film company that polled moviegoers on whether they liked advertising with or without adjectives. It turned out that one out of three didn't know the meaning of *adjective.*

Don't misunderstand me. I'm not saying that most people are morons. Some students have jumped to that conclusion, but I don't agree with them. If a person doesn't know much, that doesn't necessarily mean he's unintelligent. After all, intelligence is the ability to learn. Remember John Beck, who had never heard of Berchtesgaden but was smart enough to rise to the rank of major in the Air Force. And remember the often quoted saying by the late Glenn Frank: "We often overestimate the stock of information readers have, and underestimate their intelligence."

Here's a good example of what happens if you overestimate people's information. The Department of Agriculture puts out thousands of leaflets to help farmers in their work. As a test, a county agent once asked a 14-year-old boy to write down how he tanned a goat pelt by following a government bulletin. The boy wrote this:

Mr. George Adams gave me a goat pelt if I would write about how it was tanned. He said it was from a crossbred Angora. The pelt was fresh when I got it Monday.

Mr. Thornton sent me a bulletin about tanning. I was a long time finding the place that told how to tan a goat pelt. It is on page 12 about furs and hair robes. It told about tanning 100 pounds of hides but not about a goat pelt. Another paper by Mr. Thornton told about tanning 2 sheepskins in a ½ barrel.

Clean off flesh and fat was the first thing to do. Daddy did most of that. He didn't seem to know much about it and cussed a little and tried to phone Mr. Thornton to cuss him and find an easy way to get the red meat and fat off, but Mr. Thornton had left town. Daddy worked about three hours at it with the pelt over a barrel in the garage at night. He said the dam goat never had been skinned yet. So he skinned it all over again a little piece at a time. The fat fell on the concrete floor and Daddy slipped down in it and spoiled his good pants.

The bulletin, No. B-86, says to use just enough water to cover the hide. We used the ice-cream freezer bucket. The paper says use 1 gal. water for 2 skins. We used 1½ gal. but did not know how much salt was 6% and 5% alum of a 1½ gal. Daddy did not know how many ounces in a gallon. The dictionary said $\frac{1}{10}$ liter was 35.274 oz. and there are 3.7853 liters in a gallon. Daddy figured that on a slide rule to be 133.5 oz. per gal. Our dip bucket measured 100 oz. or ¾ gal. Daddy figured that at 5.4 lb. with a slide rule but he made a mistake because I figured 6.25 lb. but too late. He put in 2 buckets that he called 10 lb. but was 12½ lb. of water. Then we put in a ½-pound can of salt and a little over ½ lb. of alum, that should be ¾ lb. So I guess we had 4% alum instead of 5% and 5¾% salt instead of 6%.

Then the freezer bucket began to leak. Two hoops were off. Daddy put on wire hoops. It stopped leaking some time in the night. But the pelt was still under water in the morning. We put a window weight on it to hold it under.

After the freezer was fixed it was way past bedtime but we made the paste to tan with. The paper said use 1 lb. of alum, 1 lb. of salt, 1 lb. of flour, ¼ lb. of egg yolks, ¼ lb. of neat's-foot oil and 1 gal. of water for 2 skins.

For one skin we measured 64 oz. of water in the dip bucket and poured in the rest of the alum and salt. We woke up Mother to find out how much flour is ½ lb. She fussed and said 2 cups but for goodness sake to go to bed, and told Daddy he had better be working on his annual reports. Then Daddy didn't know how much 4 oz. of egg yolk was.

Neat's-foot oil was the same so we poured out the oil and filled the bottle with water. Then we poured the water in a cup to measure it. It took 8 yolks to make enough, all that Mother had for breakfast. When it was all mixed it was not a paste but thin as milk. We figured up the cost and went to bed . . .

The thing to do, of course, is to find out what people know and what they don't know, and then to write accordingly. You'd think, for instance, that a good cookbook—in contrast to a government bulletin—would always be understandable to the average housewife. Well, one women's magazine found that it isn't so: the cookbooks take a great many things for granted that are baffling to this generation of brides. So the magazine plunged into a new style of recipe writing and came up with this:

Old Style Recipe:

*Chocolate Roll*

Beat eggs until thick and lemon colored. Add ¾ cup sugar gradually. Mix and sift together flour, baking powder and salt. Add all at once and blend thoroughly. Melt chocolate over hot water. Remove from fire. Add remaining sugar, water, and baking soda. Stir until thick. Fold into cake mixture and add vanilla extract. Line greased 16"x11"x1" pan with greased wax paper. Pour in batter. Bake in moderate oven 350F 20 minutes.

New Style Recipe:

*Chocolate Roll*

Set oven at 350F which is moderate. Line the bottom of a 16"x11"x1" pan with brown or waxed paper. Grease both bottom and sides. Sift flour; measure it into a cup *lightly* with a spoon. Don't shake it down because extra flour makes a cake dry. Return this flour to sifter; add baking powder and salt. Melt chocolate over hot water and leave on the stove until you need it. Break eggs into a good-sized bowl. Beat until they're so thick you can actually lift them up with the beater. Beat in sugar, a tablespoon at a time. Sift flour into eggs and sugar mixture all at once. Mix thoroughly. Take chocolate off stove; stir in vanilla extract, baking soda and water. Add immediately to cake mixture before chocolate stiffens. Mix very well. Pour batter into pan. Bake 20 minutes.

[ 19 ]

If you study this closely, you'll see that the magazine must have done quite some research to find out what housewives know and what they need to be told. There's hardly anything more important for readable writing: the more you know about the kind of person you are writing for, the better you'll write.

Naturally, it isn't always possible to go into research studies, surveys, and polls. But a good estimate is better than nothing at all. Nowadays lack of information usually goes hand in hand with little education and low income; so if you are writing for people in the lower income brackets or people who haven't gone to college, it's a good guess that they won't have much background knowledge. Or, if you want to conduct your own miniature Gallup poll, make it a habit to try your stuff on the cleaning woman or the elevator man.

Amount of information is important, but it isn't the only thing to consider. People can be classified in many other ways—most obviously by age and sex. You'll have to write one way for young and another way for older people, one way for men and another way for women.

Aristotle—who, as I said, *did* use the scientific approach—had this to say about the difference between the young and the old:

> Young men have strong desires . . . they are fond of victory, for youth likes to be superior . . . they are sanguine . . . they live their lives in anticipation . . . they have high aspirations . . . are prone to pity . . . fond of laughter . . .
>
> Elderly men . . . are cynical . . . suspicious . . . they aspire to nothing great or exalted, but crave the mere necessities and comforts of existence . . . they are not generous . . . they live in memory rather than anticipation . . . they are mastered by the love of gain . . .

Or, to put it in more modern terms, young people like romance, adventure, and daydreams, and old people like practical, down-to-earth, bread-and-butter stuff. Check any public library, and you'll find that preference for fiction or nonfiction is mostly a matter of age.

So when you want to convey information to young people, take a hint: make it a story—with a happy ending.

Then, of course, there's always the difference between the sexes. You know all about that, but a little reminder will do you good next time you write a piece for women (if you're male) or for men (if you're female). Remember that in intelligence tests, boys do better in mathematics, science, economics, and spatial relation tests, and girls in so-called "social intelligence"—understanding of people and intimate problems of everyday life. And remember that according to newspaper surveys, most readers of business news and sports are men and most readers of society pages and local news women. In other words, to make a wild generalization, men love figures, gadgets and things, and women love talk, sentiment and people.

Here is a little specific evidence. Not long ago, a farm paper ran a story "Nylon is Here Again." It started like this:

> Nylon doesn't always mean just a precious pair of sheer stockings any more. It can mean any number of bright, new garments that are made of nylon.
>
> There are blouses, slips, children's clothes, coats and such things as curtains, rugs and upholstery materials.
>
> Nylon is one of the new-comers in the field of textiles. Production for civilian uses was practically stopped during the war, but now nylon is again being made on a large scale. And it won't be long before much of our new clothing will be made of this material.
>
> There are a lot of things about nylon materials that will make the fabric welcome to the homemaker . . .

As an experiment, the paper printed the same story also in a different version, which started as follows:

Edna, my neighbor, was lucky. She has a big family. In 1940, she bought a pretty green nylon and wool coat for Bonnie, her eldest daughter.

Bonnie wore the coat for two years. Then, when she became a war bride, she got a new coat that would match her wedding suit.

Marilynn, a pretty blonde, was next in line for the coat. She looked lovely in its bright green color. It gave her good service, too, for she wore it two years.

When Marilynn made up her mind to spend money she had earned for a new coat, Donna got the green one. Donna is a brunette. But she looks well in the coat and is still wearing it.

The surprising thing is how well the coat holds up . . .

Result of the experiment: for every two women who read the first version, there were three who read the second one.

Or here is some evidence on the male side: in 1947, the editor of *The Scientific Monthly*—clearly a men's magazine—looked through his requests for reprints to find out which of his articles had been a "bestseller." The subscribers—many of whom doubtless play with their sons' electric trains—promptly showed their preference for mechanical toys and gadgets (and their sense of humor). Overwhelmingly they had picked a satirical article "On the Mathematics of Committees, Boards, and Panels," chockful of mock formulas, ironical graphs, and fanciful equations.

What it all amounts to is that everything you write has to be slanted toward your audience. That doesn't necessarily mean that the simpler version is always the better; it all depends on who you are writing for. Let me give you two more examples:

Some time ago an expert in corporate finance gave an address on "Interstate Tax Barriers in Marketing" before the American Marketing Association. His listeners obviously expected something rather on the scholarly side and so he started with a dignified glance at history:

The subject of interstate tax barriers to marketing is a very important one, for if there had been no interstate tax barriers, there might never have been a United States of America. As we know, during and after the Revolutionary War, the colonies operated under the vague and loose arrangement called the Articles of Confederation. Every state could and, in fact, did tax any shipment that passed through its contiguous waters . . .

The editor of a business newsletter discovered this address in *The Journal of Marketing* and rewrote it for his subscribers. *His* version was called "Interstate Marketing—Undersell by Minimizing Taxes." It started like this:

You can shout about modern merchandising until the cows come home; perfect your product, popularize your prices; line up your markets, employ the shrewdest buyers, the sharpest advertisers, most enterprising salesmen, keenest accountants. But withal, you must inevitably recognize this: in today's highly competitive market the business that gets by with the lowest tax bill is the one that will undersell the rest!

Or consider the difference between the stately *New York Times* and the tabloid *New York Daily News* with its tremendous circulation. Editorials on the same topics in the two papers are apt to be light-years apart in their approach. In 1941, when Lord Halifax arrived as British Ambassador and President Roosevelt sailed out to greet him off Annapolis, the two editorials read:

| *New York Times* | *New York Daily News* |
|---|---|
| His (Roosevelt's) extraordinary action in going personally to Annapolis for the purpose will be interpreted everywhere as it was intended to be interpreted: as a tribute to the courageous people whom Viscount Halifax has come to represent and a testimonial of the ties which bind us to them in this time of crisis. | Lord Halifax must have felt from Mr. Roosevelt's manner of receiving him that the United States was saying to Great Britain, in our breezy American idiom, "Pal, the joint is yours." |

But let me add this: when I say, study your audience and slant your writing toward it, I don't mean that you should write only what people want to read. Lately, what with radio and the movies taking more and more to audience research, there's been quite some discussion about following poll results in writing. I'm on the side of Lee De Forest, who said of today's radio with its Hooperatings and audience measurements: "What have you gentlemen done with my child? He was conceived as a potent instrumentality for culture, fine music, the uplifting of America's mass intelligence. You have debased this child. You have made him a laughing stock to the intelligence."

And this goes for movies, books, magazines, newspapers, too. Never mind writing what the public wants—or what you suppose the public wants. Study your audience and then write what you want to say in the *form* that is most likely to appeal to them. Don't worry about your literary friends who will say you should have been more artistic. Let me quote a review of that best-selling novel against anti-Semitism, *Gentlemen's Agreement:* "There will be those who will object to this book because it is tastelessly written. They will be overlooking one of its greatest assets. *Gentlemen's Agreement*, exactly as is, can perform a tremendous service . . . Women who wouldn't touch *The Nation* or *The New Republic* with a ten-foot pole are going to read *Gentlemen's Agreement* as they sit under the dryer, and they're going to urge their husbands to read it."

If a worthwhile idea or work of art is skillfully popularized, everybody stands to gain. After Iturbi had played Chopin's "Polonaise in A-Flat" in *A Song to Remember,* people bought two million copies of the record. Which was a good thing for Iturbi, for Chopin, and for two million American families.

PS

Now that I reread this chapter with the advantage of hindsight, I see that I overdid it. It's *not* easy—and almost impossible

[ 24 ]

for a beginner—to pinpoint your audience and fashion your style for the exact level of information and background you think they have. You'll be doing fine if you simplify your style just as much as you're able. Fine-tuning comes much later.

*Time, Newsweek,* the *Wall Street Journal* and many other well-written publications serve up the news in a breezy style that suits their college-educated readers just fine. And in the 25 years that I've trained the editors of an information service for lawyers, accountants and other experts and technicians, I've never heard of a single complaint that the style of the newsletters and reports was too elementary or undignified.

The thing to do is to keep your audience in mind. By that I mean, exert your imagination and mentally *talk* to this fellow—informally, on the phone, during lunch, in any kind of quick, casual conversation about the subject in hand. He won't be upset if you chat with him on a sort of mental first-name basis. On the contrary, he'll be happy if you spare him the effort of unraveling long, solemn, heavy-footed sentences, filled with elaborate, superprecise words. Remember, your reader may be well informed—but more likely than not, he may also be busy, or lazy, or tired, or just inattentive. Bore him and you've lost him.

James Marlow, whom I quote elsewhere in this book, used to say, "Always write for the fellow who *hasn't* read yesterday's paper." A golden rule.

## CHAPTER 3

# THE IMPORTANCE OF BEING TRIVIAL

---

*"Unimportant, of course, I meant," the King hastily said, and went on to himself in an undertone, "important—unimportant—important—" as if he were trying which word sounded best.*
LEWIS CARROLL, *Alice in Wonderland*

---

SCHOPENHAUER said: "The first rule for a good style is to have something to say; in fact, this in itself is almost enough." The British diplomat Harold Nicolson wrote: "The first essential is to know what one wishes to say; the second is to decide to whom one wishes to say it." And the Hungarian mathematician George Polya came up with this one: "The first rule of style is to have something to say. The second rule of style is to control yourself when, by chance, you have two things to say; say first one, then the other, not both at the same time."

No doubt Nicolson and Polya made valuable additions; but, as you see, Schopenhauer's first rule still stands. It is likely to be put in first place by anybody else who may want to draw up rules of style.

But, you will say, that doesn't help much. That just passes the buck back to the person who wants to know how to write. "Have something to say" sounds much like saying "Be smart" or "Have a mind of your own."

In the main, that's true. But having something to say also means having a good stock of facts; and there are ways and means of getting at facts and keeping them handy. Most people who do any writing (without being professional writers) are handicapped by simply not knowing how to collect their material.

Let me tell you a little story:

It was a Sunday evening. I was putting the finishing touches on a research report I was working on. Suddenly I realized that I didn't have certain figures on magazine circulation that I had meant to use. If I couldn't get these figures at once I would miss my deadline. I was on the spot.

The solution was as simple as can be: I called the Public Library and had my information within two minutes.

The moral of this tale is that I knew something about libraries and didn't hesitate to get my taxpayer's money's worth out of them. I knew that a reasonably well equipped public library can furnish the answers to most practical—and impractical—questions, and that librarians make it their business to be helpful.

Most people don't seem to know this. They forget that great American institution, the public library, and when they want to know who invented the zipper they are apt to interview a dozen top-rank zipper executives instead of simply looking it up.

Using a library is easy as long as you remember three basic rules:

(1) Try the handiest source of information first.
(2) Look for something that's specially designed to answer your question.
(3) Let the librarian help you.

For example, if you want to know the meaning of a legal term, try first an ordinary dictionary, then try a legal dictionary, then ask the librarian whether she has anything else. (She may give you a book on law for laymen.)

But this isn't a book on how to use a library. Let's suppose you have found your source of information—in the library or somewhere else—and are ready to collect your raw material. If you want to come up with a piece of readable writing, you must lay the groundwork right then and there.

For ordinary writing, it may be enough to have assembled your facts; for readable writing it is not. At the same time as you gather your facts, you must also get hold of two more things: first, your framework, and second, your verbal illustrations. Your reader will need a firm framework and colorful verbal illustrations to enjoy and remember what you have written.

The framework—the slant, the angle—will often become clear to you while you are taking notes on your facts. Trouble is, ideas of this kind are apt to be vague and fleeting; by the time you are through with taking notes, they have usually disappeared. That's why Graham Wallas, in his *Art of Thought,* recommends putting these "fringe thoughts" down (in square brackets) so that you have some record of them right among your notes. That's why it is a good idea—if you are using books you own—to put random ideas on the margin. When your writing job reaches the stage of creative thinking, these seemingly irrelevant stray thoughts will be most valuable to you. Any device to nail them down is good— as long as we haven't yet got Dr. Vannevar Bush's imaginary thinking machine that will perform this function at a push-button signal.

What it comes down to is that you must concentrate on getting your facts, but not too hard. There's always the chance that your wandering mind will hit upon a good "angle" while you are copying a sheaf of statistics.

The importance of good verbal illustrations is even greater. Your facts may be complete and convincing, but your reader won't remember them ten minutes afterward if you haven't bothered to find specific illustrations. Whenever you write about a general principle, show its application in a specific case; quote the way someone stated it; tell a pointed anecdote. These dashes of color are what the reader will take away with him. Not that he will necessarily remember the illustration or anecdote itself; but it will help him remember the main idea.

Of course, direct quotations are the stock in trade of any good journalist. Albert Deutsch, for instance (in his article "Unnecessary Operations") uses them skillfully to set the stage:

Ten years ago the American Foundation made a survey in which hundreds of reputable doctors throughout the country were polled. The findings were published in a report entitled *American Medicine: Expert Testimony Out of Court*. Here are some excerpts:

A member of the American Surgical Association said: "It is probably true that at least half of the surgical operations in this country are done by physicians without special qualifications."

An obstetrician in the South commented on the many small hospitals in his region owned by a single doctor with overaverage ambition and business acumen, who "takes a short course in surgery and returns as owner and chief surgeon. In time he trains himself as a fairly efficient operator, but not before lives are sacrificed, and useless surgery is done."

A midwestern doctor, certified in both surgery and clinical pathology (examining the excised parts of the body after operations) said: "I put in three mornings a week as pathologist in one of our large hospitals. I have a choice collection of organs which have been removed, if sincerely then unconsciously, for revenue only."

And here is how a *New York Times* reporter uses direct quotations to point up a piece about the Hunter College Elementary School for gifted children:

A 4-year-old child in the nursery class was asked what he does in school. He answered very simply: "I fight and take tests." And when a student-teacher urged a 5-year-old to put on his own rubbers, he replied majestically: "Of course I can put them on myself, but a student-teacher's job is to help little boys put on their rubbers, isn't it?"

On another occasion a student-teacher was trying to quiet some children during the rest period. In exasperation she said to one of the 5-year-olds: "If you don't get quiet I'll send you back to your room." To which the alert youngster corrected her: "You shouldn't say that! You should say: 'Which do you prefer, to get quiet or to go back to your room?'"

Both these examples show how important it is to take notes of the exact words in such verbal illustrations. Neither Mr. Deutsch nor the *New York Times* reporter could have made their points so effectively if they hadn't used *the exact words that were said.* Sometimes the words used are practically the whole story, as in this little excerpt from a United Nations session:

> After it had become clear that most of the delegates opposed Manuilsky's announcement that the Argentine resolution had not been carried, the Liberian representative . . . demanded that a vote be taken on the chairman's ruling. Mr. Manuilsky passed over the Liberian request . . . until Senator Connally said emphatically:
>
> "A vote must be taken now, immediately. Immediately, not tomorrow. Immediately, not after more speeches from the chair. Immediately, not after Mr. Manuilsky gets some more advice from his advisers. Immediately."
>
> The vote was taken immediately.

Tracking down illustrative material and copying the exact words of quoted matter is often a nuisance, but it pays. Anecdotes are useful for all sorts of purposes.

Here is an excellent example from the late Professor Wertheimer's book *Productive Thinking*, showing the solution of a problem by sudden insight:

> Now I shall tell the story of young Gauss, the famous mathematician. It runs about as follows: he was a boy of six, attending grammar school in a little town. The teacher gave a test in arithmetic and said to the class: "Which of you

[ 30 ]

will be first to get the sum of $1+2+3+4+5+6+7+8+9+10$?" Very soon, while the others were still busy figuring, young Gauss raised his head. "Ligget se," he said, which means, "Here it is."

"How the devil did you get it so quickly?" exclaimed the surprised teacher. Young Gauss answered—of course we do not know exactly what he did answer, but on the basis of experience in experiments I think it may have been about like this: "Had I done it by adding 1 and 2, then 3 to the sum, then 4 to the new result, and so on, it would have taken very long: and, trying to do it quickly, I would very likely have made mistakes. But you see, 1 and 10 make eleven, 2 and 9 are again—must be—11! And so on! There are 5 such pairs; 5 times 11 makes 55." The boy had discovered the gist of an important theorem.

This may sound like a mild anecdote, but in a scholarly book on psychology it is striking enough. Less restrained is this one, used by Bennett Cerf to show the principles of terse, economical newswriting:

Stanley Frank and Paul Sann tell a classic story about a cub reporter in Johnstown, Pa., at the time of this disastrous flood in 1889. The first flash reached the nearest big-time newspaper office late at night when only the newest addition to the staff—a droopy youth just out of school—was on tap. The editor hustled him to the scene of the catastrophe, and spent the next hour in a frenzied effort to get his veteran reporters on the job. By then it was too late, however. All wires were down, and the valley was isolated. For twenty-four hours the only reporter in the devastated area was one green beginner!

The press of America waited feverishly for his first report. Finally it began to trickle in over the telegraph. "God sits upon a lonely mountaintop tonight and gazes upon a desolate Johnstown. The roar of swirling waters echoes through . . ." The editor tore his hair and rushed a wire back to his poet laureate: "Okay. Forget flood. Interview God. Rush pictures."

Finally, here is an anecdote that was used well to advertise a book on farming:

> Last spring we had an author with zest for what he was doing—B. F. Bullock, who wrote *Practical Farming for the South*. He had suggested certain illustrations, and we'd been collecting them. When he came to the Press to look them over, he'd hardly put his briefcase on the table before he asked, "Could you get a picture of Spring Brook Bess Burke?"
>
> Apologetically we admitted we couldn't. We knew he'd be disappointed. Spring Brook Bess Burke was a cow he'd said some especially nice things about. "Not Spring Brook," we repeated, "but we do have one of her daughter, Spring Brook Bess Burke II." We took the picture out of a folder and handed it to him.
>
> There was a silence while he scrutinized it. Then he laid it down on the table—gently—and gently said, "Well, she isn't the cow her mother was."
>
> No wonder reviewers found *Practical Farming in the South* full of valuable information, written with sympathy and understanding.

At this point you may possibly say that I am using this chapter to dish out a bunch of miscellaneous anecdotes I happened to like. But I am not. I am simply following my own recipe, hoping that you will remember these little stories and, with and by them, this chapter's main lesson: that for readability you need not only basic ideas and solid facts, but also a good collection of seemingly useless information.

PS

All of this is true but I'm afraid the emphasis is wrong. After all, the cute little stories and anecdotes are only the frosting on the cake—indispensable, to be sure, but useless if there isn't a solid foundation.

The foundation, of course, is a heap of facts. Or a mountain of facts. Or, best of all, an iceberg of facts, only one-ninth of which will eventually be visible to the reader of your piece of writing. The amusing little bits will come to you while you're digging for the important stuff.

It's interesting that 25 years ago I put the emphasis on library research. I wouldn't do that today. Information from printed sources is good, but information out of the horse's mouth is vastly better. Now that we live in the age of TV, when everything that happens is followed by a TV reporter holding a microphone to someone's mouth to "get his reaction," we've all learned that the art of writing is largely the art of interviewing. Pulitzer prizes are not given for excellence in prose style, but for ingenuity in getting information out of *people*.

Let me recap the lesson of this chapter by reprinting a story from the *New York Times*. It's not a great or famous story—it didn't even carry a by-line—but it shows beautifully how the thing is done:*

Corsicans of France Are Feeling the Sting of Publicity
Given to Criminals

Paris, Jan. 6 [1973]—The Corsicans of France, much like the Italian-Americans in the United States, are becoming increasingly sensitive about their collective reputation.

Usually it is bad Corsicans who make the news, and this week was no exception. When the French narcotics squad seized 300 pounds of heroin, one of those arrested with the drug was Corsican.

* © 1973 by the New York Times Company. Reprinted by permission.

The seizure followed the announcement by the Government that voting machines would be installed at Ajaccio and Bastia, Corsica's two major cities, to limit electoral fraud.

Mayor Pascal Rossini of Ajaccio, the capital, endorsed the measure, although he charged "discrimination" against urban voters since voting machines would not be used in the countryside.

There are about three million Corsicans in France, of whom fewer than 300,000 live on the island. About 600,000 have settled in and around Marseilles, making it the largest Corsican city.

In Marseilles there is a saying: "Un Corse, c'est tout bon ou tout mauvais"—"A Corsican is either all good or all bad."

Corsica has been held by Greeks, Vikings, Arabs, Spaniards, Genovese, and now the French. Corsica has given France Napoleon and most of her gangsters.

Corsicans have a taste for oratory and some of France's greatest lawyers have been Corsican, such as Antoine de Moro-Giafferi.

The oratorical inclination has also led many Corsicans into politics. The Cabinet member in charge of youth and sports is a Corsican surgeon from Marseilles, Joseph Comiti, while another Corsican, a one-legged war hero, Alexandre Sanguinetti, heads the military committee of the National Assembly, whose Speaker is another Corsican, Achille Peretti.

There are also many Corsicans in the Civil Service, notably in the police and in state social insurance.

Another strong characteristic of the Corsicans is their family loyalty. There is a story in Marseilles of a gangster who one noon receives the surprise visit of a nephew. "My boy," he says, "I will look after you, but not before 4 o'clock. Now we are robbing a bank."

Even with names like Colombani, Nicolai, Casanova, Peraldi, Mariani and Morelli, Corsicans consider themselves

French. They do not refer to mainland France as "France" —because that would indicate Corsica is not France—but as "the continent."

Although Corsica was acquired by France in 1768 from a Genoa bank that had bought it from the Pope, the Corsican dialect is heavily Italian and understood by most of the Corsicans living in France proper.

On the island itself the rhythm of life is still easier, despite the tourists. The Corsicans themselves chuckle over such jokes as this: "What is the flag of the Corsican Communist party? The same as the Soviet one—but without a hammer or sickle."

You see the principle? The writer of this 410-word story— destined to appear inconspicuously on page 54 of a Sunday paper —collected an astonishing amount of facts to give *Times* readers a compact, encyclopedic article on Corsica, filled to the brim with names, quotes and dates, and seasoned with two funny stories.

If you can come up to the standard of this model in your writing, you'll be doing fine.

## CHAPTER 4

# THE SHAPE OF IDEAS

---

*Success in solving the problem depends on choosing the
right aspect, on attacking the fortress from its accessible side.*

GEORGE POLYA

---

WHEN the *Saturday Evening Post*, in its article series on
American cities, got around to St. Louis, it assigned Asso-
ciate Editor Jack Alexander to the job. Alexander went to St.
Louis, spent ten days collecting material, and returned to his desk
in Philadelphia. But he wasn't yet ready to write. He wasn't even
ready to draw up an outline. According to the *Saturday Evening
Post,* this is what he did: "His first job was to organize all his
information and ideas. It was partly a mental and partly a
mechanical process. He spread out his typewritten notes on a big
table. Gradually he sorted his notes—and, more important, the
facts and ideas in his head—into classifications. This process is
hard for Jack to explain; he doesn't know just what happened.
Somehow, after a day of work, he got to the point where he
could think through the whole mess. He was ready to start
planning the actual writing job."

Think of what this means. *After* he had collected his raw
material, and *before* he felt ready to make an outline, Mr.
Alexander put in a full day's work getting his ideas in shape.
This seasoned professional writer assigned a full work day to
what amounts to just sitting and thinking.

This may seem strange to you. Yet actually it isn't strange at
all. Every professional writer knows that this period of just-
sitting-and-thinking between legwork and outline is the most

important part of the whole writing process. It's what makes a piece of writing what it is.

You won't find anything about this in the textbooks. Students are not supposed to just sit and think. Open any English composition textbook and you'll find that note-taking is followed by outlining without even a five-minute break for a smoke.

If you want to find out about this mysterious business of just-sitting-and-thinking, you have to go to the psychologists. They know quite a bit about it; but the trouble is that they don't write English but their own special language. They talk about *re-centering, restructuring,* and *configurations,* and the whole school of psychology that deals with these matters goes by the formidable name of *Gestalt Psychology.*

Let me do a little translating for you. In the original German, the word *Gestalt* means nothing particularly exciting; it simply means *shape.* And that's what this whole business is about: when you do this job of just-sitting-and-thinking, you are trying to grasp the *shape* of your ideas. The *configurations,* the *recentering,* the *restructuring*—all these words mean that your mind is operating just like your eye—or your camera—when it is looking at an object. To see the object clearly, you have to find the right focus, the right perspective, the right angle of vision. Only when all these things are taken care of do you really see what the object is like.

The same way, in your writing you must first go over your material in your mind, trying to find the focus, the perspective, the angle of vision that will make you see clearly the shape of whatever it is you are writing about. There has to be one point that is sharply in focus, and a clear grouping of everything else around it. Once you see this clearly, your reader will see it too. And that, the shape of your ideas, is usually all he is going to carry away from his reading.

I know of course that all this still sounds vague. But don't worry. From this point on we are getting down to brass tacks.

The most widely used device for getting ideas in shape is to buttonhole some unsuspecting victim—the kind of person who is apt to read later what you have written—and to rehearse your ideas aloud. This has two advantages: first, it forces you to funnel your ideas into a limited number of words; and second, the other person will tell you what your ideas look like from where he sits. Allan Nevins, the historian, puts it this way: "Catch a friend who is interested in the subject and talk out what you have learned, at length. In this way you discover facts of interpretation that you might have missed, points of argument that had been unrealized, and the form most suitable for the story you have to tell."

This is fine, except that Mr. Nevins says "at length." Actually, the rule here is, the shorter the better. If you can manage to spring your ideas on your friend in one sentence, then you have found the sharpest focus of them all. Everything else will arrange itself around this one sentence or phrase almost automatically.

Let me give you a few examples of this. The most famous editorial on the atomic bomb was written by the editor of the *Saturday Review of Literature,* Mr. Norman Cousins. It was firmly built upon an inspired title: "Modern Man Is Obsolete." The best-known advertisement of the same year was run by the Chesapeake & Ohio Railway. It proceeded straight from an unbeatable headline: "A Hog Can Cross the Country Without Changing Trains—But YOU Can't!"

Or think of the remarkable sentence-building career of Mr. Elmer Wheeler, the author of *Tested Sentences That Sell.* This man spends his life thinking up sentences that will bring sales talk into sharp focus. In his book he proudly tells of the millions of square clothespins that were sold with the words: "They won't roll!"

But to come back: a good way of using someone else for focus and perspective is to put such a person right into your piece of writing. You present your facts and ideas as seen by an observer with a detached point of view. This will make things clearer to yourself and will help your reader in catching on. Take, for instance, the following "Duet on a Bus" by Douglas Moore:

I overheard a bus conversation the other day. It was a long one, lasting from Grant's Tomb to Forty-second Street. A young Frenchman, recently arrived, was apparently being shown the city by a lady of middle age who took her culture as a heavy responsibility . . . It went something like this:

"I shall be happy to attend the opening of the opera."

"Yes, it couldn't be nicer. 'Faust,' you know."

"It will be amusing to hear 'Faust' in English."

"Oh, this won't be in English. All our operas are done in the original language."

"Why? Do American audiences understand French?"

"No, but it is much more artistic that way and the singers' French is usually so poor even French audiences wouldn't be able to understand them."

"The singers aren't French then?"

"Only one or two. Albanese will be Marguerite and Pinza Mephistopheles. They are both Italian."

"What happens in the Italian operas? Are they sung by Italians?"

"Well, now let's see. In 'Rigoletto' there's Tibbett, Kullman as the Duke, Antoine as Gilda, and Kaskas as Maddalena."

"They're all Americans, aren't they?"

"So they are. Well, they sing Italian anyway. Isn't it wonderful so many of our best singers are American now."

"It is an amusing idea, operas in the original language. Is 'Boris Godounov' sung in Russian?"

"No, that would be too hard except for Kipnis. He's

Russian. The rest of them sing Italian."

"You mean at the same time?"

"Yes, most of them are not Italians but it seems a good language to use."

"Why?"

"Well, you see in the old days there were really two companies at the Metropolitan, the German and the Italian. I suppose when this opera came into the repertory the Italian wing sang it."

"Why don't they sing it in English? That is closer to the Russian in sound and the audience might understand it better."

"Well, we have tried some operas in English but I don't believe the public likes it."

"Why not? Are they afraid they might catch a few words?"

And so on. (Sorry I can't print the whole thing here.) You see how useful the stooge with another viewpoint is to a writer.

But of course you can't do this sort of thing all the time. What else can you do to gain focus and perspective?

It depends on the material you are working on. Often the answer will suggest itself. Whenever you are writing about a group or an organization, for instance, the natural thing to do is to focus on a typical member of the group. Start by describing him (or her) and go on from there.

This sounds simple, but there is a pitfall in it. It's hard to look away from the eye-catching, outstanding—and therefore *not* typical—members of the group. I once talked to a writer who was working on an employee pension-plan booklet. He had all details worked out for a "given case"—but his "given case" was a $10,000-a-year man! This meant that he got nice round figures when it came to working out percentages but it also meant that the example didn't mean a thing to the average $3,000-a-year employee.

So keep your eyes on the ground when you use the typical-person device. See what Bernard DeVoto did when he had to cover an American Medical Association meeting:

> Back home—which might have been Iowa or West Virginia or Oklahoma—they probably called him Doc, and most likely Old Doc; for he would be close to seventy, his untidy Van Dyke was white, his shoulders were stooped and there was a slight tremor in his fingers. Seersucker will not hold a crease and God knows how old his straw hat was. He liked to stand in a corner at one of the pharmaceutical exhibits in the Technical Exposition. Behind him were large charts showing the molecular structure of the firm's newest product, photographs three feet by four showing how it was synthesized, and equally large graphs with red and green lines curling round the black to show its results in the treatment of anything you please—rheumatic fever, hypertension, duodenal ulcer.
>
> Doc stood there and talked with the young man from the drug house who had all the statistics by heart and because he had been trained in public relations never gave a sign of boredom but went on smiling and nodding. Doc described his cases back home and told how he handled rheumatic fever or hypertension, and said he had always got good results from potassium iodide, and ended by taking out a pad and writing down his favorite prescriptions for the young man's consideration.
>
> It must have been a different Doc from hour to hour and from exhibit to exhibit but he always seemed the same. One observer remembers him as clearly as anything else at the Centennial Celebration (and ninety-seventh annual meeting) of the American Medical Association, at Atlantic City in the second week of June.
>
> Everybody else was there too . . .

Sometimes this device is strikingly effective in a situation where you wouldn't think it possible to arrive at any average. Look at this (from John Gunther's *Inside U.S.A.*):

*Composite Portrait of a New England Legislator*

He is tall, gaunt, wrinkled, and there are great reserves of character in the face and raspy voice. He earns a living in a garage, and also owns a bit of real estate. His salary as legislator (which in New Hampshire would be two hundred dollars a year plus traveling expenses; in Vermont four hundred) is an important addition to his income. His wife is a farmer's daughter from the next county; they have been married twenty-four years and have three children. The eldest son was a carpenter's mate first class, another son is in his third year in the public high school, and is crazy about gliders; the daughter wants to go to Vassar. Our legislator has two brothers: one is a lobster fisherman in Stony Creek, Connecticut, and the other left Massachusetts many years ago, and is believed now to own a small farm in Iowa. Several generations back there were some complex marriages in the family; one distant relative is Greek born, and another married a Finn; but also our legislator is related to no less a personage than a former governor of the state. He believes in paying his bills on the dot, in the inherent right of his children to a good education, and in common sense. He gives ten dollars a year to the Red Cross, believes that "Washington ought to let us alone," knows that very few Americans are peasants, and feels that the country has enough inner strength to ride out any kind of crisis. In several respects he is somewhat arid; but no one has ever fooled him twice. He is a person of great power. Because, out of the community itself, power rises into him. What he represents is the tremendous vitality of ordinary American life, and the basic good instincts of the common people.

[ 42 ]

So much for groups and types. How about describing a series of events? The principle is the same: focus on one point that is so significant that you can hang your story onto it. Invariably there *is* such a point—the turning point, the key event that explains everything before and after. The only problem is to find it; and it is important, with events just as with people, not to overlook the simple because of the more glamorous or spectacular. Turning points have a way of happening long before the big fireworks start.

Early in 1945, for example, when everybody was talking about Beardsley Ruml and his pay-as-you-go tax plan, *The New Yorker* ran a profile on Ruml by Alva Johnston. But the profile was not written around the pay-as-you-go tax. Instead, after a few introductory paragraphs, the writer focused on an earlier turning point in Ruml's life:

Ruml was projected into commercial life by a quirk in the mind of the late Percy Straus, head man of Macy's. Unlike most businessmen, Straus spent much of his time mixing with the intelligentsia. He knew that Ruml was regarded as a two-hundred-and-forty-pound imp and *enfant terrible* because of his habit of challenging established ideas and cross-examining everything. "I want to get Ruml in as treasurer," Straus said to Delos Walker, then general manager of the store. "We need somebody to challenge our thinking. We're in danger of becoming too self-satisfied. It's good to be shaken up."

Ruml was thirty-nine at the time and had a distinguished academic berth—Professor of Education and Dean of the Social Sciences at the University of Chicago. He had no training to fit him for a job like that of treasurer of a department store. "You'll have no duties whatever," said Straus, "except to annoy me." This was an irresistible offer, particularly since Ruml felt that his accomplishment in

[ 43 ]

three years as dean had been disappointing. One of his colleagues at Chicago said that Ruml was suffering from the occupational disease of university executives which was described by President Gates of Pennsylvania as "being pecked to death by ducks." Mrs. Hutchins, wife of the president of the University of Chicago, was the author of Ruml's academic epitaph. "He left ideas for notions," she said.

Or take this passage from a *Reader's Digest* article on Federal Mediator Ching. The writer goes even further back to find his focal turning point:

> One day in 1904 a husky young trouble shooter was trying to fix a loose shoe fuse on a stalled Boston subway train. As he leaned over he slipped, and a terrible voltage flashed through his body. It enveloped him in blue flame, blew the powerhouse and stopped the entire subway system.
>
> Six days later the young man regained consciousness. The doctors thought he had a chance to live but would be permanently blinded. Actually, within four months he was well recovered and his sight restored.
>
> This obscure happening more than 40 years ago has had a pervasive influence on labor relations in America. The young man, Cyrus Stuart Ching, survived for a long and useful career as an industrial peacemaker and sage. And he remembered something. During the long weeks of his convalescence, nobody from the company management came to see him. There was no workmen's compensation in those days, but when he returned to his job the company magnanimously gave him a new suit of work clothes. This treatment set his ruminative mind to work on the queer chasm between the boss and the worker. He has been thinking about it ever since.
>
> And now Mr. Ching—71 years old, but still carrying his six-foot-seven-inch frame with jaunty vigor—has taken over the touchy post of director of the Federal Mediation and Conciliation Service, as set up by the Taft-Hartley Act.

Proper focusing becomes difficult when you have neither a group of people nor a series of events. Then what? There is a way, but it's rather hard to put in simple words. Let me try.

What you are after, as you are turning your material over in your mind, is something like the one-sentence headline, the typical group member, the turning point in the chain of events— some one thing that will point up the significance of the subject as a whole. Even if your material looks at first like a shapeless mass of totally different items, there must be one point at which they all converge—otherwise you wouldn't, or shouldn't, treat them all together in one piece of writing. The trouble is that this common denominator is usually so simple and obvious that it's practically invisible. It's the thing you take so much for granted that you never bother to give it a second thought. And that's exactly the trick: find the underlying feature that you have taken for granted and try to give it a second thought.

To come back, for instance, to Jack Alexander's *Saturday Evening Post* article on St. Louis. Alexander's problem was this: he had returned from St. Louis with a heap of notes but didn't know how to pull them together into an understandable whole. After having spent a day in thinking, he hit upon the solution. The obvious way to describe a city is to stress the things in which it is outstanding; but somehow, in the case of St. Louis, these things were hard to find. Alexander gave that a second thought and decided to write his piece around the theme that St. Louis made a virtue of *not being outstanding in anything*. He wrote:

> The spell which the city exerts is paradoxical . . . St. Louis pursues the commercial strategy of limited objectives. It has no vast industries . . . (Its) citizenry is simultaneously hospitable and suspicious of the East, gay and stubborn, serious about living and yet fun-loving . . . A booster crude enough to preach the common American gospel of giantism achieves no more than a dry rattle in his throat . . . St. Louis has never fallen for skyscrapers . . . St. Louis might have grown

up to be another Chicago or Detroit—a fate which now seems
to St. Louisans to be worse than death . . .

In this fashion, Alexander wrote a memorable article by turning the underlying theme upside down.

Of course, there are all sorts of ways of doing this, and I cannot
possibly show you exactly how the principle applies in every
case. But I can give you a few more examples:

Shortly after Hiroshima and Nagasaki, there appeared an
unforgettable article on the atomic bomb. It was written by Bob
Trout in the form of an imaginary news broadcast of the day
atomic bombs hit *the United States.*

In 1947, *Harper's Magazine* printed a highly illuminating article
about the British crisis by the economist Barbara Ward. It too
started "upside down"—by explaining that there was not one
British crisis but four: "the country has been struck by *four
different crises simultaneously.*"

Another frequent topic of magazine articles in 1947 was the
community property law which gave married couples in certain
states the advantage of splitting their income tax. Before Congress
incorporated this feature in the federal income tax law, the subject
was a natural for popular presentation—provided the writer
could really make it interesting. One writer (Bernard B. Smith
in *Harper's Magazine*) was highly successful; his piece was widely
read and quoted. Let's compare it with an example of the garden-
variety approach (by John L. McClellan in the *American* magazine):

| *Divorce Is Cheaper Than Marriage* | *Where You Pay Less Income Tax* |
|---|---|
| by Bernard B. Smith | by John L. McClellan |
| Only one marriage in three these days winds up in the divorce courts, which must mean that two-thirds of America's husbands think it is worth paying the Collector of Internal Revenue a substantial premium for the | Although there has been much debate about it in Congress, few persons realize how the community-property law in a few lucky states has perpetrated a system of special privilege that has reduced the federal income |

privilege of maintaining the institution of the family. For that is precisely what they are doing. The amendments to the Internal Revenue Code enacted by the 78th Congress in 1942 made it cheaper for a man to get a divorce and pay alimony than to stay married, and this is economically practical for anybody whose net taxable income is more than $2,000 a year . . .

. . . .

It's high time for Congress to set this absurdity straight, and make the institution of marriage as attractive financially as the institution of divorce.

taxes of a favored minority at the expense of a majority.

Most husbands and wives assume that if they live in New York, Illinois, or Wisconsin, for instance, they pay the same federal income tax that is paid by couples with the same income in California, Texas, or Oklahoma. They are wrong. They pay more. Frequently a great deal more.

. . . .

It is the duty of the Federal Government to provide an equitable system of income taxes, and it is the responsibility of the Congress to amend present law, so as to remove this injustice and provide equality under the law to all citizens alike, irrespective of their state domicile.

There can hardly be any question that Smith's upside-down treatment of the subject is more effective than McClellan's conventional approach. Mind you, I am not saying that the McClellan article is bad: it's a good, craftsmanlike popular-magazine piece. But the divorce-is-cheaper-than-marriage idea is the kind of thing that sticks in the mind; it's that extra something by which we remember what we have read.

## PS

Again, I now think I was going too fast in this chapter. For the beginner, the basic lesson is simply this: whatever you're writing—an article, a report, even a business letter or memo—first of all make sure you have a clear lead. (That's pronounced *leed*, and it's the opening, summarizing paragraph newspapermen start an article with.) You *can't* produce a decent piece of writing without a clear lead, and it's well worth spending some time on working it out before you start writing. Normally, as I explained in this chapter, the lead will be a brief statement of the main thought

[ 47 ]

you want to convey. Once you've formulated that, you're on your way.

Of course, more sophisticated, imaginative leads are more striking and will often have more effect. But save them up for the rare occasion when, for some reason or other, an ordinary lead won't work, or won't work as well.

On page 46 I wrote about Bob Trout's memorable piece on the bombing of Hiroshima and Nagasaki in which he described an imaginary atomic bomb attack on the United States. Almost 30 years later, on January 3, 1973, shortly after the American bombing raids over Hanoi, an article by Herbert Mitgang appeared in the *New York Times*. It was called "The Bombing of Queens." This is how it began:

> QUEENS, N.Y.—For the first time in history, an American city came under direct enemy aerial bombardment yesterday. The main target, according to the official Hanoi spokesman, was the Sunnyside marshaling yard in the Borough of Queens, now in shambles, but other damage to nonmilitary structures is reported. There are 185 known dead . . .

## CHAPTER 5

## ALL WRITING IS CREATIVE

*Theoretical insights flourish best when
the thinker is apparently wasting time.*

J. ROBERT OPPENHEIMER

"SOMEHOW it wouldn't come around. He couldn't sleep.
One night an idea suddenly came to his mind; he leaped
out of bed and started writing. He wrote six pages that night . . ."

What do you think the man wrote? A poem? A story? A chapter
of a novel? You're wrong: he was working on a magazine article.
The quotation refers to Mr. Maurice Zolotow, a contributor of
articles to the *Saturday Evening Post.*

Don't think that this method of writing nonfiction is unusual.
It isn't. In fact, it's rather typical. And that's why, in this down-to-
earth book, you are now going to read a chapter on the unconscious mind.

Ordinarily—not always, but more often than not—writing
proceeds like this: collecting material—trying to find a good
approach—spending some time on something else—getting a
sudden bright idea—planning and organizing—writing—revising.
The most mysterious—and most fascinating—part of the whole
process is the one you don't read about in the handbooks: the
search for a good approach, the period when you abandon the
search, and the moment when, out of nowhere, an idea pops into
your mind.

Maybe you won't believe me when I say that this is common
experience. All right, I'll cite chapter and verse. This is the way
the human mind works in creating *anything*—whether it's the

mind of a poet or a mathematician, a philosopher or a historian, a scientist or an advertising man. Let's hear a few among hundreds of witnesses:

A poet (Rainer Maria Rilke): "During a few days, when I really meant to do something else, these sonnets were given to me . . . One little song came to me when I woke up, quite complete up to the eighth line . . ."

A mathematician (Sir W. Rowan Hamilton): "After I had been haunted by the problem for fifteen years, the solution started into life, or light, full grown, on the 16th of October 1843, as I was walking with Lady Hamilton to Dublin and came up to Brougham Bridge. That is to say, I then and there felt the galvanic circuit of thought close."

A novelist (Louis Bromfield): "One of the most helpful discoveries I made long ago in common with some other writers is that there is a part of the mind, which the psychologists call the 'subconscious,' that works while you are sleeping or even while you are relaxing or are engaged in some other task far removed from writing. I have found it possible to train this part of the mind to do a pretty organized job. Very often I have awakened in the morning to find a problem of technique, or plot, or character, which had long been troubling me, completely solved while I had been sleeping."

A philosopher (Bertrand Russsell): "I have found that if I have to write upon some rather difficult topic, the best plan is to think about it with very great intensity—the greatest intensity of which I am capable—for a few hours or days, and at the end of that time give orders, so to speak, that the work is to proceed underground. After some time I return consciously to the topic and find that the work has been done."

An engineer (John Mills): "When I started engineering, I used to rely on the work of the subconscious. If my chief called me up and presented a short engineering problem on which he wanted a reasoned recommendation, I would ask how soon and hope it wasn't the same day because I wanted to sleep on it. If the next noon would be soon enough, I would go back to my desk, look over the papers in the case but try to do so casually and without reaching any conclusions. That evening at home I would be very careful not to get started on any serious mental effort—I would make my reading casual and mechanical instead of purposive study. Just before I went to bed, which was synchronous with sleep, I would say to myself: Tomorrow I've got to tell so-and-so about such-and-such. Of course, subconscious didn't always come through with the answer, but a surprising percentage of the time it did or with something so near that neither I nor my superior could tell the difference."

A historian (Allan Nevins): "I read exhaustively around every angle I intend to treat and make full notes. But I put my notes aside before I start to write. . . . It is a matter of digestion."

An advertising man (James Webb Young): "Out of nowhere the idea will appear. It will come when you are least expecting it—while shaving, or bathing, or most often when you are half awake in the morning. It may waken you in the middle of the night."

And a scientist (Nobel-prize winner Otto Loewi) tells this story: "One night, after falling asleep over a trifling novel, I awoke possessed by a brilliant idea. I reached to the table beside my bed, picked up a piece of paper and a pencil, and jotted down a few notes. On awakening next morning I was aware of having had an inspiration in the night and turned to the paper for a reminder. To my consternation I could not make anything of the scrawl I found on it. I went to my laboratory, hoping that sense would come to what I had written if I was surrounded by familiar apparatus. In spite of frequently withdrawing the paper from my pocket, and studying it earnestly, I gained no insight. At the end of the day, still filled with the belief that I had had a very precious revelation in the night before, I went to sleep. To my great joy I again awoke in the darkness with the same flash of insight which had inspired me the night before. This time I carefully recorded it

[ 51 ]

before going to sleep again. The next day I went to my laboratory [and brought proof to the chemical mediation of nerve impulses]."

So, I repeat, getting ideas out of the unconscious is the rule rather than the exception. It is so commonplace among creative writers that nobody ever bothered with collecting scientific evidence. But somebody did bother once to poll a group of research chemists on whether they relied on sudden inspirations. Eighty-three percent said they did.

The question is, of course: just how do these sudden inspirations happen? Do they really come out of nowhere? And why are they apt to appear at night? Is there anything we can know or do about their mechanism?

So far, the answers to these and similar questions aren't very satisfactory, but we do know this: bright new ideas are always combinations of old ones; they come to us usually after our mind has had a rest after a concentrated effort; and if we do it right, we can sometimes coax them to the surface.

That there are no really brand-new ideas is a fact every psychologist knows. Creative thinking is just another name for finding new idea-combinations.

How do you hit upon new combinations? The recipe is obvious: have a large number of ideas and experiences on hand; put them together; stir vigorously. Or, more concretely: have a well-stocked mind; and, as William James put it, "get your mind whirling and see what happens."

Still more concretely, here is the process as described by another mathematician (Henri Poincaré): ". . . Ideas rose in crowds. I felt them collide until parts interlocked, so to speak, making a stable combination." And another poet (William Ellery Leonard) puts it this way: ". . . Suddenly something organized itself inside me and called for instant expression . . . Organization had taken *verbal shape* . . . a subconscious linking of ideas, of emotional tensions, of imagery, of memories . . ."

So, what you have to do is to draw upon all your ideas, experi-

[ 52 ]

ences, memories, and move them about until you feel the click, the electric spark, the sensation of "That's it!" If you keep your mind always in apple-pie order, you'll probably never have that feeling. The combinations will always be the old, well-established ones; your mind will always run in fixed grooves. That's why there is such a thing as a too strict classification or a too orderly outline. If you are the kind of person who loves neat card files, try dropping all your cards on the floor some time. It will do you no end of good. Or if you are used to starting every writing job by making an outline, don't. Wait until you have felt the click. Before that, any outline will tie your ideas down.

The conscious mind, of course, is always more orderly than the unconscious. That's why the unconscious is so much better at combining ideas in a novel way. It puts things together that we never would put together "in our right mind." As long as we pay attention to what we are doing, we just cannot make ourselves combine two ideas that, offhand, don't seem to fit together. But when the mind is busy with something else, or when we are relaxing or asleep, anything goes. Our unconscious just keeps toying with idea-combinations regardless of whether they make sense or not. And then—"out of nowhere"—comes the flash of inspiration.

That doesn't mean that all good ideas come to us while we are asleep. But it does mean, as one psychologist said, that to have ideas we must "think aside."

I don't know, of course, whether the examples I used in the last chapter were written in that fashion. But I rather think they were. In one way or another, almost all of them are examples of novel idea-combinations—the kind of thing I have just been talking about. And I don't suppose that the combination of bus ride and opera, or the traits of several legislators, or community-property taxes and divorces, could have been thought of gradually. They must have come to the writers' minds all at once.

There are innumerable ways of combining ideas; the types I

listed in the last chapter are just a few of the most common. In fact, the more unusual a combination, the more striking it is, naturally. This is not a recommendation of sensationalism and cheap effects. On the contrary. Let me give you one more example which clearly must have been the result of a sudden inspiration. (For all I know, the lightning struck the author while he was shaving.) This was written in December 1944, when everybody was thinking about the progress of the war—and about Christmas. But E. B. White in the *New Yorker* managed to write an unforgettable piece about *both*. It began with these words:

> They are not wrapped as gifts (there was no time to wrap them), but you will find them under the lighted tree with the other presents. They are the extra gifts, the ones with the hard names. Certain towns and villages. Certain docks and installations. Atolls in a sea. Assorted airstrips, beachheads, supply dumps, rail junctions . . .

And it ended like this:

> Gifts in incredible profusion and all unwrapped, from old and new friends: gifts with a made-in-China label, gifts from Russians, Poles, British, French, gifts from Eisenhower, de Gaulle, Montgomery, Malinovsky, an umbrella from the Air Forces, gifts from engineers, rear gunners, privates first class . . . there isn't time to look at them all. It will take years. This is a Christmas you will never forget, people have been so generous.

Probably you will never write such a prose masterpiece. But the basic recipe applies to all writing jobs—even to your most humdrum business letters, memoranda, and reports. Get your facts, think hard of the best way of presenting them, and then "think aside." Let the matter drop for a while until you suddenly hit upon a striking combination of ideas.

[ 54 ]

If you don't believe that this method works for such matters as business correspondence and reports, think of all those letters you could have written twice as well had you waited until the next morning. And think of all those you did improve after you had taken time out for something else.

But probably you know exactly what I am talking about. Probably your bright ideas, like almost everybody else's, come to you in a flash too.

## CHAPTER 6

# FROM FALSE STARTS TO WRONG CONCLUSIONS

*Write the way an architect builds, who first
drafts his plan and designs every detail.*
SCHOPENHAUER

ALMOST all reading matter in this country gets off to a false
start. This is not an exaggeration; it is a statement of fact
which I am going to prove.

Let me first define my terms. What is a false start? It's a beginning that doesn't do what a beginning *ought* to do. Psychologists
tell us that an effective piece of writing should start with something that points to its main theme. In other words, you must put
your reader in the right frame of mind; you must start by getting
him interested in what's going to come.

Look around you and you'll find that most reading matter
doesn't start that way. It usually starts in routine fashion—with
a stale, humdrum opening that does *anything but* whet your
appetite for the main dish.

Take the three most common pieces of writing in American
life: the business letter, the newspaper report, and the magazine
short story. Each of them has a standardized opening; each of
these openings is wrong.

Ninety-nine out of a hundred business letters start with an
acknowledgment of the addressee's last letter. Have you ever
asked yourself why? The only plausible answer I found is that
it's always been done that way. It's an old, old custom. There's a
quaint, sixty-five-year-old composition textbook on my shelves
that contains the following model business letter:

[ 56 ]

*4 Park St., Boston, Mass.,*
*May 26, 1882.*

*Mrs. M. E. Dawson,*
*Jacksonville, Ill.*

*Dear Madam,—Your letter of the 23d inst. is at hand. We do not sell single poems from the Leaflets in quantity, but we have published "The Building of the Ship" in a pamphlet with "Evangeline," and supply teachers with the same at the rate of fifteen cents per copy. There are notes to the poems, but no illustrations.*

*Yours truly,*
*Houghton, Mifflin & Co.*

I purposely copied the letter here in the original form; I hope this will remind you of the fact that "Your letter of the 23d inst. is at hand" is something that goes back to pre-typewriter days. It's time to stop furnishing your letters with this shabby antique.

Of course, people who have the souls of file clerks always say this stock opening is needed for filing purposes. But that's no argument: there's always room for a reference somewhere in a corner of the letter; and quite often it doesn't make a bit of difference to anybody who wrote what on what date. Mrs. Dawson didn't need to be told that Houghton Mifflin & Co. had "her

[ 57 ]

letter of the 23d inst. at hand"; she knew that before she opened the envelope.

There's been some progress since 1882, but not much. Before I started this chapter, I conducted a little survey: I went through my files and assembled all the answers I got when I asked for permissions to quote in my book *The Art of Plain Talk.* (I had written the same letter to about two dozen writers and publishers.) Result: two-thirds of the replies began by acknowledging my letter, one-third began by saying yes or no.

At one end of the scale was a letter from a textbook company that began like this:

> Dear Mr. Flesch:
> We have your letter of July 21 and note that it is your intention to include—in your book on modern English prose style, to be published by Harper & Brothers under the title THE ART OF PLAIN TALK—a few brief passages from our Wirth's THE DEVELOPMENT OF AMERICA.

After reading these fifty words, I knew exactly as much as before.

At the other end of the scale was the reply from the well-known writer on popular science, Mr. J. D. Ratcliff, who returned my letter with the following note on it:

> By all means.
> J. D. Ratcliff

Naturally, you can't always follow Mr. Ratcliff's method in your correspondence, but the basic principle is sound: say what you have to say, and then stop. Watch your letters perk up once you've thrown the acknowledgment phrase out the window.

Now let's look at newspaper reports. The trouble here is different—but not very different. They too start with an antique: the typical news lead is a Civil War relic. In those days the telegraph wasn't too reliable and war correspondents invented a writing technique that made the story look complete even if the wire service broke down in midstream. This is the famous 5-W lead: it tells Who, What, When, Where, and Why in the opening paragraph, then starts all over again and tells Who, What, When, Where, and Why in the next couple of paragraphs, then retraces its steps and goes into more details about Who, What, When, Where, and Why, and so on and on in a vicious circle.

Obviously this is an upside-down method of telling a story; newspapermen call it aptly the inverted-pyramid formula. But they still use it every day; and now that bad wire service isn't a good excuse any more, they rationalize some other way. For instance, they say this method is easy on the copyreader who wants to save space: he simply snitches the tail end off the inverted pyramid and the story still looks intact. True; but that would be a good reason for writing shorter stories rather than for crowding everything into one sentence at the top.

Here are a few gems from my newspaper lead collection:

> Fifteen unkempt Greek guerrillas who helped shell Salonika six weeks ago were executed by firing squads today as a clammy dawn routed the shadows from a sixth century citadel frowning down on the death scene. . . .

> China's Northwest and its unclimbed, unphotographed and unmeasured peaks of the Amne Machin mountains— which are believed to be the highest in the world—may yet place the country on the map as one of the major possessors of uranium should the hopes nursed by a group of American scientists be realized this month, when they plan to explore this range by air with special equipment designed to tell whether there is any of this precious metal deposit in the mountains. . . .

> After missing two of four preliminary questions and getting on the program in the first place by a partial misunder-

standing, a thirty-two-year-old Valley Stream, L. I., bride of six months won merchandise worth more than $17,000 at 9:45 o'clock last night by solving the "secret sentence" on the Columbia Broadcasting System program "Hit the Jackpot" in the C.B.S. Playhouse at 1697 Broadway, near Fifty-fourth Street. . . .

Does this sort of thing put the reader in the frame of mind for reading on? It does not. It puts him in the frame of mind for stopping right then and there and going on to the next item. Studies have shown that newspaper readers have a habit of nibbling at stories rather than reading them. Probably our crowded Civil-War-type lead sentence is the main reason.

On this front too there's some progress to report, however. Whether it's the competition from the radio, or the newsmagazines, or the newspapers' own drive toward more readability, the fact is that these monstrous leads are getting rarer. More and more openings now simply point out the significance of the story and prepare the reader's mind for details to come. Here are two such good examples from the same newspaper page:

> Wisconsin's restrictive legislation on oleomargarine was under fire today from one of the state's own dairy co-operatives.
>
> The Golden Guernsey Co-operative, consisting of milk producers and distributors, adopted a resolution . . .

And:

> Apparently it isn't very hard to fly a B-17.
>
> Two American sergeants who took an unauthorized 1,700-mile joy-ride in a Flying Fortress said today that they didn't have much trouble, although neither had ever been at the controls before.
>
> Master Sergeant Glen D. Woods, of Muncie, Ind., and Staff Sergeant Theodore S. Havens jr. of Washington, N.J.,

arrived here last night and took up residence in the guard-house . . .

Finally, let's take a look at the typical opening of that great American institution, the magazine short story. Fortunately, Mr. Jack Woodford, in his brilliant book *Writing and Selling*, has analyzed it for us. Here is what he tells the beginning writer: "Pick up the nearest 'slick-paper' magazine to hand and, opening to the first story written by one of the veteran trained seals of commercial fiction, note how the story begins with action and dialogue, continues on until the reader is firmly hooked, and then 'cuts back' to expository matter: the bringing up of background, atmosphere, characterization, etc. . . . You can always get a good start by, after you have written into the story, arbitrarily yanking out a good beginning somewhere and putting it at the start of the story. . . . Of course, many writers in the commercial fiction racket no longer have to use the middle of their stories as the beginning. Their names have become so widely acceptable that they can put the beginning where it belongs and leave it there; but that is a luxury which you will not be able to command for a long time to come . . ."

If you follow Mr. Woodford's suggestion and pick up the nearest slick-paper magazine, you will find that his analysis is right. But the magazine writers have gone him one better: they don't bother any more to yank a piece of dialogue out of the middle of the story. They now preface their stories with *any* old piece of dialogue, even if totally irrelevant. In fact, it's *apt* to be totally irrelevant. For example:

A few minutes before the train pulled into Back Bay, Sarah Affleck turned from the window and said aloud, "Its webs of living gauze no more unfurl; Wrecked is the ship of pearl!"

The man across the aisle looked up from his magazine. "Excuse me, madam?"

Almost as startled as he at the sound of her voice, Sarah

managed to smile composedly at him. "Nothing," she said. "Just a piece of a poem I happened to think of."

He nodded as if it were the usual thing for passengers on the New York-Boston train to speak suddenly in verse, and returned to his magazine. But a few minutes later, when the train slowed for South Station, he watched her with an inquisitive eye as she rose and got into her coat. It would make a neat story to tell at the office: "There was this woman, around thirty-five, I would say, sitting across the aisle from me, and just as we were getting into Back Bay, out of a clear sky she began reciting poetry. A little touched, maybe. You never can tell . . . The poetry? I can't remember. Something about a wrecked ship—a ship of pearl."

On her way from the train to the gate into South Station, Sarah Affleck tried to remember the name of the poem and who had written it, but she had forgotten it, forgotten everything except those two lines. Twenty-three years ago, when she was Sarah Bennet, nearly eleven years old . . .

And then the story starts. If you expect anything more about the fellow passenger, the poem, or the ship, you are mistaken: they were just gadgets to crank up the story.

Here's another example:

"The truth is," said Hilda at dinner, "if I'm going to be in something at all, I might as well be the head of it."

"You usually are," said Warren.

They smiled at each other with complete good humor. Two days before, Hilda had received a letter asking her co-operation in the annual Community Chest drive. She had called up to say yes indeed, they could count on her. And now, today, they had invited her to be chairman.

"I didn't give them a definite answer," she told Warren. "I said I'd have to talk to you about it. And I certainly won't take it if you don't want me to."

"Why on earth should I not want you to, darling?"

"Well, I don't know."

Hilda and Warren Parrish had been married for twelve years . . .

You think this story is going to be about the Community Chest drive? Of course not. Such a topic would be much too drab for the slicks. The story is about "The Woman Who Dreamed About Humphrey Bogart."

Naturally, as Mr. Woodford points out, this trick isn't often used in the higher literary brackets. But for the mass of current fiction it is standard equipment.

Let me hasten to add that there are plenty of exceptions. To cite one beautiful example, here is the beginning of a story ("Mr. Whitcomb's Genie" by Walter Brooks) which appeared in the *Saturday Evening Post*. The introduction does exactly what it should do: it points to the main theme and establishes the mood.

There was this old couple and their names were Mr. and Mrs. Jethro Whitcomb. They had a small farm up back in the hills with a few cows and some chickens and usually a pig. They sold most of the milk and eggs, but they smoked and pickled the pig. They had a garden and some fruit trees and every summer Mrs. Whitcomb put up three hundred cans of vegetables and fruit. So they always had plenty to eat and the milk and eggs brought them coffee and tea and flour and gas for the old truck. Of course they rolled up a total of working hours that would have put the average industrial worker on the ash heap in a couple of months. But it seemed a comfortable life to them, though naturally no fiesta.

This ends my indictment of standard openings. As I said, psychologically speaking, the opening should interest the reader, prepare his mind for what's going to follow, but not give away the show. The standard letter opening is dull, the standard news lead spills the beans, and the standard short story beginning is an arbitrarily dragged-in chunk of dialogue. And this in spite of the fact that every subject contains material for a good beginning: a striking fact, a vivid quotation, a question to the reader—anything that will serve to transform an indifferent stranger into an interested reader.

Standard endings are just as bad as standard beginnings. For a definition of a good ending, let's turn again to the psychologists' findings: they say that a good ending should echo the main theme, just as a good opening should sound it in advance. Or, according to the famous recipe of the legendary old Negro preacher: "First, tell 'em you're goin' to tell 'em; then tell 'em; then tell 'em you've tole 'em." In other words, a good ending ties everything together; a bad ending peters out.

In business letters, petering out is the most common fault. (I suspect that not one person in a thousand plans the ending of a business letter before he starts dictating.) And that unnatural inverted pyramid of the newspaper story peters out by definition. So here again, the accepted standard procedure is psychologically wrong.

With popular-magazine stories it is different though. They don't peter out but each has its neat happy ending. To be sure, there is a strong literary trend to make story endings too as psychologically unsatisfactory as is humanly possible, but so far popular-magazine editors have blocked it. As one of them recently wrote: "The literary sketch, the story with its conclusion implied (as developed by the *New Yorker*), and the reminiscence do not readily find acceptance." And that's that.

What it all comes down to is this. Good openings and endings don't just happen. And you can't produce them by applying mechanical rules either. The best way to convey your ideas to a reader is to plan carefully the beginning, middle, and end— sounding the main theme at the beginning, echoing it at the end, and developing it by natural steps in the middle. This is the point at which most textbooks go into pages and pages on how to make an outline, laying down rules and formulas and whatnot. I don't think anybody has ever profited from these rules. Usually they deal with Roman numerals and lower-case letters rather than writing.

There's nothing wrong with outlining. But if you have waited until your ideas have taken shape in your mind, chances are some sort of outline has already taken shape with them. All you have to do is "to follow your nose through to an outline," as Van Wyck Brooks put it. Once you have clearly focused on what you want to tell, you'll know the natural way of telling it too. Follow it, and your reader won't have much trouble.

If you don't follow the natural order of your subject, the result is invariably confusion. Take any book review section that's handy and look at the criticism of some novel with literary pretensions. You will usually find that the novelist has experimented with an artificial arrangement of his material instead of telling his story in natural chronological sequence. The critics, almost to a man, resent it. Why? Because anything with an unnatural pattern is hard to read. (Some time ago John Beecroft, of the Literary Guild, was asked whether he had any basic rule for his selection of bestsellers. "Yes," he answered. "Most readers don't like flashbacks.")

As an amusing instance, here is what Malcolm Cowley wrote about Thomas W. Duncan's novel *Gus the Great*:

> The movement is something like that of the frog jumping out of a well, in the old riddle. This time, however, the frog is out of the well when the story begins, and he has to fall in again by easy stages. On page 1 Gus Burgoyne is a man of sixty. He teeters there for a whole chapter; then his foot slips and he tumbles into the past.
>
> On page 23 Gus is a big, blustering man of forty. On page 65 he is a youngster of twenty-two, getting ahead in the news-

paper game. On page 80 he is only a gleam in his mother's naughty eye as she looks into a saloon and catches her first glimpse of his father.

He is born on page 97. "Ah," we say to ourselves, "the practice jumps are over now. The story will move ahead"—and it does move, for a time, until Gus is out of high school, on page 159, and is asking for a job on "The Tamarack Beacon." But on page 163 he is back in high school, president of the junior class, and on page 174 he is suddenly a little boy going to his first circus. It isn't until page 373, a little more than half way through the novel, that he is again a grown man owning and managing a circus of his own—*the* circus that we have been led to expect as the central theme of the novel.

And this kind of criticism isn't confined to the current crop of novels. In a recent book of literary criticism, the author blames Aldous Huxley for "compelling the reader to spend his time in trifling detective work" in *Eyeless in Gaza,* and takes Joseph Conrad to task for "puzzling the reader by the confusing sequence" of *Lord Jim.*

Mind you, I am not blaming the novelists for not always following the calendar arrangement. Sometimes another order may serve their purpose better. But if so, they should go out of their way to prepare the reader's mind very carefully for the shock of the unnatural order.

How does all this apply to nonfiction? you will ask. The answer is clear: whenever you can, present a series of events in chronological order; and where there is no story to tell, follow at least the most natural development of the subject.

Some time ago, the newspapers provided a perfect demonstration of all I have said in this chapter. In the fall of 1947, the *New York Herald Tribune* carried this obit—complete with 5-W lead and petering-out inverted pyramid:

NEWARK, N.J., Oct. 16.—Dr. Vivian Inez Douglas, twenty-seven, of 130 South Fourteenth Street, who was to have become the first woman doctor at Lincoln Hospital, Durham, N.C., died Tuesday at the Newark Eye and Ear Infirmary, a death certificate disclosed when it was filed today.

Dr. Douglas, a Negro, had dreamed of entering the medical profession since she was a small girl. She received her medical degree last June from Meharry University School of Medicine, Nashville, Tenn., and never practiced.

Dr. Douglas was to have begun her internship at Lincoln Hospital this summer but she contracted spinal meningitis just before she was graduated from Meharry.

Dr. Douglas was born in Newark and educated in public schools. She attended Newark University evenings for a year and was graduated from Fisk University in Nashville.

She was an only child and her father, Elijah Douglas, a shipyard worker, took odd jobs to make extra money to help her. Her parents and her grandmother, Mrs. Jeannette Watson, survive.

A reporter on another paper, Mr. Jay Nelson Tuck, saw what could be done with this story if it was told as it should be told— with a beginning, middle, and end. His version appeared that same afternoon (October 17, 1947) on the front page of the *New York Post*:

> Under the best of conditions, it's hard enough for a student to obtain a medical degree. Imagine, then, how the difficulties are multiplied if the student has to face additionally the triple barrier of poverty, sex prejudice and race prejudice.
>
> That's what Vivian Inez Douglas was up against. She worked as a receptionist for Dr. Hutchins F. Inge of Newark, studying books in every spare moment and studying at the University at Newark at night.

Her parents, Mr. and Mrs. Elijah Douglas of 130 S. 14th St., Newark, made every sacrifice for her. Mrs. Douglas worked as a house servant at backbreaking domestic labor. Douglas was a shipyard laborer and besides that he shoveled snow, drove a truck, did anything he could to earn another dollar to pay his daughter's medical education.

Dr. Inge said the girl herself couldn't ever have slept much, what with doing his work, attending evening classes and studying through most of the night. In spite of that, he said, she was always pleasant and jolly, and was popular with his patients. She went on to Meharry University, Nashville, Tenn.

Inch by painful inch, she moved nearer to her degree of M.D. But last spring, the blow fell.

Vivian, 27, was stricken with spinal meningitis. Even that could not stop her.

In her bed at Hubbard Hospital, Meharry University, she continued her studies, received her M.D. degree and learned of her appointment to an internship at Lincoln Hospital, Durham, N.C., where she was to be the first woman physician.

Then her condition grew worse and she was transferred to the Newark Eye and Ear Infirmary.

There, last Tuesday, Dr. Vivian Inez Douglas, a Negro, died.


PS

This is the chapter where I made a mistake. I underrated the value of the spill-the-beans newspaper opening.

Let's look once more at business letters and news reports. Sure enough, the old-style business letter—with its standard "your letter of . . ." opening—is hopelessly old-fashioned. That much is clear. But how should it be changed? Answer: by using the example of the spill-the-beans, inverted-pyramid news report.

Start your letter with the main item of information and you can't go wrong.

The upside-down newspaper story is here to stay. As I said 25 years ago, this doesn't mean that monster 5-W lead sentences are a good thing. They were getting rarer then and they're actually hard to find now. But the principle of spilling the beans stands. Examples of those snappier-type leads I mentioned on page 60 can now be found in any newspaper any day. For instance:

> Auto theft is decreasing across the country.
> Statistics for 1972 that will be released by the FBI later this month will show . . .

> The White House admitted today that it had erred. The error will not shake the Republic but it cost a retired colonel more than $10,000 a year and the Administration a bit of face.
> Here is what happened: . . .

> Can the sane be distinguished from the insane in psychiatric hospitals?
> Eight individuals decided to find out. Each feigned symptoms of mental instability and was admitted to a mental hospital. The result: doctors labeled them as schizophrenics despite their best efforts to convince the hospital staff of their sanity.
> Results of this three-year experiment appear in the latest issue of *Science* . . .

The inverted-pyramid newspaper story can and should be used as a model for any kind of writing—business letters, memos, reports, factual material of any kind. Start with a brief spill-the-beans lead and follow it up with more and more details, in descending order of importance. When you've said what you wanted to say, stop. (I was also wrong in recommending prepared, elaborately summarizing endings.) Here's a typical example of such a story (from the *New York Times,* March 3, 1973): *

The granddaughter of an 83-year-old widow murdered on the Upper East Side last week was arrested yesterday and charged with homicide.

The 24-year-old suspect, like two others previously accused in the slaying, was described by the police as a narcotics addict.

The victim, Mrs. Mary Hample, was found dead in her apartment in a housing project at 405 East 92d Street on Feb. 22. The police said her throat had been slashed and $1,400 and a jewelry box had been taken from the apartment.

Yesterday's arrest was that of Jeannette Hample of 1581 First Avenue, granddaughter of the victim and, according to the police, niece of Mrs. Charles Hample, the victim's daughter-in-law, who found the body while making a customary daily visit.

Previously charged were Catherine Thorne, 26, roommate of Miss Hample, and Alfred Ernest, 34, of 437 East 82d Street. The police said that all three suspects had narcotics records and that Mr. Ernest also had a previous record of arrests on assault, forgery and weapons charges.

Homicide detectives reported that the victim had kept $1,400 in cash in her home as an emergency fund, a circumstance they said was known to the suspects, who, the detectives contended, duped her into admitting them to the apartment and then attacked her.

The money and the murder weapon—a knife—have not been recovered, the police said. But scuba divers of the Police Department last Wednesday found the discarded jewelry box at the bottom of the East River, off the 92d Street pier.

* © 1973 by the New York Times Company. Reprinted by permission.

Never mind some of the language, which could have been improved by following the rules given in this book. But study the organization. The story starts with a lead paragraph telling nothing but that the girl was arrested for killing her own grandmother and that the grandmother was 83 years old. The names, the addresses, the details of the crime—all that is left for later. What matters most, and what makes it a newsworthy story, is the murder of an old woman by her own granddaughter.

The exact details follow, in the order of less and less interest. First the girl's age and the fact that she was a drug addict. Next, how the murder was done and how much was taken. Next, the girl's name, her address, her two accomplices' names and addresses. Next, how they got into the apartment. Finally, the empty box at the bottom of the river.

This is the way factual writing is organized today. Follow this model in your own writing.

## CHAPTER 7

# HOW TO BE HUMAN THOUGH FACTUAL

---

*Don't write about Man, write about a man.*

E. B. WHITE

---

O NLY stories are really readable.

Some time before I started to write this book, I asked one of the *Reader's Digest* editors how they came by their easy, readable style. There was no special recipe, he said; they just naturally wrote—or edited—that way. But he added something else that was far more revealing. "Whenever we want to draw attention to a problem," he said, "we wait until somebody does something about it. Then we print the story of how he did it."

I also asked *Time* magazine about *its* readability formula. Again, I didn't get much of an answer. "Writers are instructed," I was informed, "to make their stories as complete, as readable, and as interesting as possible. Of course, the language of *Time* is the idiom of American speech. We try to render concrete, vivid, and human all the events on which we report, and consistent with that effort is the clear language of a spoken idiom." A little later, however, in *Time*'s twenty-fifth anniversary issue, I got a much clearer answer in print: "The basis of good *Time* writing is narrative, and the basis of good narrative is to tell events (1) in the order in which they occur; (2) in the form in which an observer might have seen them—so that readers can imagine themselves on the scene. A *Time* story must be completely organized from beginning to end; it must go from nowhere to somewhere and sit down when it arrives."

And that's the secret of America's two largest factual maga-

[ 72 ]

zines: they print stories. Why? Because only stories are really readable.

Let's see how this works. Let's take a news story at random and see what happens to it when it appears in *Time*. Here's the *New York Times* report on the famous Supreme Court decision on anti-Negro real-estate covenants:

> WASHINGTON, May 3 [1948]—Covenants to bar Negroes or other racial groups from owning real estate were held legally unenforceable by a 6 to 0 ruling in the Supreme Court today.
>
> Chief Justice Fred M. Vinson handed down two opinions advancing the long fight made by Negroes against such covenants and against their enforcement by courts in the states and federal territory.
>
> One of the opinions, neither of which prohibited the making of such agreements, dealt with cases arising in Missouri and Michigan, while the other originated in the District of Columbia.
>
> The state court issue was decided on that part of the Fourteenth Amendment to the Constitution that forbids any state to deny to any person within its jurisdiction the equal protection of the laws. . . .

And here is *Time*'s story:

*A House With a Yard*

During World War II, tall, stringy J. D. Shelley made good money as a construction worker. His wife Ethel Lee had a job as a maid. Like many other Negro families, the Shelleys scraped and pinched to get every possible nickel into the bank. They had six children. They lived in a savage St. Louis slum, and they ached for quiet, decency and a home of their own.

They finally found it—a two-story house of rust-colored

brick on the border between white and Negro districts in mid-St. Louis. The place was 50 years old, but it had a lawn and stood on a quiet, elm-shaded street. They made a down payment, signed a mortgage and moved in one day in October 1945. That evening a process server notified them that they had been sued by a white neighbor. The neighbor wanted to throw them out.

Then the Shelleys discovered that their house was covered by a restrictive real-estate covenant which a "neighborhood improvement association" had drawn up in 1911. It prohibited any owner from selling it to a Negro.

The Shelleys were not surprised. Like every Negro, like Jews, Chinese, Mexicans and those of many another racial group in the U.S., they had lived their lives behind opaque, flint-hard walls of prejudice. But they could not bear the idea of going back to the noisome streets they had left behind. They went to their minister and asked for help.

They got it. A Negro attorney agreed to represent them. Their church, Negro real-estate dealers and the American Civil Liberties Union contributed money. The National Association for the Advancement of Colored People incorporated their case into a pool of similar cases from all over the nation. With mingled hope, doubt and embarrassment, the Shelleys suddenly found themselves one of the spearheads of a great legal battle.

They won their case in St. Louis' circuit court, but the Missouri supreme court reversed the decision. Finally the Shelleys' case went to the Supreme Court of the United States, to be considered with those of two other families from Washington, D.C. and Detroit.

Last week Chief Justice Vinson delivered the opinion of the court. Its essence: restrictive real-estate covenants are lawful—as private agreements—but under the terms of the 14th Amendment and the Civil Rights Act of 1866 they cannot be enforced by either state or federal courts. Without doubt, this was a momentous decision in U.S. judicial history. It would set off no violent upheaval in the pattern of city life. But it removed one of the weapons by which segregation is enforced, and would give the Negro an increasingly better chance to make a decent life for himself.

Said Mrs. Shelley, when she heard that she could keep her house: "My little soul is overjoyed. Wait till I get by myself. I'll tell the Lord of my thankfulness."

Of course, the story principle has been used by popularizers for a long time. For instance, ever since De Kruif's *Microbe Hunters*, science has been explained to laymen in the form of dramatized stories. A typical article on science in the *Saturday Evening Post* starts like this:

> The story begins with the flutter of butterfly wings in the laboratory of Dr. Frederick Gowland Hopkins, who later carried out pioneer dietary studies which earned him a knighthood, the Nobel prize in medicine and the title of "father of the vitamin theory." But in 1889 Hopkins was simply a young research fellow at Guy's Hospital, London, eager to learn the chemical make-up of some of nature's wonders. Dabbling one day with the wings of several dozen brimstone butterflies, he found that the yellow color washed off and dissolved in hot water. After concentrating the pigment, he analyzed it, noted its chemical resemblance to uric acid, and made his discovery the subject of his first research paper.

> The butterfly report gathered dust for the next thirty years, while Doctor Hopkins and the vitamin theory gathered momentum without their benefit. Then, in 1925, a German scientist, Dr. Heinrich Wieland, who later won the Nobel prize in chemistry, picked up the pigment again . . .

If you think that this method of writing about science isn't respectable—a sort of cheap, undignified trick—then I recommend to you the study of the book *On Understanding Science* by James B. Conant. The book was published by the Yale University Press; its author was president of Harvard, no less. Understanding science, the book says, is a matter of understanding highlights of scientific history; therefore, science education should rely on the case study method. Dr. Conant seems to think that this method of approaching science is rather novel; but it certainly isn't novel to anyone who has ever read an article about science in a popular magazine. In his examples, Dr. Conant mentions such things as the twitching of a frog's leg in Galvani's laboratory; in the *Saturday Evening Post* it's the flutter of butterfly wings in the laboratory of Dr. Hopkins.

All of which goes to show that factual exposition is done best by story-telling. If you want to convey information effectively, you'd better make sure of characters, drama, conflict, a plot, and a denouement.

There's nothing on earth that cannot be told through a hero— or heroine—who's trying to solve a problem in spite of a series of obstacles. It's the classic formula; and it's the only one you can rely on to interest the average reader.

Most subjects have obvious stories and plots, ready for use. The scientist who struggles for a solution, the practical man who is trying to lick a problem, the little fellow who is the living example of an abstract idea—all these make natural fact-stories. Journalists write that sort of thing every day. Sometimes the method is tremendously effective: John Hersey made Americans understand the meaning of the atomic bomb by writing about half a dozen people who lived through Hiroshima.

But what do you do if there simply is no human-interest story connected with the subject? Give up? Present the bare, dry facts and let it go at that? Not at all. If there are no people visible on the scene, it's your business to put them there. If there's no story to tell, you'll have to invent one.

Now you will say that some things don't lend themselves to

fictional treatment, that some subjects are too serious anyway, that the story method is apt to distort the facts. But it all depends. There are degrees of humanizing; even a little often goes a long way.

The historian Arnold J. Toynbee, for instance, can hardly be accused of overshooting the mark as a popularizer. But here and there the scholarly pages of his *Study of History* are enlivened by something like this:

> In the middle of the seventeenth century, when [the English, the Dutch, the French, and the Spaniards] had found their first footing on the fringes of the American mainland, it would have been easy to predict the coming conflict between them for the possession of the interior, but the most farsighted observer then alive would not have been likely to hit the mark if he had been asked, in 1650, to pick the winner . . . "France," he might have said, "seems likely to be the winner . . ."
>
> Let us suppose that our imaginary observer lives to see the turn of the century. By 1701 he will be congratulating himself on having rated French prospects higher than Dutch . . .
>
> Shall we endow our observer with superhuman length of life, in order that he may review the situation once more in the year 1803? If we preserve him alive till then, he will be forced to confess that his wits have not been worthy of his longevity. By the end of 1803 the French flag has disappeared off the political map of North America altogether . . .

This little by-play isn't an exciting human-interest story, I'll admit. But it does help. For comparison, here is an example from a first-rate popularizer, George Gamow, who is tackling the driest of all subjects, statistics:

> In order to understand [the Law of Statistical Behavior] let us turn our attention to the famous problem of a "Drunk-

[ 77 ]

ard's Walk." Suppose we watch a drunkard who has been leaning against a lamp post in the middle of a large paved city square (nobody knows how and when he got there) and then has suddenly decided to go nowhere in particular. Thus off he goes, making a few steps in one direction, then some more steps in another, and so on and so on, changing his course every few steps in an entirely unpredictable way. How far will be our drunkard from the lamp post after he has executed, say, a hundred phases of his irregular zigzag journey? One would at first think that, because of the unpredictability of each turn, there is no way of answering this question. If, however, we consider the problem more attentively . . .

And then follows the best explanation of statistical reasoning that I have ever found anywhere.

Or, for another example, here is a top-notch advertising man who knows that human interest has a place even in selling neckties:

> White men's settlements began, here in the mountains of New Mexico, before the Pilgrims ever set foot on Plymouth Rock.
>
> Coming up from Old Mexico, at the beginning of the 17th century, these Spanish settlers found fertile little mountain valleys, watered by rushing streams, surrounded by timbered slopes, and by grassy mountain meadows which would support large flocks of sheep . . .
>
> Spinning, dyeing, and weaving of wool became part of the activities around every big *hacienda*. The dyes were there— ready to be yielded by native plants, as neighboring Pueblo Indians showed them. With these dyes and a vast colorful landscape and skies to learn from, these people became natural artists.
>
> These are the people whose weavers continue to this day

to use their skill with wool, with colors, and with hand-weaving to produce for me such ties as I show you here . . .

There's one flaw, however, in all these examples: the people mentioned don't have names. Yet nothing adds more realism to a story than names; nothing is as unrealistic as anonymity. Imagine a story whose hero has no name! If you ever read Franz Kafka's nightmarish novels about "K.", you will know what namelessness does to a story.

So name your characters. Don't just call them A, B, C, like a textbook in elementary algebra, and don't call them John Doe or Joe Doakes either. Such names are *almost* mathematical symbols by now. Give your characters real-sounding names—names they could or might have in real life. Advertising copy writers know well how to do this naturally:

> Take the case of the family I'll call the Martins. Ted Martin had read item after item about school kids getting into trouble. Ted didn't like that sort of thing in the city where he was raising a son. And when he read one more story of a school boy in a jam, he exploded.
>
> "Confound it," he roared, "why doesn't somebody *do* something about this? Why aren't these kids kept busy at decent things?"
>
> So Jimmy said, "There *is* a boy's clubhouse, Dad. But it's dying on its feet . . ."

You see how simple it is? After a few sentences "the family I'll call the Martins" doesn't sound artificial at all.

Of course, if you want to have some fun, you don't need to stick to "possible" names like Ted and Jimmy Martin, but you can let the names help tell the story. If your story illustrates the workings of accident insurance, you might call the victim of the accident Mr. Hardluck; if your topic is installment buying, you might write about Mr. and Mrs. Weekly. A well-known example is Emily Post's famous book on etiquette, which contains a whole cast of characters named Mr. and Mrs. Worldly, Bobo Gilding and Lucy Gilding (née Wellborn), Colonel Bluffington, Hector Newman, old Mrs. Toplofty, Jim Smartlington, Clubwin Doe, Mr. and Mrs. Kindhart, Grace Smalltalk, and so on and so on. Symbolic names are, in fact, one of the most ancient literary devices: in the commentaries on Roman Law the creditor (plaintiff) was traditionally called Aulus Agerius, the debtor (defendant) Numerius Negidius—names that, to Romans, must have sounded like Randolph Richfield and Peter Paynix.

Psychologically speaking, the main character in your story should be someone the reader can identify with. So maybe the best name for the hero of your story is simply "you." That again is an old, old trick; it can put life into practically anything. Even an abstruse topic like reciprocal trade agreements can be made clear and interesting with it. Here is proof (by James Marlow of the Associated Press):

> If you're a housewife or clerk it's hard to think of "foreign trade" as something that affects you.
>
> But it does, sooner or later, because a lot of our prosperity, and world prosperity, is wrapped up in foreign trade.
>
> If you are an American businessman or farmer, with things to sell here or abroad, foreign trade affects you directly.
>
> And now once more, as in other years, Democrats and Republicans are quarreling over the way we handle our foreign trade.
>
> The root of the argument goes deep. But it is not hard to understand if you look back a bit into American history. Here's the background:
>
> You made shoes. A man in France made shoes. He was able to sell his shoes here cheaper than you. He was ruining you.

[ 80 ]

You appealed to our government for help. The government set up a tariff to protect you from the foreign competition.

Which meant: there was a tariff or duty or tax on every one of the Frenchman's shoes coming in here for sale.

If that tariff was high enough, he'd have to sell his shoes here at a higher price than yours, if he wanted to make a profit.

So you got a break, called tariff-protection, because the tariff put him at a disadvantage in selling in this country. That's an old story . . .

"Humanizing" doesn't even stop with the human race. Animals have been characters of stories ever since Aesop's fables. It's still a handy device for all sorts of purposes. The Army fought malaria with a little booklet about Ann, the anopheles mosquito; Alabama spreads health information with a pamphlet about Hubert Hookworm. And there's always the possibility of personifying *things*. After all, we do speak of a car, a train, a ship as "she." Why not go a step further and breathe life into other things? *Time* magazine once explained its punchcard system to subscribers by telling them about machines with such names as Choosey, Tabby, and Clinky.

So there is a human-interest story in everything. And if you make use of that story, your piece of writing will be full of names and personal pronouns like *he* and *she* (or *I* and *you* if you use yourself or the reader as "characters"). This makes a simple yardstick for the human interest you have managed to get into your writing. If you want to measure it, here is what you do:

Count all personal names in your text. Then count all personal pronouns (except the *its* and *theys* that don't refer to people). Next, count all masculine and feminine words like *uncle* or *spinster* (but not masculine *or* feminine words like *teacher* or *employee*). Finally, for good measure, count the two words *people*

[ 81 ]

and *folks*. Altogether, the percentage of these words (their number per hundred words of text) will give you a fairly good human-interest yardstick. In a dull scientific treatise the percentage may drop to zero, in a lively novel it may be over twenty (every fifth word a reference to a character). In good, readable nonfiction (say, *Time* or the *Reader's Digest*) it's usually around six or eight.

"An abstract style," said the French philosopher Alain, "is always bad. Your sentences should be full of stones, metals, chairs, tables, animals, men, and women."

PS

Since I wrote this chapter, the technique of explaining difficult subjects through little human stories has become almost routine. Every newspaper reporter worth his salt knows he must fill his reports with examples, practical applications, things that happened to *people*.

In the winter of 1973 food prices went sky-high and both the *New York Times* and the *Wall Street Journal* ran stories about it. The one in the *Wall Street Journal* (February 28, 1973) opened like this:

> An elderly man and his wife shake their heads as they rummage through the margarine cooler in a Dallas supermarket to find the cheapest brand. In DeKalb, Ill., a young mother meticulously maps the floor plans of four supermarkets so she can zip in and out to buy just the items she wants and not be tempted by more appealing and more expensive foods.
>
> And in Atlanta, Mrs. Winnie McPhedran calls a family conference and announces to her husband and four sons: "Either we change how we eat or change how we live. If you want to keep on eating the way you have been, we will have to sell the boat."

[ 82 ]

Five days later, the *New York Times* (March 5, 1973) echoed:

> In Mineola, L.I., a well-to-do orthodontist served fried chicken at a dinner party last week after discovering that his first choice, filet of sole, was up to $3.60 a pound.
>
> On the Upper West Side, two elderly women burst into tears when they saw the prices at their supermarket's meat counter.
>
> In Forest Hills, Queens, two women chipped in to buy a side of beef because, they said, it was the only way they could afford to get shell steaks.
>
> In White Plains, a housewife who used to do all her marketing at one supermarket now spends an hour going from shopping center to shopping center, searching out the advertised "specials."
>
> In the Bedford-Stuyvesant section of Brooklyn, a machinist decided that with ground beef at $1.29 a pound, he might have to start getting his protein from cereal.

As you see, the two reporters not only used exactly the same approach, but even the same technique in showing the general nature of the problem. With their small samples, they included old people (in Dallas, on the Upper West Side), a housewife (in DeKalb, Ill., and in White Plains), a man (again in Dallas and in Brooklyn) and a well-to-do family (the Mineola orthodontist and the McPhedrans of Atlanta who own a boat).

Naturally, both reports were based on the same government statistics, but both reporters instinctively felt the story could only be told by way of real people, young and old, rich and poor, male and female, confronted with the problem in their own daily lives.

## CHAPTER 8

# DRAMA IN EVERYDAY PROSE

*Honest John Bunyan was the first that I know of who mixed narration and dialogue,—a method of writing very engaging to the reader who in the most interesting parts finds himself, as it were, brought into the company and present at the discourse.*

BENJAMIN FRANKLIN

THERE were many more questions Mr. Bannerman wanted to ask the insurance agent. He leaned forward and said: "Does the contract have value if I die before retirement?"

The agent, Mr. Fitzsimmons, nodded. "Yes. The full accumulation, as explained in my answers twelve and thirteen, will be paid as an equivalent income to the beneficiary you have named. A lump sum will be paid if an estate is the payee."

This seemed to satisfy Mr. Bannerman. "Are there various income options for the death benefit?" he asked, with unflagging interest.

Mr. Fitzsimmons was prepared for that one. "Yes," he said and continued smoothly: "You or your beneficiary may elect one of the following income options: one, an annuity payable during the lifetime of the beneficiary with payments ceasing at death; or, two, installments for ten or twenty years, as elected, and if the beneficiary survives such a period, continuing thereafter during the lifetime of the beneficiary. Three, a series of installments for a fixed period as elected."

Mr. Fitzsimmons seemed pleased with himself, but Mr. Bannerman didn't seem to respond to the explanation. Instead, he was ready with another question: "Does the annuity contract help out in my life insurance program?"

Without the slightest hesitation, Mr. Fitzsimmons replied: "Yes. The full accumulation payable as a death benefit is small in early years but as premium payments are continued and as interest accumulates the death benefit in later years may become quite substantial and a valuable part of your estate."

Mr. Fitzsimmons smiled encouragingly. But Mr. Bannerman stonily fired his next question: "Does this affect the type of life insurance I need?" . . .

In case you haven't already guessed it, you have just read a typical piece of Q-and-A booklet conversation. (I've always wondered what it would look like written out, and so I sat down and did it. You'll admit it looks awfully silly.)

The basic idea of the Q-and-A booklet is sound. The trouble lies with the Q-and-A writer's method. Usually, what he does is this: he takes the prepared information and carves it up into medium-sized chunks, each of which he labels "A." Then he wedges between these chunks little questions that are really nothing but Edgar Bergen's cues for Charlie McCarthy's answers. These he labels "Q.", and there you are.

Unfortunately, the result doesn't read like any dialogue anyone ever listened to. People are not ready with answers in smooth, well-rounded sentences; and most of the questions people ask are uncertain even in their phrasing. The typical Q-and-A booklet isn't effective because you can tell from miles away that its conversational tone is faked.

Genuine dialogue is the most readable thing there is. Everybody knows that. Let me quote just two witnesses, 3,000 miles and a generation apart. Benjamin Sherbow, an American typographer, wrote in 1916: "Have you ever watched people at a library selecting books for home reading? Other things being equal, if they see enough pages that promise interesting dialogue, they are much more apt to put the book under their arm and walk away with it, than if they see too many solid pages, which always suggest hard work." And in 1947 Phyllis Bentley, a

[ 85 ]

British novelist, wrote this: " 'What is the use of a book without pictures or conversations?' thought Alice just before the White Rabbit ran by, in condemnation of the book her sister was reading, and this childish comment is supported by novel-readers of all degrees of intelligence. Long close paragraphs of print are in themselves apt to dismay the less serious readers and their instinct here is a sound one, for an excess of summary and an insufficiency of scene in a novel makes the story seem remote, without bite, second-hand . . . A great part of the vigour, the vivacity and the readability of Dickens derives from his innumerable interweavings of scene and summary; his general method is to keep summary to the barest essential minimum, a mere sentence or two here and there between the incredibly fertile burgeoning of his scenes."

Naturally, dialogue is the fiction writer's stock in trade. But well-handled dialogue can be amazingly useful in nonfiction too. It's a splendid tool in explaining almost anything: soil erosion, philosophy or income taxes. Let me show you:

From a U.S. Soil Conservation Service pamphlet:

> When we got the map that day, I remember a curious kind of expression coming over Camilo's face. He said, "That's what I have wanted for this farm for a long while." And then almost in the same breath, "But we'll never get it done on the land, I'm afraid."
>
> "Why?" someone asked him. "You like the idea. Perhaps John will, too."
>
> "Sure, I know perfectly well we have washes on this farm. I know we ought to stop them. And see," he said, pointing to the map, "they suggest we put trees in that corner . . . and over here, bad spots to plow! It's good, this map. But John will think he can't afford to follow it." . . .

From a book about philosophy by Irwin Edman:

> "Mr. Jeremy," I say without preamble, "I suppose you believe you exist."

Young Jeremy looks at me quizzically. I feel he is wondering if this is what professors of philosophy are paid to do.

"Of course I exist," he says, and I detect the slightest tone of impatience in his courteous and somewhat surprised tone.

"What makes you so sure?" I ask.

The large football player in the second row shifts his bulk impatiently in the seat too small for him, as if suddenly wondering what is going on here.

"Well," says Jeremy, "it's me. I mean I. I brought myself in here." The class smiles a little at that.

"How do you know it's you?" I say.

"I can pinch myself," he says. The football player does that very thing. Then he pinches his neighbor. I tap warningly on the table with a piece of chalk.

"I can feel my hands if I press them hard and I have a pain in the crick of my neck."

"You mean you have sensations," I say. "But how do you know they're yours?"

"Well, whose else would they be?" asks Jeremy in great surprise.

"But who are you?" I insist. "Simply this cluster of sensations at the present moment?"

From a lawyer's newsletter on taxes:

## DEDUCTION FOR DEFERRED PAY

Section 23 (a) of the Internal Revenue Code seems clear enough to most people. It allows an income tax deduction for—

"All the ordinary and necessary expenses paid or incurred during the taxable year in carrying on any trade or business, including a reasonable allowance for salaries or other compensation for personal service actually rendered."

But there's a controversy over what that language means. In down-to-earth talk, here's the argument:

[ 87 ]

*Employer:* "I want a deduction for large sums I am irrevocably putting away for employees' retirement annuities and for contributions to a profit-sharing fund. True, each employee's right is forfeitable and he cannot be sure of getting anything until he has performed services in the future, but I can never get anything back."

*Tax Court:* "No, the law sets up *special* requirements as to deductions for deferred pay, but first you've got to get by the *general* section—23 (a). You have not paid, as Sec. 23 (a) requires, anything as 'compensation for services actually rendered.' It's compensation, all right, but it's for *future* services—to induce the employees to stay on the job."

*Employer:* "Maybe. But I'm not insisting it's compensation. Let's just say it's an 'ordinary and necessary expense' of business. If it is, then it's deductible. At least, that's the way I read section 23 (a)."

*Tax Court:* "No. If the payment is 'compensation'—and it is—it can't be deducted unless it is for services actually rendered."

*Employer:* "I'll leave it to the Circuit Court."

*Circuit Court:* "The employer is right. The payment is 'necessary' in the company's business and is an 'ordinary' means of operating profitably in a period of labor unrest. Therefore, it's deductible as an ordinary and necessary expense and it's not necessary to decide whether or not it's compensation."

*Tax Court:* "We are compelled to settle this employer's taxes as the Circuit Court directs. But we still think we were right and we will deny the deduction to other employers in like situations."

Now of course you will say that you can't turn everything into dialogue. There must be a limit to this form of presentation. How much dialogue will factual writing stand?

[ 88 ]

The answer to this question will surprise you. If you analyze a random collection of well-written popular magazine articles, for instance, you will find that most of them are shot through and through with snatches of conversation and bits of direct quotation from what was *said*. The seasoned popular nonfiction writer knows that to interest his readers he must not only turn most of his material into narrative, but must then go one step further and turn a large part of that narrative into dialogue. All exposition needs some story; all needs some drama.

To make this graphically clear to you, I took a fairly typical article from the *Reader's Digest*, which I am going to reprint here in full. I made no changes except to print all direct quotations (dialogue) in *italics*. You can see at a glance that the writer has used dialogue to tell about half his story. In fact, I worked out the exact ratio. The dialogue amounts to 48 percent of the sentences.

## LET'S HELP THEM MARRY YOUNG
### by Howard Whitman

I'd hate to be 22, and in love, these days. *How could I support a bride? How could I find a place to live? How could I train for a profession—in a day when more and more training is essential?*

Without financial help I couldn't.

That is the spot thousands of young Americans are in today. *"I'll have a gray beard by the time I'm able to marry," says Hal Smith.* Hal makes $30 a week in a gas station. *"Marriage is a luxury we can't afford," remarks Jean Foster, whose boy friend is a medical student.*

The case for making marriage available to hundreds of thousands of the blocked generation is not built on sentiment: it is a serious business of saving young people from frustration, of preserving the American home, of stemming the tidal waves of promiscuity, delinquency and divorce.

[ 89 ]

We surround boys and girls in their late teens and early twenties with ideals of marriage and home building. We admit that our Hal Smiths and Jean Fosters are biologically mature, that they possess growing and compelling urges toward mating and parenthood. We lure them toward marriage in our movies, our fiction, in the whole romantic gloss with which we daub youthful life. *Then we snatch away this illusion with: "Don't be a fool, Alice. It's ridiculous to marry a boy who's making only $30 a week!" Or, "Out of the question, Ned. You can't marry until you've finished your internship!"*

The result is a sexual dilemma. Psychiatrists' offices teem with men and women suffering from guilt complexes because they indulged in premarital sex relations, and with equal numbers who are frigid or impotent because they were too long repressed.

From the files of Dr. Janet Fowler Nelson come these case histories:

Tom and Lillian were in love and wanted to marry, but couldn't because Tom, an architect, was working out his apprenticeship at $28 a week. Faced with a wait of five years or more, Tom and Lillian realized that they had to make a decision. Either they would (1) have extramarital relations, thus breaking the rules of society, or (2) stifle their emotional and physical drives, with the resultant frustration. They chose the first alternative.

*When they finally married, Lillian was oppressed with the fear that "Tom only married me because he thought he ought to," and Tom unhappily remarked, "If she was that way with me, maybe she'd be the same with any man."*

Equally bitter is the case of conscientious Arthur and Margaret, who chose the second alternative. Margaret's parents refused to allow her to marry until she had a college diploma and had taught school for at least a year. She and

Arthur "went steady" from the time she was 19 until she was 23. Then they were married. A few years later Margaret was in Dr. Nelson's office relating a sorrowful story of their failure to reach mature sexual adjustment. *"You see,"* *Margaret said, "we ruled out all petting before we were* *married. We knew that was the only way to keep out of* *difficulty. I suppose it was puritanical, but anyway we prided* *ourselves on never showing any signs of physical affection."*

Arthur and Margaret had fallen into a familiar trap. They had reined in their impulses by labeling them evil and tawdry. *"This carried over into their married life and com-* *pletely blocked a happy adjustment," Dr. Nelson explains.*

If we gave young people hope that they could marry at 20 or 22, they could cope with their growing urges. *"Early* *marriage," declares Dr. James F. Bender, director of the Na-* *tional Institute for Human Relations, "leads to far better* *marriage adjustment both physically and psychologically.* *The cases of incompatibility which come to my office are* *not the couples who married early but the late-marrieds who* *are crippled by stunted and repressed emotions or by previous* *furtive experiences."*

Promiscuity, sociologists agree, is the greatest foe of successful marriage. But a YMCA poll among men in their early 20's indicated not only that extramarital relations were "greatly increasing" but that 80 percent of the young men blamed financial bars against early marriage for the upward trend.

Our communities, up to their necks in delinquency, scream alarm at the number of wayward girls, young sex offenders, unmarried mothers. *"Yet what is this," asks Will* *C. Turnbladh, of the National Probation Association, "but* *an indication of the stone wall many young people are up* *against?"*

Early marriage is not merely a check against evils. It has

plentiful assets of its own. In a veterans' housing project in New York City, I visited a number of young couples. Isaac Bardavid, a veteran of three years in the Pacific, and his wife, Charlotte, were married four years ago when she was 18 and he 21. *"It's given us a chance to grow up and develop together,"* Charlotte said. *"We feel we understand each other much better than we would if we had married four or five years later."*

*"And I can tell you this,"* Isaac put in. *"Together we've got more courage to face the future than we'd ever have separately. Being a married man—with one child already and another on the way—I'm sure I'm a much better citizen than if I were single. I work harder. I have a bank account for the first time in my life. I plan for the future. I know if I were single today, I'd be running around, staying up until all hours, getting nowhere fast."*

A neighbor, Paul Malone, didn't marry until he was 33, two years ago. *"But I didn't wait through choice,"* he said. *"I was stopped twice, once by the depression, once by the war."* He glanced at six-month-old Billy, playing on the floor. *"The trouble is, I'll be 50 by the time he's 15. It's much better for kids to have young parents. If I had my own choice in the matter, believe me, I'd marry young!"*

*But do young marriages stick?*

In New York's Home Term Court, where hundreds of problems in family living come before Magistrate Anna M. Kross, cases repeatedly bear out the strength of early marriage. *"I often advise young people to get married,"* Judge Kross declares. *"The idea of waiting for 'better jobs' or 'money in the bank' is strictly materialistic. As a matter of fact, the hardship of starting out in life does not destroy marriage. It makes it stronger. The thing which really weakens our social structure is that family life starts too late!"*

*What can we do about it?* The answer is simply a return

to an idea which is as old as America—family aid to young married couples.

In the America which conquered a wilderness, it was unthinkable that a young couple should marry without being given a few acres of land, a team and wagon, or a plow, or a cow barn, or the old house by the meadow. Only in up-to-date, citified America have we come by the idea that a boy and girl must marry in the full armor of independence, forgetting the "hidden subsidies" of the 1800's which parents provided as part of the natural business of getting young people on their feet. *"We must substitute our own form of subsidy," declares Dr. Benjamin Gruenberg, eminent sociologist and educator. "In cities, this usually means assisting young couples financially until they are established. Family aid ought to be an accepted custom—in fact an obligation—just as it used to be."*

We ought to revive, too, the sadly neglected customs of the dowry and the bride's chest. In France, where the family unit is probably stronger than anywhere else in the world, no family would think of turning out a jeune fille without enough francs to keep her going for a year or two. And fathers consider it their duty to give sons a part of their business, their shop, or farm.

Finally, we need a major refocusing of our views on marriage and higher education. Thousands of parents support their unmarried sons and daughters through college, yet threaten to cut them off without a penny if they marry while at school. Thanks to the GI Bill of Rights, we are learning how surprisingly well marriage and education go together. At many of our universities one third of the students are married. And the brilliant fact is that these students, particularly the ones with children, are getting the most out of education because they can and do apply their energies more completely. *At the University of Wisconsin the married*

[ 93 ]

*veterans received significantly higher marks than the un-
married ones—and those who had children did the best of all!*

*From the dean's office of the University of Iowa comes the
statement: "Marriage has a settling influence on students.
They have someone to make good for, someone who is pleased
when their record is high, someone to encourage them when
things go wrong."*

The GI bill has shown us the light. It will be all to the
good if—through parents' aid, scholarship grants, and campus
housing plans—we continue to let marriage and higher education march forward hand in hand.

Any investment we make in early marriage is, after all, an
investment in the future families of America. There is
nothing more gilt-edged than that.

If you are an observant reader, you probably noticed that I put
not only the spoken dialogue in italics, but also a few other sentences like *But do young marriages stick?* or *What can we do
about it?* Before you jump to the conclusion that I cheated in
figuring my statistics, look again at the sentences between quotation marks. You'll find that a large number of them are questions
(*"Yet what is this but an indication of the stone wall many young
people are up against?"*), commands (*"Don't be a fool, Alice."*),
exclamations (*"It's ridiculous to marry a boy who's making only
$30 a week!"*), incomplete sentences (*"Out of the question Ned."*),
or sentences addressed directly to the audience (*"And I can tell
you this."*). So I think it's justified to consider *all* sentences of
these types "conversational" sentences, even if they are part of the
running text and have no quotation marks around them. After
all, these questions, exclamations, and commands are really
nothing but a one-sided conversational exchange between author
and reader.

At any rate, you can use the percentage of the types of sentences
I put here in italics as another statistical measure of reader interest

in your writing. Let's call it the percentage of "personal sentences" —like the percentage of "personal words" in the last chapter.

Such a count immediately shows the difference between fiction and nonfiction or the degree by which nonfiction has approached fiction. In fiction, the figure will usually be over fifty percent; on the other hand, in technical papers or dissertations, it will regularly be zero. In popular magazine articles the typical ratio is between twelve and fifteen percent—about one "personal sentence" in eight. (The count of 48 percent in our example is very high, of course, but not exceptional for a professional popularizer.)

Whatever you write, there's no excuse for using the indirect approach instead of the direct quotation or direct address to the reader. In fact, I know of only one occasion where you can't address another person directly—a Congressional debate—and only one where you can't use direct quotation—a press conference at the White House. In any other case, it's up to you to make things as interesting to read as you can.

PS

Here again, the principle explained in this chapter has since become routine. Today interviews are a must. Exact quotes from what people said are now indispensable for all nonfiction writing, just as they've become indispensable in fiction. So if you want to write good reports and articles, use direct quotations to the utmost. Use a tape recorder, a notebook, your memory—how you do it is up to you. But write what people *said*.

Here's a typical story that appeared on February 21, 1973, in the *New York Times*:\*

The Road to a Bank Robbery Charge—at 13
by George Goodman, Jr.

A 13-year-old boy, whose poverty-ridden parents are deaf and unable to speak, will go on trial in Buffalo tomorrow on

\* © 1973 by the New York Times Company. Reprinted by permission.

charges involving a $700 armed robbery of a bank there last Wednesday.

Described as a "fairly typical product" of Buffalo's Lower East Side slum by a spokesman for the Erie County Probation Department, the black child could be sent to a state training school if adjudged guilty in Family Court.

But in the words of his 15-year-old brother whose own involvement in a variety of juvenile problems has resulted in run-ins with probation authorities:

"It really don't make no whole lot of difference what they do. If they don't put him in reform school, he's got to go right back out in the street. The street ain't nothing but some trouble."

Ralph (which is not the boy's real name) was arrested, soon after the bank robbery, in a dismal district of factory buildings and old two-story frame houses. According to the police, Ralph walked into the Marine Midland bank, thrust a paper bag before a woman at a teller's window, demanded she fill it with "twenties," and brandished a loaded revolver.

Neither the revolver nor the estimated total of $700 in loot has been recovered, and the police have said they expect to arrest two other juveniles in connection with the robbery.

Through interviews with school officials, a relative and a neighbor of the family, a picture—though sketchy— emerged, of a boy and a family trying unsuccessfully to cope with problems beyond their ability.

Ralph attended Clinton Junior High School, which has an all-black student body of 850. Assemblyman Arthur O. Eve described the school as one of the area's best, with dedicated teachers, small classrooms and a variety of extracurricular activities.

"But," said John Fahey, the school's attendance officer, "youngsters bring problems affecting the community into

their classrooms." The most serious problem, he said, is un-
employment. Ralph's father worked on part-time jobs as a
mechanic, and his mother worked occasionally as a domestic,
a relative said. Poorly dressed, unclean and unkempt, Ralph
usually came to school unprepared with even the basic sup-
plies for his school work, school officials said, adding that the
family received welfare assistance. Though the parents visited
the school at the request of Ralph's teachers and seemed eager
to help the boy when problems arose, others said there were
frequent and bitter fights between the parents that resulted
in one or both leaving the home for days or weeks at a time,
leaving the three boys and one girl to fend for themselves.

"There is a grandmother who lives in the home," said
Susan Pritchard, Ralph's former eighth-grade teacher, "but
she seems incapable of supervising the children."

"In September," she recalled, "he started out trying so
hard other teachers talked about him. He was so bright. So
sharp."

Ralph had problems that usually involved a lack of interest with school work, Miss Pritchard said.

"There were no discipline problems as such," Philip Lafornara, the school's principal, said, "although the boy was
an occasional truant."

Other teachers complained he would sometimes walk out
of his classrooms. At other times, Miss Pritchard said, he
would "throw up his hands" over some private exasperation
that he refused to discuss.

"I became a second mother for a time," Miss Pritchard
said. She even discussed taking the boy into her home, but
Mr. Fahey counseled against it.

"I decided it wouldn't work," she said, "because never did
he trust me enough to share any confidence whatsoever."

Ralph was switched from Miss Pritchard's class to a special
intensified instruction course, Mr. Lafornara said. But by the

end of last semester, Ralph failed all his courses except industrial arts.

In fact, on the day Ralph first appeared in Family Court on the bank robbery charge, he was scheduled to be there in connection with the theft of a car last December.

As a "problem youngster," Mr. Lafornara said, Ralph was always accompanied during the lunch-hour by a school official.

"I sat him down at lunch around 12:15 on Wednesday," he said, and some time after that, Ralph walked out of the school.

"Usually the children go downtown," Mr. Fahey said, "hang around in the public housing projects," which, with about 50 percent vacant apartments, are a favored gathering place for truants, he said.

Mr. Lafornara said there was no drug or alcohol problem among the students, but a lot of "petty thievery, shoplifting and things of that sort."

In a talk with a reporter last week, Cross Fredericks, Ralph's court-appointed lawyer, who has been in practice since the 1930's, said:

"I've seen some sharpies in my day but this youngster is the sharpest yet. With this boy, none of my approaches tell me anything about him."

To write this 800-word story, Mr. Goodman interviewed at least ten people—someone in the County Probation Department, Ralph's older brother, a police officer, a relative, a neighbor, Assemblyman Eve, Mr. Fahey, Miss Pritchard, Mr. Lafornara, and the school official who accompanied Ralph during the lunch hour. Probably the total number of people he interviewed was closer to 15 or 20. Some of them he quoted indirectly, but six he quoted directly, plus the quotation of what Mr. Fredericks said to another reporter the week before. The quotes from Miss

Pritchard and the older brother are especially illuminating, clearly showing the brother's sullenness ("It really don't make no whole lot of difference what they do") and Miss Pritchard's affection for Ralph ("He was so bright. So sharp.").

Without the direct quotes, Mr. Goodman's story would have been insignificant and almost meaningless. With them, it gave the reader not only the facts, but also understanding, insight and compassion.

PPS

After I'd written this postscript, I talked to Mr. Goodman. He turned out to be a 33-year-old reporter who had studied this book when he was in journalism school.

He said he spent two days in Buffalo, walking around the area and soaking up the atmosphere. "You have to do this kind of article on a 24-hour basis," he said.

He'd talked to at least twice as many people as were actually mentioned in his piece. In particular, he had a long interview with the woman judge who handled Ralph's case, but eventually the *Times* cut the article to about two-thirds its original length and the interview fell by the wayside.

After the article appeared, one woman reader, in helpless sympathy, sent in $50.

## CHAPTER 9

# AN EAR FOR WRITING

---

*Spoken language is the primary phenomenon, and writing is only a more or less imperfect reflection of it.*

E. H. STURTEVANT

---

THE newest thing these days in college English teaching is something called communication. The idea is that writing shouldn't be treated any longer as a poor relation of English literature but as something that has to do with the way we talk.

That's no great discovery, of course. Everyone who reads his fair share of newspapers, magazines, and books, must realize that "literary" writing, for all practical purposes, is a thing of the past. Almost all professionals are now on the side of colloquial writing. Take any magazine story and you'll find spoken English not only in the quoted dialogue but also in the paragraphs *without* quotation marks. In fact, more often than not nowadays, stories are written as if they were told by one of the characters.

And the conversational tone isn't limited to fiction. It has spilled over into almost everything else. Nowadays you find it not only in popular articles but in serious editorials, foreign correspondence, intellectual discussions and literary essays.

The *New York Herald Tribune*, for instance, devoting an editorial to the situation in Finland, calls it "You Can't Win" and winds it up this way:

> What it all adds up to is that the Finns know that if they don't sign a treaty, they lose; if they do sign, they may be allowed to go on playing for a while; but still, they can never win . . .

Meanwhile, the paper's correspondent in Greece reports in this style:

> . . . Early in the engagement it became fairly obvious that the business of advising the Greeks how to fight won't work when you get down to battalion level. It's all right when you stick to planning in the higher echelons, but no Greek combat officer worth his salt is going to listen to any foreigner telling him how to flush a nest of rebels.
>
> What it all boils down to is that American officers can't do much good out front in this situation, and they can easily do a lot of harm . . .

Or listen to Max Lerner, reviewing a book on Russia:

> Maynard's book . . . will occupy you for the evenings of two or three weeks, working at it pretty steadily . . . I have seen nowhere a better analysis of the intellectual tradition in Russia and the role of intellectuals, on which Maynard does a sort of Vernon Parrington job . . .

In short, the centuries-old struggle between literary and colloquial English is almost over and *Write as You Talk* has become the almost universally accepted rule.

But what does it mean to "write as you talk"? That's where the trouble starts. It's a good rule as long as you understand that, like the Golden Rule, it's really unattainable. You can't actually write the way you talk. You can, however, put a reasonable facsimile of your ordinary talking self on paper. You can purposely put into your writing certain things that will make it sound like talk.

In English, the handiest and most conspicuous device is the use of contractions. Maybe you even think that it's mainly words like *don't, won't,* and *it's* that make writing sound colloquial. Well, they are not the whole story, but they come into it. If you want to write informal English, the use of contractions is certainly essential.

I have a notion that many people don't use contractions often because they are not quite sure which of them are conventionally used. (In the same way, many people shy away from using direct quotations in their writing because they are not quite sure how to handle quotation and punctuation marks. The best advice is to look closely at a piece of written dialogue and learn the mechanics once and for all.) So maybe it is worthwhile to list the contractions that are generally used. Here they are:

I'm, I've, I'll, I'd
you're, you've, you'll, you'd
he's, he'll, he'd
she's, she'll, she'd
it's, it'll
we're, we've, we'll, we'd
they're, they've, they'll, they'd
aren't, isn't, wasn't, weren't
haven't, hasn't, hadn't
won't, wouldn't, shan't, shouldn't
can't, couldn't, mustn't
don't, doesn't, didn't
here's, there's, where's, how's, what's, who's, that's, that'll
let's

But let me add a warning. Don't start using the contractions on this list at every single opportunity from here on. It's not as simple as that. Contractions have to be used with care. Sometimes they fit, sometimes they don't. It depends on whether you would use the contraction in speaking *that particular sentence* (e.g. in this sentence I would say *you would* and not *you'd*). It also depends on whether the contraction would help or hinder the rhythm that would suit your sentence for proper emphasis. So don't try to be consistent about this; it doesn't work. You have to go by feel, not by rule.

Just to show you how subtle this business can be sometimes,

here is a sentence from an editorial in the *New York Times* that contains both *cannot* and *can't*:

> The conclusion is that the stopped private car is a luxurious nuisance that the city *cannot* afford in the mid-town panel, that it serves too few people to warrant the inconvenience it causes a great many more people who do not use private cars, and that the loss to business and trade just *can't* be sustained.

My own explanation of the inconsistent *can't* here is that the editorial writer unconsciously tried to preserve the rhythm of his three emphatic verbs:

*cannot afford, serves too few people,* and *can't be sustained.*
He couldn't have used such a subtle means of emphasis at the time when contractions were not yet acceptable on the *Times* editorial page.

But after all, this is a minor matter. What really does make talk sound authentic? What are the things by which we immediately spot spoken English when we see it on paper?

There are a number of answers. There are differences in grammar, in usage, and in idiomatic phrasing. But the main characteristics of spoken English seem to be two: loose sentence structure and a great deal of repetition.

Real ad-lib talk is hard to find in print, but occasionally one does find examples. For instance, when President Truman talked for a few minutes to a group of radio news writers, the papers printed his "impromptu remarks":

> . . . You have a very great responsibility. I can say that I don't think I have met as many soft-voiced gentlemen in my life as I have here. You have a very great responsibility in that by reporting facts, making broadcasts to the people generally, you have a very powerful effect on public opinion,

and public opinion in a free country is vital to the welfare of the government of that country.

. . . I think I have myself, according to the Hooper survey, talked to as many as 40,000,000 people at one sitting. Now that's a responsibility, a very grave responsibility—to see that that ability and power are used for the welfare of this great republic.

You gentlemen can make a great contribution to our future, by being careful and factual, and remembering always that you and I are living under the Bill of Rights. This and the Declaration of Independence are the greatest documents ever put out by the hand of man. And that is what has made our country great, and that is what we want to keep and implement, so as to keep our country great.

Now you can make a great contribution to that, and I hope you will do that. I am sure you will.

Another more spectacular occasion was a press conference General Eisenhower gave after his victory in Germany. The papers printed the questions and answers verbatim. For example:

Q. From the enemy's viewpoint which day and what event would you say constituted the last straw that broke the camel's back? When was it perfectly obvious that the jig was up?

A. From everything that we can find, from their own statements, they knew it—the professionals knew the jig was up— on the third day after the Rundstedt offensive had started in the Ardennes. He knew then that he could not go where he intended. If he could not get complete surprise and drive clear through to Liège and drive on behind Antwerp, then there was not much he could do.

At the end of the third day we found that he still hoped then, according to their own statements, that he might get to Liège, where there was a terrific supply base, and cause us embarrassment and loss, and loss of time. From that time on, and when they found their forces destroyed in the Eiffel and in the Saar with that terrifically swift movement down from the north, they knew that it was confirmed. Then they knew they could not even fight a defensive battle . . .

A good source for verbatim statements is also the transcripts of hearings. There you often find bits like this:

> But it got along in the winter, and then it came February, as I seem to recall it, of 1934, and my company got a telegram, the General Motors people got a telegram, and all the companies that were in the automobile manufacturers' code got telegrams; and the same telegram went to the President of the United States, and the same telegram went to General Hugh Johnson, the head of the National Recovery Administration. It was like these telegrams that go about now.

I take this passage from a little *Saturday Evening Post* editorial that compared its language to the prose of Gertrude Stein. And Gertrude Stein, who all her life experimented with the possibilities of spoken prose, did write a remarkably similar style:

> It's funny about honey, you always eat honey during a war, so much honey, there is no sugar, there never is sugar during a war, the first thing to disappear is sugar, after that butter, but butter can always be had but no sugar, no not sugar so during a war you always eat honey quantities of honey, really more honey than you used to eat sugar, and you find honey so much better than sugar, better in itself and better in applesauce, in all desserts so much better and then peace is upon us and no one eats honey any more, they find it too sweet and too cloying and too heavy, it was like this in the last war '14-'18 and it is like this in this war, wars are like that, it is funny but wars are like that.

In fact, most writers with a good ear who try really hard to catch the essence of spoken English, come up with something of the sort. Jimmy Cannon, the sports writer, can do it beautifully when he is in the mood (*New York Post,* September 19, 1947):

> ... Mr. Strauss, a real estate attorney who has been running the 20th Century Sporting Club since Jacobs fell sick, was describing the great future of what he calls the sport when Harry Markson, the publicity man, came into the room. Mr. Markson said there was a newspaperman on the telephone who wanted a comment from Mr. Strauss on a story which came out of Cleveland ...
>
> "Cheap publicity," Mr. Strauss said. "All they're looking for is cheap publicity. Who are they?"
>
> Mr. Strauss answered his question in a deeper voice, the way the character actors do on the radio when they play all the parts in a sketch.
>
> "Out-of-towners," Mr. Strauss said. "Out-of-towners. So Mr. Atkins had to run to Cleveland to make this offer. .... They're all alike. Larry Atkins, Harry Voiller. All out-of-town guys. All looking for cheap publicity."
>
> Mr. Strauss sat very straight in the chair and spaced his words slowly, as though he were reading them as they were flashed on a screen one at a time.
>
> "Where are the New Yorkers?" asked Mr. Strauss and the question had the sombre quality of the verse of those songs which describe what New York is like. "Why should out-of-town guys come to tell us what we should do here? I am a born New Yorker. I was a member of the New York State Assembly. I was also the Superintendent of Reindexing and Records in the County Clerk's office."
>
> "The last title was the Superintendent of Reindexing and Records in the County Clerk's office," I said because Mr. Strauss is a man who likes to be quoted correctly.

"That's right," said Mr. Strauss. "It was a big job in those days."

I said I was sure it was.

"Who are they, these out-of-towners?" asked Mr. Strauss, "to tell a born New Yorker what to do in New York? I'll tell you who they are. They are out-of-towners."

The reason why I am giving you all these examples is to remind you of all the repetitiousness and loose-strung sequence that goes on in your and my and everybody's talk. I hope you agree with me by now that direct quotations and informal talk-to-the-reader are necessary for readable writing. Well, if that's so, repetition and loosely built sentences are part of the secret of readability.

If you ever took seriously what you learned in school about English composition, you were probably shocked by this last sentence. According to conventional English teaching, it is sheer blasphemy. If there are any rules of style an American school child carries into his adult life, they are the rule of thumb against repetition of the same word and the taboo against so-called sentence fragments and run-on sentences. Quite often they are the only things people know, or think they know, about the rules of rhetoric.

There's hardly anything more ruinous to good writing than the rule of thumb against repetition of the same word. Fowler, in his *Dictionary of Modern English Usage,* has this to say about what he calls "elegant variation":

> It is the second-rate writers, those intent rather on expressing themselves prettily than on conveying their meaning clearly, and still more those whose notions of style are based on a few misleading rules of thumb, that are chiefly open to the allurements of elegant variation . . . The real victims . . . terrorized by a misunderstood taboo . . . are the minor novelists & the reporters. There are few literary faults so widely prevalent . . .

[ 107 ]

> The fatal influence is the advice given to young writers never to use the same word twice in a sentence—or within 20 lines or other limit . . .
>
> Sentences in which the writer has carefully *not* repeated a word set readers wondering what the significance of the change is, only to conclude disappointedly that it has none . . . A dozen sentences are spoilt by ill-advised avoidance of repetition for every one that is spoilt by ill-advised repetition.

There is little anyone can add to this—except one or two examples from current American writing. Here is one where the same country is called by three different names within the same sentence:

> LAKE SUCCESS, L.I., Sept. 29 [1947]—(UP)—Palestine's Arabs swore before the United Nations special Palestine committee today to drench the soil of that tiny country "with the last drop of our blood" in opposing any big power scheme to partition the Holy Land.

Here's another that manages to mention four people while talking about two:

> READING, Pa., Feb. 12 [1948]—(AP)—Descendants of Mordecai Lincoln gathered here today to pay tribute to their ancestor's famous great-great-grandson, Abraham Lincoln, on the 139th anniversary of the Civil War President's birth.

Ordinary colloquial repetition would have helped these sentences no end.

The school teachers' taboo against sentence fragments and run-on sentences is even more of a superstition. Human speech teems with these constructions. In fact, on the average, it probably contains more sentence fragments and run-on sentences than standard-brand "grammatical" sentences. There would be more fragments and run-on sentences in writing too if we didn't disguise the true state of affairs by tricks of punctuation. Actually, the punctuation of anything that is freely spoken is purely an arbitrary convenience for the reader—as anyone can testify who has ever tried to punctuate the transcript of an ad-lib radio program. People just don't speak with commas and periods—they make themselves understood by forming words in sequence.

Gertrude Stein deliberately used almost no punctuation because she wanted people to read her as if they were listening to her words with close attention. Over at the other side of the literary scene Damon Runyon did much the same thing in putting the idiom of Broadway on paper. Like this, for instance:

> Well, even in the confusion I notice that the hole that is once a cellar looks as if somebody recently clears it out and does a lot of digging as if to make it deeper as there is much fresh earth around and about and there are steps dug in one wall as if to enable whoever does the digging to climb in and out and I also notice that there are light boards across the hole like a flat roof, and it is plain to be seen that these boards give way under some kind of weight in the middle so I figure this is where Cleo the calf and Cleo the pretty and Henri drop through into the hole.

I don't mean to say that you could or should write this way for serious, practical purposes. But with a good dose of punctuation it sounds fine and is often very effective. Writing by ear, if done properly, makes good business letters, advertisements, and almost everything else.

Here is an example from a Christmas letter a broker wrote to his customers:

Dear Mr. Scott:
Alone in the office; doing a bit of night work. Outside, the clanging of street cars, the voices of the scrub women banging

their buckets about and stopping to exchange a bit of blarney with the night watchman. Mind began to wander from one thing to another. Forgot the work. Thought of Christmas, of the year gone by, thought of you. A year ago; took the bull by the horns and started a brokerage business. A little nerve, a few accounts, and a lot of friends. Those were the only assets. Here it is Christmas and still in the ring. Nothing to brag about, haven't set the world on fire, but going better every day. Every reason to be happy and merry and joyful just as people are supposed to be at this time of the year.

Been thinking about all of this . . .

Here's another from a Macy's ad:

You're not a cigar store Indian. You're not stiff and wooden and unyielding. You're a mass of muscles and joints that were made to move. Effortlessly. Easily. Gracefully. But many suits won't let your body enjoy that free play. They throttle it at every turn. Limit its field of freedom. Suppress its natural impulse to get up and go.

A Gort & McLeod "Soft Contour" suit brings you a world of difference for only $63. It won't limit your stride—or your Spring clothing budget. It won't rebel when you reach. It *caters* to your ease. It *frees* your movements.

That's because the tailoring is fluid, soft. Because the cloth is supple and yielding. Because the cut is ample and unrestraining. It's a suit that's easy to wear. Easy to look at, too. It's a suit that makes your $63 travel a long, long way.

Here is a third example from the insurance field. It is from the unique book *Risk Appraisal* by Dr. Harry Dingman—an insurance man who knows how to write:

Applicant age 50 is the applicant of experience. He has bought before. He has talked with many agents. He has talked with many buyers, policyholders. He has, possibly, talked with many doctors. He knows the value of personal insurance and he knows how to present himself. By contrast, the applicant of 20-30-40 buys casually, even grudgingly, and lapses easily. He cannot imagine age 60 or 70. For dodoes? Yes. For grandfathers? Yes. For elderly executives? Yes. But for him? No. He will buy tomorrow, or tomorrow, or tomorrow. And so tomorrow he will be 50 in age and 50 in thousands of insurance, and 50-50 chance it will be—not literally, but might be—degenerative changes have developed. When he does apply, his application is a brief autobiography. He got born, and there's family history. He got schooling, and there's economic status. He got sick, and there's personal history. He got a job, and there determined his earnings. He got a wife and established his community status. He got careless and laid bare his habits. What is ascertainable on all these points determines his appraisal. What the applicant tells us is informative. What he does not tell us may be more informative. He is checked and double checked by information obtained from agent, inspector, insurance physician, his own physician, and any other source that may seem pertinent. Court records, for example. His attorney. His banker. Having told his name, age, address, occupation, marital status, his experiences with alcohol, doctors, hospitals, insurance companies, he signs his name. His statements become the basis of the contract. He errs if he does not tell the truth, all of it.

When I discovered *Risk Appraisal* I wrote Dr. Dingman a letter and asked how he had acquired his style. His answer is worth quoting in full:

Dear Mr. Flesch:
    You were kind to write your letter of five days ago. If you like RISK APPRAISAL, I am flattered. It ought to be better than it is, I've spent enough time, Lord knows. Two other books I wrote and various articles. All trade stuff. That's my

experience in writing. No academic training. No studies in literature, nor English, nor composition. My loss, of course. I like short words, even four letter words. I like short sentences. Verbless sentences on occasion. Single word sentences. Why not? We use words to express thoughts. If one expresses, why use two? Too many of us, including me, use too many adjectives. Many too many articles. Yet I hesitate not to use an extra adjective or article if it adds rhythm. Prose that scans easily is prose that reads easily.

Any style that I have—if I have—is influenced by two things: Bible English; newspaper English. Any style that I have— if I have—insists on two principles; use the fewest words possible; use the simplest words possible. AND, I refuse to take myself too seriously. Some of my readers are smarter than I am. BUT, none of my readers is more interested in my subject matter. If I adhere to basic principles, dumb as this author may be, smart as my readers may be, they can't lick me. Two plus two equals four, whether Einstein says it, or Dingman.

Sincerely,<br>Harry Dingman

PS

There's been vast progress here. Writing by ear has really taken hold.

As to contractions, they're now everywhere. Even the conservative *Wall Street Journal* has a rule that says "It is our style to make contractions of negative words, i.e., didn't, won't, wasn't, etc., as this makes it less likely the 'not' will be dropped by a tape puncher, changing the whole meaning of the sentence." As soon as this rule was adopted, the *Wall Street Journal* went fully colloquial. Open it any day and you'll find items like this:

> Joseph E. Cole, 58-year-old chairman and chief executive of Cole National Corp., Cleveland, gets a 25-year "employ-

ment agreement" expiring in 1997 when *he'll* be 83. *He's*
guaranteed at least $135,000-a-year base salary for the first
10 years, adjusted to the consumer price index. Then salary
and time on the job will taper off.

On the other hand, the curse of "elegant variation" is still with
us in full force. As I said, the superstition that you must never,
never repeat a word in the same or the next sentence is the one
thing people remember from their school days and stubbornly
cling to. And why shouldn't they? The false rule is still hammered
into their minds in classrooms and textbooks. Here's what I found
in the widely used handbook *Errors in English and Ways to
Correct Them* by Harry Shaw:

> *Vague:* He took the books from the boxes and placed them
> on the floor.
>
> *Better:* He took the books from the boxes and placed the
> volumes on the floor.

Let me say with all the strength I can muster that Mr. Shaw's
"vague" version is the way anyone would speak this sentence
normally (except that he'd probably use *put* instead of *place*) and
his so-called "better" version sounds terrible. When we talk about
books, we call them books. We *don't* call them volumes, just as
we normally don't call a judge a jurist, a pope a pontiff, a king
a ruler, or an elephant a pachyderm. These are words used only
by "elegant variationists" whenever they can't resist the itch for
a synonym.

And don't tell me that in the sentence about the books and the
boxes the reader would think the boxes rather than the books
were put on the floor and needs the word *volumes* to avoid confusion. It isn't so. In context, anyone reading "He took the books
from the boxes and put them on the floor" would naturally think
that the books rather than the boxes were put on the floor.
Otherwise the sentence would have read "He took the books from
the boxes and put the boxes on the floor."

[ 113 ]

I hope you see the point. After thirty years of trying to cure my students of this bad habit I know it's a tough problem.

Finally, let's get to verbless sentences. Again, they're now found everywhere. Here are three recent newspaper examples:

> The street floor of Gimbels East blossomed with flowers yesterday. *With good reason.* The store was celebrating its first birthday.

> When she got to Gatwick Airport, she tried to do what most travelers do from Gatwick—take the train into London. *No trains.* The locomotive engineers in England were on strike.

> Under the reform atmosphere of the 1960's many people in Yugoslavia had begun to think more about new cars, weekend houses and vacations abroad than about the intricacies of ideology. *Not any more.*

In 1926, when 70-year-old H. W. Fowler published his famous *Dictionary of Modern English Usage,* he mentioned neither contractions nor verbless sentences. Obviously he didn't feel that such ultra-colloquial forms of expression were worth mentioning in a book on how to write. .

By 1965, when a second edition appeared, things had changed. The editor, Sir Ernest Gowers, felt he had to include two newly prepared articles on contractions and verbless sentences. But Sir Ernest, an 85-year-old retired civil servant with rather fastidious tastes, couldn't bring himself to give his unqualified approval to these newfangled ways of writing. Of contractions, he wrote: "The printing of these forms in serious prose will no doubt continue to grate on some old-fashioned people." And of verbless sentences he wrote: "Overdone, as it [this style] is in the sprightlier sort of modern journalism, it gets on a reader's nerves."

My advice is simple: disregard such quaint Victorian sensibilities and use contractions and verbless sentences freely.

# DID SHAKESPEARE MAKE MISTAKES IN ENGLISH?

---

*It is well to remember that grammar is common speech formulated. Usage is the only test. I would prefer a phrase that was easy and unaffected to a phrase that was grammatical.*

W. SOMERSET MAUGHAM

---

THE other day, glancing through a book on English usage, my eye fell on this: "only, misplaced . . . Shakespeare makes this mistake in *The summer's flower is to the summer sweet Though to itself it only live and die.*"

Did Shakespeare really make mistakes in English? I don't think so. You probably don't think so either. But most of our English teachers do.

There are about a dozen or so points of English usage on which most teachers differ with the rest of the population. People make these "errors" day in day out in their speaking and writing, while English teachers spend a goodly portion of their lives correcting them. And yet, these so-called mistakes have been committed by almost all the great men of English literature—including Shakespeare.

Of course, you may say, everybody makes mistakes now and then and even geniuses slip. But that's no valid argument here. The point is that the rules of English usage are not immutable natural laws, but simply conventions among English-speaking people. If enough people insist on making a "mistake," then it isn't a mistake any more and the teachers might as well stop wasting their time correcting it.

Progressive English teachers realized this situation long ago. In some classrooms and textbooks students are now taught that certain usages are permissible in informal or colloquial speech. But that's not enough. If you want to write readable, natural-sounding English, you need more than these halfhearted waivers from "liberal" teachers. You need the assurance that these so-called mistakes are good English, that their literary standing is equal to the so-called correct usage, and that they are sometimes actually preferable.

I said *sometimes* preferable. That's what makes this whole business so difficult. Actually, you can't say that a split infinitive or *different than* is good or bad: it all depends on the particular sentence. There's hardly a rule in English usage that holds good in all possible situations; in fact, wherever there is a choice, the mechanical application of a rule of thumb will be more often bad than good. So don't take what follows as a blanket endorsement of every so-called mistake in every possible situation. I am not trying to draw up rules in reverse; I simply want to tell you a little about the facts of language.

And now let's get back to Shakespeare's "mistake" in "misplacing" the word *only*. This is simply an example of the trend in idiomatic English toward leaving some leeway for shifting words within a sentence—especially adverbs, which seem to be a little more movable than other words. The most famous battleground here is the so-called split infinitive. Sticklers insist that you mustn't put an adverb between the word *to* and the infinitive of a verb. But everybody else has been doing it for centuries whenever it made better sense.

Before I give you a few out of the millions of examples of good, idiomatic split infinitives, I want to show you two examples of infinitives that were *not* split because the writers couldn't get over that old rule of thumb. Result: the sentences just don't sound right.

From the column "Matter of Fact" by Joseph and Stewart Alsop:

[ 116 ]

The only real means of regaining Northern [Democratic] mass support in present circumstances, is *actually to put through* the social and other measures which the President has advocated.

From a book review by Supreme Court Justice Robert H. Jackson:

Hope for enduring peace was revived by two expedients—the effort *better to organize* international society through the League of Nations, and the Kellogg-Briand Pact.

I don't think anybody will deny that these sentences would have been more idiomatic if the Alsops had written *to actually put through,* and Justice Jackson *to better organize.*

And now look at a few examples from writers who did *not* shy away from the split infinitive—and improved their sentences: *New York Times* correspondent John MacCormac:

The [Austrian] Government wished and intended *to greatly develop* the nation's hydroelectric power system but was hindered by lack of capital.

An advertisement:

When run through a magnetic recording device known as the Soundmirror, the tape's surface becomes magnetized in such a way as *to faithfully pick up* any sound.

A *New York Post* editorial:

The basic mistake was *to even consider* making a treaty with the inhabitants of the home of the Nazi-Fascist terror.

*Washington Memo* by Charles van Devander:

In a speech on the House floor Gearhart advocated a new constitutional amendment *to forever prohibit* the income tax, which he called "the most unfair, the most unjust and the most unequal tax ever devised by man."

[ 117 ]

A film review:

> *The Search* is a picture for everyone *to see, feel and deeply understand.*

Another film review:

> While the film keeps alluding to the swelling divorce problem, it doesn't really tackle it until the principals decide *to thus terminate* their marriage after Mrs. Hunter's innocence is established by the jury.

And, speaking of the movies:

> The motion picture is the only art at which we of this generation have any possible chance *to greatly excel.*

I found this last example in an article by Raymond Chandler in the March 1948 *Atlantic Monthly.* Since I had read somewhere that the *Atlantic* considers the split infinitive taboo, I wrote a letter to the editor, Mr. Edward Weeks, and asked how come. His answer was interesting:

> Dear Mr. Flesch:
> In accordance with Atlantic usage, we do not encourage our authors to split infinitives. In fact, we try to prevent them from doing so. Mr. Raymond Chandler, however, was obdurate, and when our Proof Reader raised the question on the galley margin: "Is split infinitive okay?", Mr. Chandler replied: "Yes, dammit."

Which proves that the *Atlantic* is considerably stricter than Shakespeare was. His Henry V, at any rate, is on the side of infinitive-splitters, when he says:

> My learned lord, we pray you to *proceed*
> *And justly and religiously unfold . . .*

Another famous controversy rages about expressions like *it's me* or *that's him*. Winston Churchill went out on a limb by committing himself publicly to *it's me,* but Shakespeare was there long before him. Cleopatra says of Octavia, "Is she as tall as *me?"* and Macbeth cries:

> Lay on, Macduff;
> And damned be *him* that first cries, *Hold, enough.*

When it comes to *who* and *whom* too, our perverse English idiom often prefers the nominative *who* to the "grammatically correct" *whom.* For instance, *Time* quotes the mayor of New Orleans: "After we heard Sam Jones speak we knew *who* we wanted for governor." Or the *New Republic* writes: "I don't know *who* Twentieth-Century-Fox think they're fooling with their spurious English and cockney accents." Or Herblock captions one of his cartoons in the *Washington Post: "Who* are you going to vote against?"

All these examples would surely sound artificial if *whom* had been used instead of *who.* So would Shakespeare's noble verse (from *King Henry VI,* Part I):

> *Who* joinst thou with, but with a lordly nation,
> That will not trust thee, but for profit's sake?

Now let's look at a third idiomatic construction grammarians don't like. Take for instance this sentence from an article by James Reston in the *New York Times*: "There is no possibility, Stassen sources declare, of Stassen accepting the vice presidency under Taft." Grammarians would correct this and make it "of *Stassen's* accepting," muttering something about a fused participle or a possessive case with the gerund. Most Americans, of course, are quite unable to tell a gerund from a hole in the ground and pay no attention whatever to this matter. They are like Billy Rose who has not the slightest hesitation in writing

[ 119 ]

"I don't object to other people drinking." Or like Shakespeare, for that matter, who wrote, in *Twelfth Night,* "Journeys end in lovers meeting." (Of course, in Shakespeare's time apostrophes were not used. But I rather doubt that he would have written *lovers'* in any case.)

Ordinary people also show more sense than grammarians in the use of the plural. Their current idiom follows a simple rule: use the plural, regardless of grammar, whenever you are talking about more than one. This goes for group words like *family* or *police* as well as for indefinite words like *everybody, anyone, neither, none,* etc. For example, the *New Yorker* writes: "The management of the hotel *haven't* wanted anything said about it, but we convinced *them* that it was too big a thing to keep secret." Or the *New York Times* headlines a picture: "Where the Council of Foreign Ministers will hold *their* meetings." Or *Time* quotes a fashion designer: "I used to tell everyone when something wasn't becoming to *them.*" Or Elliot Paul writes (in *Linden on the Saugus Branch*): "Deacon Parker, who lived way up on Revere Street, had one set of keys to the church. The Reverend K. Gregory Powys had the other. Neither of them *were* at home."

English literature literally teems with examples of this usage. Dr. Samuel Johnson wrote: "Neither search nor labour *are* necessary." Lord Chesterfield wrote. "If a person is born of a gloomy temper *they* cannot help it." Dryden wrote: "None *have* been so greedy of employments as they who have least deserved their stations."

You insist on an instance from Shakespeare? All right, here it is (from *Cymbeline*):

> Thersites body is as good as Ajax
> When neither *are* alive.

Spoken English doesn't care either for subtle distinctions in verb forms. For centuries, pedants have repeated the rule that *can* stands for ability and *may* for permission. But the ordinary person disagrees. He reserves *may* for possibility and uses *can* for ability *and* permission. A good example is the following anecdote from John Gunther's *Inside U.S.A.:*

> After two hours of sturdy talk with Erwin D. Canham and R. H. Markham in the *Christian Science Monitor* offices I wanted a cigarette badly.
> "Can I smoke?" I asked.
> Mr. Canham, executive editor of the *Monitor*, replied gently: "Of course. But no one ever has."

Another grammatical distinction that's dying out is the use of the subjunctive. In fact, for most practical purposes, the English subjunctive has been dead and buried for centuries; but the old-guard grammarians pretend it's still alive in the "condition contrary to fact." Again, most speakers and writers disagree. Here are two neat examples:

From a mystery story by Rex Stout:

> "For God's sake," the inspector said finally in bitter disgust. "As if this case *wasn't* enough of a mess already. All it needed to make it a carnival was Nero Wolfe, and by God here he is."

From Judge Goldsborough (during the John L. Lewis trial):

> If this court *was* to use its individual judgment it would impose a prison sentence.

There doesn't seem to be a handy Shakespearean example for this usage, but if you want authority, there *are* examples from Marlowe, Pepys, Bunyan, Defoe, Swift, Burke, Sheridan, Fielding, Austen, Charlotte Brontë, Byron, Thackeray, Dickens, Hardy, Meredith, Wilde, and countless others. (A prize exhibit is this, from the eighteenth-century writer Sidney Smith: "When I have the gout, I feel as if I *was* walking on my eyeballs." No grammarian can possibly deny that this is a condition contrary to fact.)

A similar fossil is the fine art of distinguishing between *shall* and *will,* or *should* and *would.* In this country the truth is that nobody cares; anyway, in conversation we all say *I'll* and *I'd* and *we'll* and *we'd* and let it go at that. But in England the distinction is supposed to be still alive; Fowler, in his *Dictionary of Modern English Usage,* tells us that some people there know it instinctively since they are "to the manner born." Well, Shakespeare apparently wasn't, since Hamlet tells Osric: "Let the foils be brought, the gentleman willing, and the king hold his purpose, I *will* win for him if I can; if not, I *will* gain nothing but my shame, and the odd hits."

As to adverbs, the natural English idiom is impatient with the syllable *ly* and likes to get rid of it. Street signs tell us to *go slow,* soap boxes promise that we will *wash easier.* An advertisement in the *Saturday Review of Literature* starts like this: "One of our editors says that sometimes, if he stops whatever he is doing and listens *real hard . . .* " and a *New York Times* advertisement begins, "If you work a little harder and advertise a little better and *stronger . . .*" Shakespeare's *Midsummer Night's Dream* opens:

> Now, fair Hippolyta, our nuptial hour
> Draws on apace; four happy days bring in
> Another moon; but oh, methinks, how *slow*
> This old moon wanes!

And *The Tempest* ends:

> Sir, I invite your highness, and your train,
> To my poor cell: where you shall take your rest
> For this one night; which (part of it,) I'll waste
> With such discourse as, I not doubt, shall make it
> Go *quick* away . . .

The normal English-speaking person also has a deep urge to monkey around with connectives and make them clearer or simpler. For instance when there is some distance between the words *the reason is* and the following clause, we sometimes like to start that clause with *because* to make it a little clearer for the reader. Like this, for instance (from Anne O'Hare McCormick of the *New York Times*): "His early experience as the Irredentist Deputy representing an Italian district in the Austrian Parliament—a high school of political maneuver—helps de Gasperi in Parliament, but *the chief reason* he was able to throw out the Communists and weather a series of governmental crises *is because* the country at large, including his political opponents, believes in his honesty and disinterested patriotism." Or this from Arnold J. Toynbee (who is speaking of expressions like *The Bronze Age* or *The Iron Age*): "*A second reason for* regarding the technological classification of social progress with suspicion *is because* it is a manifest example of the tendency of a student to become the slave of the particular materials for study which chance has placed in his hands."

After such verbs as *to doubt* or *to know*, we don't like to bother with the "correct" conjunction *whether* but prefer the simple *if*. For instance, in *The Merchant of Venice*, when the Prince of Morocco is confronted with the three caskets, he asks Portia: "How shall I know *if* I do choose the right?"

We also like simplified connectives when we compare situations that are different or alike. *Different from what* is cumbersome; we rather write *different than*. For example, the literary magazine *Encore* writes: "Before Japan attacked Manchuria and was revealed as a savagely aggressive military dictatorship, our impressions of her were ironically *different than* they are today." Elliot Paul writes: "The daily life of a Linden man [in 1900] was not essentially *different than* it had been at the time of the War of 1812." And Winston Churchill, in the preface to his *Gathering Storm*, writes: "I write from a *different* standpoint and with more authority *than* was possible in my earlier books."

[ 123 ]

Shakespeare somehow never used this construction, but everybody else who was anybody in English literature did. A particularly fine specimen from Oliver Goldsmith is this: "The [Roman] consuls had been elected for very *different* merits *than* those of skill in war."

Finally, we come to the use of *like* as a conjunction. Here we are way out at the frontier of English usage. There is a lively battle going on, and the fighters against the old iron rule are still very much on the defensive. True, H. L. Mencken includes *"like* for *as"* when he writes in *The American Language*: "Many of the forms that the grammatical pedants rail against most vehemently—for example, the split infinitive, the use of *between, either* and *neither* with more than one, the use of *than* after *different,* the use of *like* for *as,* and so on—are so firmly established in the American vulgate that the schoolmarm's attempts to put them down are plainly hopeless. Most of them, in fact, have crept into more or less elegant usage . . ." But there are plenty of people who are not schoolmarms but do wince whenever they encounter *like* as a conjunction.

Nevertheless, the use of *like* as a conjunction nowadays *seems practically indispensable for anyone who wants to preserve the flavor of spoken English in writing.* Characters in mystery stories say, "It looks *like* the man was murdered"; never anything else. When *Time* wants to quote an average person, it writes: "Honest, it's a sin to buy so much with prices *like* they are," carefully avoiding *as.* Even without trying to be colloquial, the *New York Times* writes: "London now looks more *like* it did before the war than it did when it swarmed with troops of the Allied nations." The Associated Press writes: "It looks *like* the appeal of New Yorkers interested in maintaining genius row will not prevail." A court decision says: "It becomes impossible for the Tax Commissioner to follow Federal income tax rules and to treat the trust income *like* the same is done under Federal statutes." And the American Federation of Labor, in full-page newspaper ads, cries: "Don't let *NAM* kid you—*like* they did on 'lower prices.' "

Today, Americans in all walks of life are using *like* rather than *as*:

Mr. Joe Axelrod, a manufacturer (quoted in *Time*): "We have the biggest backlog of employment applications we've ever enjoyed, and it now looks *like* we can get the cream of the textile workers."

Mrs. Laura Gorton, a women's club leader (quoted in the *New York Times*): "Are we going to have these controls going on and on *like* they do in France?"

Mr. Henry Peabody, of the League for Less Noise (quoted in the *New Yorker*): "It looks to me *like* the public is apathetic."

Miss Edith M. Stern, a magazine writer (quoted in the *New York Times*): "Ten million women making ten million baked potatoes is absurd. Hot meals should be delivered *like* they are to airplanes, every night."

Harold Russell, the handless veteran and movie actor (quoted in the *New York Post*): "I wish everyone would learn to treat us *like* we treat ourselves."

Bobby Clark, the comedian (quoted in the *New Yorker*): "We had a lot of good people then . . . Real funny fellows. Make you laugh *like* you meant it."

Humphrey Bogart (quoted in *Time* on his appearance before the Thomas Committee): "I acted impetuously and foolishly on the spur of the moment, *like* I am sure many other American citizens do at many times."

Joe Louis (quoted in the *New York Post*): "They've got to run a tournament to get a successor to me. That's the only way, *like* they did after Gene Tunney retired."

John Dos Passos (writing in *Life*): "Bob Garst was sitting in his accustomed corner laughing *like* he'd split about the difficulties of getting seed corn detasseled."

H. L. Mencken (quoted in the *Saturday Review of Literature*): "The minute war is declared the Communists will be treated *like* the Japs were, and a whole lot of innocent people will be roped in."

President Truman (according to a *New York Times* headline of January 7, 1949):

PRESIDENT ATTENDS ELECTORAL COUNT
AND QUIPS 'LOOKS LIKE I'M AHEAD'

But I suppose you have more than enough of this. I'll stop here—but not before I've quoted Shakespeare once more:

> *Like* an arrow, shot
> From a well-experienc'd archer, hits the mark
> His eye doth level at, so ne'er return,
> Unless thou say, Prince Pericles is dead.

PS

I remember having a lot of fun writing this chapter. I just went over it again and found that I discussed 13 "wrong" usages and gave 72 examples.

Maybe I drowned the simple point I wanted to make. "Mistakes" made by millions of people, sometimes over a period of centuries, are *not* mistakes, no matter what the teachers and grammarians say. They're idioms. And what's an idiom? As defined in *Webster's Dictionary of Synonyms*, it's a "phrase or collocation which is peculiar to the language in which it occurs either in its grammatical structure or in the meaning which is associated with it but which cannot be derived from it when the words are interpreted literally; thus, 'to keep house,' 'to center round (a person),' 'to catch cold,' 'to strike a bargain,' are homely but truly English phrases called *idioms*."

Now since any new idiom, by definition, disregards conventional grammar and literal interpretation, it is bound to upset teachers and textbook writers. In spite of the fact that everybody says "It's me" and "Who are you talking about?", they try to stem the tide and somehow make the English-speaking world abandon their comfortable idioms. Of course, they don't succeed; but they do succeed in making people feel guilty when they use their own language in a way that hasn't yet got the stamp of approval by so-called experts.

The idiom *to center round* (or *around*), quoted by Webster as a "homely but truly English phrase," makes a neat example of how the process works. Some twenty or thirty years ago, Mr. Theodore M. Bernstein, then Assistant Managing Editor of the *New York Times,* had qualms about the *Times'* use of the phrase *center around.* "The verb *center,*" he told his editors, "means to be collected or gathered to a point. Therefore, one may use *center on, center in,* or *center at,* but should not use *center around.*" (He later repeated this advice in his bestselling book *The Careful Writer.*) Ever since, *New York Times* editors and rewrite men have dutifully refrained from using *center around.* In a recent story about a campaign against caning—that is, beating —in British schools, I found the sentence "The effort has *centered on* the publication of a chilling, documented survey." Of course, the normal idiom in this sentence would have been *centered around.* But in the *Times,* because of Bernstein's decree, it's *centered on.*

Why do people use new idioms, despite the howls and protests of traditionalist grammarians? There are various reasons. Sometimes there's a gap in the language and a word that's needed just isn't there. So people fill the gap with whatever word happens to be handy, even though it's "ungrammatical." The "everybody . . . they" idiom I mentioned in this chapter is a good example. (Just the other day I found this delightful specimen: "Today everybody knows their sign of the Zodiac.") Grammarians insist the word *their* is wrong and should be replaced by *his or her.* But *his or her* is too cumbersome; other languages have a simple word for it, but English doesn't; so people use *their.*

Another example is the word *hopefully.* German, for instance, has the word *hoffentlich,* meaning "it is hoped." So, when people felt they wanted a word for *hoffentlich*—since they'd gotten out of the habit of saying "God willing"—they picked *hopefully.* (For example: "Monetary experts are searching for a better arrangement, one which *hopefully* would assign the dollar a less unique role than it had.") Wrong, the grammarians cried; disgraceful; a crime against the language. But people keep on using *hopefully,* a million times every day.

Sometimes people insist on expressing a shade of meaning they feel the approved word doesn't have. So they pick a word grammarians disapprove of. Take *disinterested,* for instance. All the textbooks say it can only be used to mean *impartial;* when you mean "without interest," you must say *uninterested,* but not *disinterested.*

But people feel there's a difference between *un-* and *dis-.* *Dis-* means more. *Disqualified* means more than *unqualified; disorganized* means more than *unorganized; dissatisfied* means more than *unsatisfied.* In the same way, *disinterested* means more than *uninterested;* it means a lack of interest that is *displayed.* In the memoirs of the playwright S. N. Behrman, he describes Alfred Lunt's acting style during rehearsals: "His readings were very casual, only sporadically vital, and in the main, *disinterested.*" Would the "correct" word *uninterested* have been better? I doubt it. It would have missed the flavor of Alfred Lunt's studied nonchalance.

Or take the expression *convince to,* as in "When Mr. Johnson was majority leader, he convinced a Senator to vote against the dividend credit to break a tie." Again, grammarians protest: you can *convince* someone that something is true, but you *persuade* him to do something. Again, people feel differently. They feel that *persuade* somehow has offensive overtones; it smacks of arm-twisting or trickery. Nobody wants to admit he's *persuading* people and playing on their emotions—or that he's being *persuaded* by them and talked into something he doesn't want to do.

So the word *convince,* implying logic and reasoning, is now our universal euphemism for *persuade*—in spite of what the grammarians say.

Finally people sometimes use an idiom simply because they like the sound of the word. Grammarians say you mustn't use *aggravate* to mean "annoy"; *aggravate,* they tell you, means to add to an annoyance rather than cause it. But people prefer *aggravate.* (Herman Melville wrote: "Nothing so *aggravates* an earnest person as a passive resistance.") Why? Because *aggravate,* like *grind, grate, gruff, growl, grim, grime, grisly, grumpy* and dozens of other words with unpleasant connotations, contains the sound of *gr. Annoy* just doesn't sound as aggravating as *aggravate.*

So stick to your guns. Use popular idioms. They'll make your writing more readable.

PPS

All the "incorrect" usages I discussed in this chapter and the postscript are listed as standard and fully accepted usages in *Webster's Third New International Dictionary* or *Webster's New Collegiate Dictionary* (8th edition)—except for the use of the subjunctive "If I was" instead of "If I were" to express a condition contrary to fact. I wrote to the editors of the Merriam-Webster Company about this question and got an answer in which they listed, for example, sentences from *Harper's Magazine,* the *Columbia Forum* and the (London) *Times Literary Supplement,* in which the "wrong" *was* was used. "We expect that Webster's Fourth will follow the practice of Webster's Third and try to record actual usage," the editors wrote.

Not long ago, U.S. Senator Sam Ervin was quoted as having said, *"If I was President,* I'd fire in not more than two minutes any aide that would not go down and testify."

He used good idiomatic English.

## CHAPTER 11

# OUR SHRINKING SENTENCES

---

*Whenever you can shorten a sentence, do. And
one always can. The best sentence? The shortest.*

GUSTAVE FLAUBERT

---

IF YOU don't mind spending a good deal of time browsing
and swallowing a good deal of secondhand bookstore dust,
you might still find somewhere a copy of L. A. Sherman's
*Analytics of Literature.* The book was published in 1893; according to the title page, Sherman was then professor of English at
the University of Nebraska. I don't know much else about him
and his work; but I have come across a few old men who still
remember him as the greatest teacher they ever had.

*Analytics of Literature* is one of the most original literary
studies ever written. Sherman combined a genuine feeling for
great writing with an unquenchable thirst for statistical data.
The result was a series of chapters on "the literary sentence
length in English prose" and what amounted to a brandnew
method of literary criticism.

Sherman's key concept is "the decrease of predication." He discovered and proved that English sentences have grown shorter
and shorter for centuries; but he also found that this development was an effect and not a cause. The cause was that English
writers gradually learned to get along without a complete subject
and predicate for each idea. First they wrote everything out in
strings of sentences connected with *and;* then they discovered the
subordinate clause; then they learned to cut clauses down to
phrases. Result: the average Elizabethan written sentence ran to
about 45 words; the Victorian sentence to 29; ours to 20 and

[ 130 ]

less. (Of course, Sherman's "current" figures were taken from the 1890's; but he predicted what happened later.)

As an example of early English prose, Sherman quotes the following from Hakluyt (written about 1600):

> And then we began to reckon amongst ourselves how many we were set on shore, and we found the number of be an hundred and fourteen, whereof two were drowned in the sea and eight were slain at the first encounter, so that there remained an hundred and four, of which five-and-twenty went westward with us, and two-and-fifty to the north with Hooper and Ingram; and, as Ingram since has often told me, there were not past three of their company slain, and there were but six-and-twenty of them that came again to us, so that of the company that went northward there is yet lacking, and not certainly heard of, the number of three-and-twenty men. And verily I do think that there are of them yet alive and married in the said country, at Cibola, as hereafter I purpose (God willing) to discourse of more particularly, with the reasons and causes that make me so to think of them that were lacking which were with David Ingram, Twide, Browne, and sundry others, whose names we could not remember.

The first of these two sentences has 118 words, the second 63. The average is 90.5.

Now let's compare a vaguely parallel passage, written in 1948:

> We were flying in an Army transport from Vienna to Istres, France, the airport for Marseille. Our route from Munich was planned to avoid the Alps. They are peculiar mountains; they have no rolling foothills but jut up out of a flat plain like a rock in the middle of a stream. At present they were just off to our left a few miles, completely obscured by the gray, misty nothingness that was nudging softly at the windows of our smooth-flying C-53. Besides

Alberta Snavely, wife of the Chief of Air Forces in Vienna, and myself, our party consisted of General and Mrs. Haynes, Colonel and Mrs. McMahon and their 11-year-old daughter, Alice Mary, and George Harvey, petroleum expert for the War Department. My son, Captain Ralph Tate, Jr., was our pilot, and there was a crew of three.

This passage has seven sentences in 139 words, averaging 20 words per sentence.

I owe another parallel example to Mr. Fred Reinfeld, the chess expert. In 1946 Mr. Reinfeld undertook the job of editing the fifty-year-old classic *The Principles of Chess* by James Mason; a year later he wrote, with U.S. chess champion Sammy Reshevsky, a book *Learn Chess Fast!* The two books cover exactly the same ground; and Mr. Reinfeld carefully preserved Mason's charmingly Victorian style. Here are Mason-Reinfeld and Reshevsky-Reinfeld on The Pawn:

### The Principles of Chess

The Pawn is the weakest, but not the least interesting, of all the forces. Its line of movement is forward only, or in one direction in file, one square at a time, save at its first time of moving, when it may advance one square or two squares at the option of the player—if he then has an option in the matter. But in moving two squares, if it passes one commanded by an adverse Pawn, it may be taken in passing by such adversary, as we shall have occasion to remark in considering the power of capture—hitherto left out of account. The Pawn's average range of movement in capturing—*i.e.* its attacking range—is less than two; but its total effective force is one-third that of the Knight or Bishop, very nearly.

### Learn Chess Fast!

The Pawn is paradoxical. Although it is the weakest of all the chessmen, it plays a vital role at all stages of the game. The beginner despises the Pawn for its weakness, but the chessmaster fully appreciates its important qualities. "The Pawns," wrote the great eighteenth-century master André Philidor, "are the soul of chess."

The Pawn is the only one of the chessmen which can move in only one direction: it moves *forward vertically, one square at a time*. White Pawns always move *toward* the Black side, Black Pawns always move toward the White side. In chess diagrams, White Pawns move upward, Black Pawns move downward.

Mason's average is 34 words per sentence, Reshevsky-Reinfeld's 13.

Sherman wrote: "The standard English of the future is sure to be close to the spoken norm . . . The written sentence is growing shorter year by year, while the spoken does not alter. This means, not that the literary sentence will continue to grow shorter and shorter as long as the language lasts, but on reaching approximately the oral form and structure will there remain . . . Literary English, in short, will follow the forms of standard spoken English."

Have we arrived at the end of the process? A typical magazine article now runs to less than 20 words per sentence; an ad-lib radio discussion on current affairs to about the same. Has literary English then reached the "spoken" stage? And if so, do we need any special effort to make our sentences readable?

If we always wrote the way we talked, we wouldn't have to make that effort, of course. But we don't. When we try to imitate dialogue or conversation on paper, we naturally stick to short sentences and our average may run to 15 or even 10 words per sentence. But as soon as we get the itch to appear more serious and dignified, up it goes and we get more and more Victorian; and when we yield to the temptation of pomposity, we get downright monstrous and write sentences no man has ever said aloud.

Our academicians write like this:

From the purely methodological standpoint, it is doubtful whether any antithesis is falser than that which has sometimes been set up as between an emphasis on the importance of a study of economic institutions and their functioning, on the one hand, and an emphasis, on the other hand, upon that type of calculation by "economizing" individuals, which represents the subject matter of the core of "traditional" economic analysis. For no economist, at least since the day

[ 133 ]

of Bagehot, ought to be prepared to deny that the whole of
our analysis is concerned with a world characterized by a
very special set of economic "institutions," which condition
at every point the economic calculations of the individuals
who live under those institutions. On the other hand, sufficient defense of the use of that part of "traditional" economic analysis which is here in question is provided as soon
as one contemplates the void left in our apparatus for explaining the events of the real world by those who would
press their insistence upon the importance of "institutions"
to such a point as to deny that "rational" economic calculation does occur, or that the particular type of "rational" calculation described in traditional economic theory does have
a counterpart in reality.

And political pundits write like this:

Ever since the general told a Senate committee that the
proposed sum of $8 billion for the first fifteen months of
the ERP was a "precision" amount, and more than implied
that Congress cannot reduce the sum without rendering
worthless the entire program, members who either want no
ERP at all or believe the "precision" amount to be merely
an educated guess, have revealed far greater confidence than
before that they can carry their points. And ever since General Marshall has firmly announced that, if the administra-
tive plan for the ERP presented to Congress is not accepted
without material change the result in effect will be "two
Secretaries of State"—implying disastrous confusion—staunch
friends of his and of the project who strongly dispute this
view have been forced into partial opposition.

As I said, this is far worse than Victorian; but even if one of
our literary writers deliberately uses the Victorian manner, it
doesn't sound right any more to our ears. Listen to this sentence
from a recent book by Sir Osbert Sitwell:

Not only was Caruso as natural a singer as the thrush he resembled, the blackbird or the conventional nightingale to which he was compared, but contradictorily, for all its lack of art, his voice, carrying in its strains, in the sound of those notes which he was able to attain and hold as could no other singer, of that or of a later day, the warm breath of southern evenings in an orange grove, and of roses, caught in the hush of dusk at the water's edge, possessed, as well as a high degree of technique, a certain kind of art.

The cure for this type of sentence elephantiasis is very simple. All you need is to stop being stuffy and talk like a human being, and that's that.

But there is one profession that thinks it can't live without long sentences: the lawyers. They maintain that all possible qualifications of an idea have to be put into a single sentence or legal documents would be no good.

I have asked dozens of lawyers whether they know of any court decision that would back up this notion, but I got only evasive answers. I did find, however, some excellent authority for my own point of view. David F. Cavers, a Harvard Law School professor, writes: "Casting all conditions and requirements into a single sentence . . . will often compel the unfortunate reader to take this sentence apart so that he can obtain an understanding . . . His task . . . would have been much easier if the author had broken the sentence down into several sentences . . ." And Benjamin Cardozo wrote: "There is an accuracy that defeats itself by the over-emphasis of details . . . The sentence may be so overloaded with all its possible qualifications that it will tumble down of its own weight. 'To philosophize,' says Holmes in one of his opinions—'to philosophize is to generalize, but to generalize is to omit.' "

A Harvard law professor and one Supreme Court Justice quoting another one—that's good enough authority for me, I should say.

It isn't, of course, for the dyed-in-the-wool legal minds. In the spring of 1946, Lowell B. Mason started his fight for plain language in the Federal Trade Commission; two years later, he had apparently hardly progressed an inch. One of his frequent criticisms against "prissy commands, written in gobbledygook" was slapped down like this:

> The paragraph to which Commissioner Mason's dissent is directed forbids the respondents to represent that Enrich (the product) is a cure or remedy or a competent or effective treatment for low vitality, morning lassitude, excessive yawning, chronic drowsiness, shortness of breath, run-down condition, anemia, headaches, lack of appetite, restless sleep, irregular pulse, fainting spells, palpitation, pale cheeks or lips, swollen ankles, tiredness and lack of energy, unless such representations be "expressly limited" to those cases in which the listed conditions are due to iron-deficiency anemia.

And now I want to present a nightmare: Section 23 (p) of the Internal Revenue Code. It is not an obscure portion of the law that I dug up for an exhibit; it's *the* tax basis for pension plans, one of the most important sections of our tax law. It begins as follows:

> (1) General Rule.—If contributions are paid by an employer to or under a stock bonus, pension, profit-sharing, or annuity plan, or if compensation is paid or accrued on account of any employee under a plan deferring the receipt of such compensation, such contributions or compensation shall not be deductible under subsection (a) but shall be deductible, if deductible under subsection (a) without regard to this subsection, under this subsection but only to the following extent:
>
> (A) In the taxable year when paid if the contributions are paid into a pension trust, and if such taxable year ends

within or with a taxable year of the trust for which the trust is exempt under section 165(a), in an amount determined as follows:

(i) an amount not in excess of 5 per centum of the compensation otherwise paid or accrued during the taxable year to all the employees under the trust, but such amount may be reduced for future years if found by the Commissioner upon periodical examination at not less than five-year intervals to be more than the amount reasonably necessary to provide the remaining unfunded cost of past and current service credits of all employees under the plan, plus

(ii) any excess over the amount allowable under clause (i) necessary to provide with respect to all of the employees under the trust the remaining unfunded cost of their past and current service credits distributed as a level amount, or a level percentage of compensation, over the remaining future service of each such employee, as determined under regulations prescribed by the Commissioner with the approval of the Secretary, but if such remaining unfunded cost with respect to any three individuals is more than 50 per centum of such remaining unfunded cost, the amount of such unfunded cost attributable to such individuals shall be distributed over a period of at least 5 taxable years, or

(iii) in lieu of the amounts allowable under (i) and (ii) above, an amount equal to the normal cost of the plan, as determined under regulations prescribed by the Commissioner with the approval of the Secretary, plus, if past service or other supplementary pension or annuity credits are provided by the plan, an amount not in excess of 10 per centum of the cost which would be required to completely fund or purchase such pension or annuity credits as of the date when they are included in the plan, as determined under regulations prescribed by the Commissioner with the approval of the Secretary, except that in no case shall deduction be allowed for any amount (other than the normal cost) paid in after such pension or annuity credits are completely funded or purchased.

I seriously believe that a 440-word sentence like this is a matter for a psychiatrist: there is something warped and pathological about it. Let's quick turn to something more pleasant.

The trouble with all these sentences is not their length but their complexity; there would be no trouble if long-sentence writers limited their efforts to *compound* sentences. But that's what they don't and won't do; sentences strung together with *ands* would sound as quaint nowadays as those by Hakluyt I quoted on page 131, or as "special" as those by Damon Runyon on page 109. However, there *is* such a thing as a modern long sentence that's easy to read. Let me explain.

Some time ago, Mr. John Crosby, the *New York Herald Tribune* radio critic, listened to a BBC program *American Letter.* The speaker in London, Mr. Alistair Cooke, was saying: "I believe there is a peculiar mythical appeal to Englishmen in the distant prospect of America. At least two generations of Britons have been conditioned by a whole childhood literature about the West, by the glittering stereotypes of the movies, by the regrettable tradition of reporting eccentric scandal from America . . . To more Europeans than I think would admit, there is always at the back of the mind this image, this myth of New York as Babylon, where anything goes, where everything has its price, where—in the voracious version current among my schoolmates in England—you rode the daring waves of pleasure to the music of Duke Ellington and at your side was always a beautiful and dangerous girl."

Mr. Crosby got quite excited about Mr. Cooke's style. Next day he wrote in his column: "As spoken English this is a far cry from that to which we Americans are generally subjected. We are cursed with colloquialism, much of it vigorous and descriptive, but when used to the total exclusion of cadenced and polished prose, a little confining. Mr. Cooke's sentences, while long, break down into speakable and almost chatty English . . ."

Exactly. Long sentences *can* break down into speakable units. They will do that if, like Mr. Cooke, you build your clauses one after the other in neatly parallel fashion: "by—by—by . . . where—where—where." Some of the best English prose is written this way; I cannot resist the temptation of quoting one such passage from Joseph Conrad. (Conrad lovers don't need to be told who wrote it, of course.)

> Few men realize that their life, the very essence of their character, their capabilities and their audacities, are only the expression of their belief in the safety of their surroundings. The courage, the composure, the confidence; the emotions and principles; every great and every insignificant thought belongs not to the individual but to the crowd; to the crowd that believes blindly in the irresistible force of its institutions and of its morals, in the power of its police and of its opinion. But the contact with pure unmitigated savagery, with primitive nature and primitive man, brings sudden and profound trouble into the heart. To the sentiment of being alone of one's kind, to the clear perception of the loneliness of one's thoughts, of one's sensations—to the negation of the habitual, which is safe, there is added the affirmation of the unusual, which is dangerous; a suggestion of things vague, uncontrollable, and repulsive, whose discomposing intrusion excites the imagination and tries the civilized nerves of the foolish and the wise alike.

I found another good example in one of Hamilton and Madison's papers in *The Federalist*. It deals with the argument for a federal union and against a loose confederacy like the old German Empire:

> The history of Germany is a history of wars between the emperor and the princes and states; of wars among the

princes and states themselves; of the licentiousness of the strong, and the oppression of the weak, of foreign intrusions, and foreign intrigues; of requisitions of men and money disregarded, or partially complied with; of attempts to enforce them, altogether abortive, or attended with slaughter and desolation, involving the innocent with the guilty; of general imbecility, confusion, and misery.

But don't get me wrong. I am not saying long sentences are excusable; I am only saying you can get away with them if you are as good as Hamilton and Madison, or as Conrad, or at least as Mr. Alistair Cooke. Otherwise, stay off them; remember that articles in *Life, Time,* the *Reader's Digest, Collier's* and the *Saturday Evening Post* average 18 words per sentence, and that average Americans like to get their information in this style.

Some people who cannot get over their years of training in the "smooth," long sentence, rationalize their defeat by saying that short sentences are apt to lead to jerky, staccato writing. But that just isn't so. In the five 18-word-sentence magazines just mentioned, jerky writing is rare: proper punctuation marks between the sentences—periods, semicolons, colons, or dashes—keep the movement at an even flow.

Other people insist that short sentences make dull reading. There are many, for instance, who would agree that the *New Yorker* is ten times as readable as the *Reader's Digest.* They are right—but the reason is not the difference in sentence length (*New Yorker* sentences average 20 words) but rather the difference in sentence *variety*; the *New Yorker* contains far more sentences under 10 and over 30 words than the *Reader's Digest.* Moral: stick to a short average sentence, but vary the pattern as much as you can.

As an example, I shall close this chapter with a little editorial from the *New York Herald Tribune.* It starts with a 50-word sentence; but by the time the writer is through, the average has come down to 16.

## No, No, No, No, No, No

A girl in a bar stuffed nickels in a jukebox for one uninterrupted hour, and during that time played nothing but a tune called "Civilization," known also to some as "Bongo, Bongo, Bongo" and to others by the sixfold repetition of the word "No" with which the first line ends. Another customer promptly shot her and then, for good measure, shot the bartender. This appears eminently reasonable, but more careful consideration of the case will convince the thoughtful that the problem goes deeper than that. The jukebox, after all, remains; so does the record; so do women with nickels. Furthermore, shootings inside a bar are always to be deplored; they disturb the customers, sometimes break bottles and are often characterized by poor marksmanship.

If there is any recourse, it must be approached in a more fundamental manner. One must proceed back through the woman with nickels, through the record, through the jukebox, to the original malefactors: the men who wrote the song. They are the guilty ones, for violence was inevitable the moment "Civilization" was published. Here is where legislation can have a substantial effect. Let us make it the law that hereafter the authors of any popular song must hear it played, without interruption, for six hours before they will be permitted to make it public. Such a restriction would make it unlikely that any such song as "Civilization" would ever be published again; it would, in fact, make it unlikely that any popular song would be published. Nothing could be fairer than that.


PS

Back in 1949, I mentioned five mass-circulation magazines whose prose style averaged about 18 words a sentence—*Life, Time,* the *Reader's Digest, Collier's* and the *Saturday Evening Post.* Now three of these five magazines are dead, but *Time* and the *Reader's Digest* are still with us and their average sentence length is no longer 18 words but something like 15 to 17. (I can't offer exact statistics but I'm pretty sure my random counts are typical.) This may not seem like much of a decrease, but if you look at it as 10 percent over a period of 25 years, you'll realize it's quite a change.

How do you go about writing 15-to-17-word sentences? My students—lawyers, bankers, government employees—usually started with sentences averaging forty words or so. After I'd taught them to split their sentences in two and make full sentences out of subordinate clauses, their averages dropped to about 20 or 21 words. But then they were stuck. To go below that figure, they had to learn to zip up their writing and put in an occasional sentence of two to five words. This they found much more difficult. It meant they had to pay attention to rhythm and force.

Not long ago I found a newspaper report on health conditions in Indonesia. It began like this:

> Health clinics have been scattered across Asia in recent years, but they are still scarce. Most people who go to them live within walking distance—a mile or two. Transportation costs money. Yet in East Java clinics are meant to serve people within a radius of 10 to 15 miles.
>
> Hospitals? They are few and are considered to be places where one goes to die. In view of the sanitary conditions, that is often the patient's fate.
>
> In the eyes of the villagers the local medicine man or woman is better.
>
> The difficulties confronting the professionals are described by Dr. Wongsokusumo Bahrawi, who directs health care in East Java. He has the best facilities in Indonesia, but he is the first to concede their inadequacy.
>
> "We have 1,250 doctors for 25.4 million people in East Java," he explained. "That sounds like one doctor for every 20,000 people, but it's a distortion because most of them are

in big cities. So really, in rural areas, there is only one doctor for every 180,000 people."

The United States has a doctor for every 700 people.

This excerpt contains 184 words and 14 sentences. The average sentence length is 13 words.

How did the reporter do it? He wasn't afraid of starting his second paragraph with the one-word question "Hospitals?" and he wrote, with the utmost simplicity, "The United States has a doctor for every 700 people."

That's the way a seasoned pro does it. To get to that point in your own writing you'll need practice, self-discipline and a deep conviction that short sentences are better than long ones.

## CHAPTER 12

# OUR EXPANDING WORDS

---

*One of your first jobs, as you write for
money, will be to get rid of your vocabulary.*

JACK WOODFORD

---

ON THE first anniversary of American independence, July
4th, 1777, an Englishman was sent to prison because his
sympathies were on our side. He was John Horne Tooke, a member of Parliament, who had asked for help to widows and orphans
of Americans "murdered by the king's troops at Lexington and
Concord."

By a curious chain of circumstances, that date became historic
in the science of language. When Tooke came out of prison, his
political career was over; he decided to take up philology, of all
things, and a few years later published a book called *The Diversions of Purley.* It was so revolutionary that some professional
philologists haven't caught up with it yet.

Tooke went into etymology, the science of word origins, with
a vengeance. He traced back the derivations of thousands of
English words and found that each one of them originally
described a simple operation. In short, he dug out of the language
what we now—175 years later—call "operational definitions." As
he put it, "that imagined operation of the mind which has been
termed abstraction is in truth only a device of language for con-
veying thought more speedily . . . What are called the operations
of the mind are merely the operations of language . . . Words
like *fate, chance, luck, saint, providence, hell* and *heaven* are all
merely participles poetically embodied . . . These participles, not

[ 144 ]

understood as such, have caused a metaphysical jargon, and a false morality, which can only be dissipated by etymology . . ."

Of truth, for example, Tooke wrote: "*Truth* means simply and merely—that which is trowed . . . It is the past participle of the verb *to trow*—*to think, to believe firmly, to be thoroughly persuaded of* . . . Truth supposes mankind: *for whom* and *by whom* alone the word is formed, and *to whom* only it is applicable. If no man, no truth. There is therefore no such thing as eternal, immutable, everlasting truth; unless, mankind, *such as they are at present,* be also eternal, immutable, and everlasting. Two persons may contradict each other, and yet both speak truth: for the truth of one person may be opposite the truth of another."

In short, Horne Tooke arrived at the same conclusion as John Stuart Mill, who called metaphysics "that fertile field of delusion propagated by language."

But all this is by the way. The significant thing Tooke found out about language is that all the structural parts of language— the prepositions, conjunctions, prefixes, suffixes, and whatnot— once were full-fledged, meaningful words that got gradually whittled down to handy little symbols. Language, as Tooke discovered, goes through a continuous process of condensation and abbreviation; through the centuries people manage to cram more and more meaning into fewer and fewer words. What once took a whole sentence or clause to express, can now be compressed into a single word; and language is full of clever devices that make for more and more speed.

Tooke's examples range from such simple Anglo-Saxon words as *tooth* (that which tuggeth) and *smith* (one who smiteth) to such Latin imports as *memorandum* (that which ought to be remembered) and *legislator* (a proposer of laws). The principle is always the same: a single participle or complex word takes the place of a cumbersome word combination.

The point is that in modern English this process has been going on *simultaneously* with the shortening of sentences. Our sentences have grown shorter in number of words, but the words themselves have grown longer and richer in meaning. And while we don't need so many words any more to express our thoughts, the words we do use carry a much heavier load of ideas. So, in a sense, our modern short sentences are an illusion; as far as ideas are concerned, our sentences are usually much longer and fuller than those that people wrote two or three centuries ago.

Take, for instance, the comparison between Hakluyt's *Voyages* and the description of a modern airplane trip on page 131. The average sentence has shrunk from 90 to 20 words; but the average word has lengthened from 1.35 syllables to 1.48 syllables. Or take the two samples from the Victorian chess manual and the modern one on page 132: the sentences have shrunk from 34 words to 13, but the words have lengthened from 1.36 syllables to 1.43.

But, you may say, the examples are not fully parallel; they don't cover exactly the same ideas in both versions. So here is the perfect illustration: a comparison between the King James Version of the Bible, published in 1611, and the Revised Standard Version, published in 1946. The text is, of course, exactly parallel; there is only a change in idiom from the seventeenth century to the twentieth. My example is taken from Paul's *Epistle to the Romans*, Chapter 13.

| *King James Version:* | *Revised Standard Version:* |
|---|---|
| Let every soul be subject unto higher powers. For there is no power but of God: the powers that be are ordained of God. Whosoever therefore resisteth the power, resisteth the ordinance of God: and they that resist shall receive to themselves damnation. For rulers are not a terror to good works, but to the evil. Wilt thou then not be afraid of the power? Do that which is good, and thou shalt have praise of the same: For he is the minister of God to thee for good. But | Let every person be subject to the governing authorities. For there is no authority except from God, and those that exist have been instituted by God. Therefore he who resists the authorities resists what God has appointed, and those who resist will incur judgment. For rulers are not a terror to good conduct, but to bad. Would you have no fear of him who is in authority? Then do what is good, and you will receive his approval, for he is God's servant for your |

if thou do that which is evil, be afraid; for he beareth not the sword in vain: for he is the minister of God, a revenger to execute wrath upon him that doeth evil. Wherefore ye must needs be subject, not only for wrath, but also for conscience' sake. For, for this cause pay ye tribute also: for they are God's ministers, attending continually upon this very thing. Render therefore to all their dues: tribute to whom tribute is due; custom to whom custom; fear to whom fear; honor to whom honor.

good. But if you do wrong, be afraid, for he does not bear the sword in vain; he is the servant of God to execute his wrath upon the wrong-doer. Therefore one must be subject, not only to avoid God's wrath but also for the sake of conscience. For the same reason you also pay taxes, for the authorities are ministers of God, attending to this very thing. Pay all of them their dues, taxes to whom taxes are due, revenue to whom revenue is due, respect to whom respect is due, honor to whom honor is due.

You see what happened here? The committee that worked on the modern version naturally tried as hard as they could not to change the meaning; on the contrary, they tried to use words that would express the same ideas exactly as a modern reader would express them himself. So they changed *soul* to *person, powers* to *authorities, ordained* to *instituted, good works* to *good conduct, praise* to *approval, him that doeth evil* to *wrong-doer, custom* to *revenue,* and *fear* to *respect.* Result: the words have become longer—in spite of the fact that we now say *resists* instead of *resisteth* and so on. The average word in the sample from King James Version has 1.37 syllables, in the sample from the modern version, 1.44.

True, all these differences are not very significant: they average only about five percent. But remember that my modern examples are all exceptionally simple: a passage from the *Reader's Digest,* a section from an elementary chess manual, and something from the Bible. All were written in very simple modern prose. When it comes to more sophisticated modern writing, the average word has not 1.44 syllables, but 1.50, 1.75, or even 2.00. After all, we have seen that words become longer the more abstract the ideas they express; and some writers seem unable to deal with the problems of modern civilization in words of less than a two-syllable average. (Remember that half the words we use are little monosyllables, like *is* and *of*; so a two-syllable average really means a parade of four- and five-syllable words.) What's more, as we have seen, our more heavy-handed writers don't care much for the modern short sentence either; and so we get prose that consists of overlong sentences packed to the brim with long, overloaded words.

What I am driving at is this. Most of the long, complex words in modern prose are not labels for things in the world around us —like *radioactivity*—but condensed expressions of abstract ideas *that can be expressed just as well in two or more shorter words.* This is proved by the fact that at one time or other our ancestors did express them that way. I am not saying that we should all go back to more primitive methods of speech; but I do say that we shouldn't stuff our sentences with tightly packed bundles of abstractions without ever choosing a simpler way of expressing the same ideas.

Mind you, I am not saying that compactness isn't a virtue. But there's a point of diminishing returns and it comes sooner than most people think. I remember a conversation I once had with a hosiery manufacturer who was working on a series of slogans for his product. One he was particularly proud of was "dimensional restorability." When I asked what in the world he meant by that, he explained that the stockings he made didn't shrink or stretch but stayed the same size. He challenged me to improve upon his two-word slogan, and I immediately suggested "back-to-size." But that sort of thing didn't satisfy him at all. "Dimensional restorability" was for him the acme of English prose.

I mention "dimensional restorability" because it seems a perfect antidote against the itch-for-the-long-word. Maybe it would have helped if the writers of the following pieces of prose had had "dimensional restorability," framed, in front of them while they wrote. But possibly not: I suspect these writers *wanted* to appear profound.

Pomposity thrives in every kind of soil. Here is a literary critic:

> The biological concept of function brings the phenomena of sentience and symbolization within the purview of experimental analysis.

Here is a music critic (Olin Downes of the *New York Times*):

> Mr. Breisach gave a musicianly and generally meritorious reading of the score. It is not to be concluded that if he continues to interpret this score he will necessarily fail to confer upon it more of the tension, fantasy and sparkle that permeate the miraculous composition [of *The Magic Flute*].

Here is a drama critic (Howard Barnes of the *New York Herald Tribune*):

> With all the latitude and sustained crescendo of a fine musical composition "The Best Years of Our Lives" moves with variety and instancy to its climax. On the way, it celebrates an experience common to most of us in recent months with such courage and eloquence that it becomes a singularly dynamic and rewarding document of the stresses and satisfactions in living.

Here is an art critic:

> No other painter [than Vermeer van Delft] with all the liberty in the world, has ever surpassed that last gravity of balance.

A nugget from the U.S. Treasury Department:

> The generally accepted view is that the additional units of effort required to earn additional income tend to have increasing disutility.

[ 149 ]

A bit of sociology:

> If distance is the disclosing concept of the meaning of the global character of the war, status has a similar value in describing the instability of the individual adolescent under war conditions.

And finally something from psychology:

> The elementary fact of actualizing the stimulational function of objects, with its consequent selectional and organizational implications, points to a satisfactory behavior relationship between the organism and its surroundings which well merits the name of control.

But of course you know that sort of thing very well. Lord knows, these examples are no rarities. I put them here because I thought that together they would serve to make the point clearly. And I am going to add two more where pomposity is shown up beautifully by the simplicity of the subject.

One of these examples was *meant* to be funny. It comes from an article by James Reston of the *New York Times* in which that serious reporter on international affairs took time out to explain the World Series to U.N. delegates:

> (1) The purposes and principles of the world series are as follows: (a) To bring about, by peaceful means, and in accordance with the principles of justice and law, a settlement or adjustment of the annual dispute over who has the best baseball team in the United States. (b) To achieve co-operation between the National and American Leagues in solving problems of a sporting character and in promoting and encouraging respect for human rights and for fundamental freedoms, without distinction as to race, sex, language, or religion (this is better known as the "Jackie Robinson clause"). (c) To provide solace and diversion for the American

people and to that end to settle disputes that might otherwise lead to a breach of the peace.

(2) Membership. There are no permanent members of the world series, as in the United Nations. Membership in the world series is open to the two peace-loving teams that accept the obligations of the National and American Leagues and beat the bejabbers out of all other opposition. . . .

The other example was *not* meant to be funny. It comes from a fat scholarly tome on *The Prediction of Personal Adjustment* and reads as follows:

It is quite possible that in many cases the assumption of linearity in combinations is not justified for composite criterion measures. Certainly there are many cases where a person may be so poor on one component of the activity that it is impossible to compensate this deficiency with any amount of excellence on some or all of the other components. On the other hand, there are doubtless many instances where a score on a given component of a criterion beyond a certain point would be of no advantage so far as success in the activity as a whole is concerned. For example, in the case of marital adjustment, there is probably a definite limit or point of diminishing returns as to frequency with which a man kisses his wife so far as it affects marital happiness.

Pomposity is often funny, but it has its serious side. Long words are hard to read; sometimes they are actually unintelligible. For example, the following letter from the Veterans Administration didn't mean a thing to its addressee:

The non-compensable evaluation heretofore assigned you for your service-connected disability is confirmed and continued.

The veterans who got this information wrote back: "What the hell does this mean?" He was told there hadn't been any change

[ 151 ]

in his physical condition and so he still wouldn't get any money.

I like this last example because it shows clearly what is the trouble with this kind of language and what isn't. The trouble is that the thoughts are bunched together in tight little bundles like "non-compensable" or "service-connected"; in other words, the trouble is the terrific *density* of the language. The things being said come too thick and fast for the ordinary reader.

The trouble is *not*, however, what is usually called vocabulary. What I mean is this: the poor, bewildered veteran who got that letter may have known perfectly well the meaning of the words *to compensate, evaluation, service, connected,* and *disability;* but that didn't help him a bit. Even if he had studied the special Veterans Administration words "non-compensable" and "service-connected" beforehand, he wouldn't have been able to decipher the letter. It simply wasn't a case of being unfamiliar with words.

In fact, if someone cannot understand a piece of writing, the trouble is rarely that his vocabulary is too small; usually he simply can't cope with *the way the words are used.*

That's a simple truth. But nowadays there is so much talk about the glories of vocabulary that maybe it's worthwhile to add a few words here. The vocabulary builders say if you have trouble with reading it simply means you don't know enough words; learn more words and you are up there with the masterminds. The facts are different: you can't really "learn words" without learning and studying a subject; and even if you could, words by themselves wouldn't help you much in reading.

Vocabulary building as a major industry dates back to some intelligence tests that were given to various occupational groups about a dozen years ago. It turned out that big executives topped everybody else in the range of their vocabulary. That's not a particularly exciting discovery since corporation officials usually get to be where they are after they have had a lot of diversified experience. But the vocabulary builders have seized upon that little experiment and quoted it in hundreds of full-page ads since. Their logic is simple: top executives have top vocabulary; hence: vocabulary means success. And so the battle cry was born: "Build up your vocabulary for quick advancement."

Of course that's all nonsense. It's simply the good old Horatio Alger formula turned cultural: from intellectual rags to material riches. What's more important, however, is the theory behind it: that by learning "big words" you will learn things you didn't know before. The trouble is that all the hullabaloo about vocabulary building gives the ordinary citizen the notion that there's a premium on rare and unfamiliar words. Indeed, he ought to realize that they work like a drug—harmless in small doses but dangerous if used too much.

The other day I glanced through one of the best known of the vocabulary-building books. The preface explained proudly that after studying the book the reader wouldn't say any more "He was busy as a bee" but "He was bustling and industrious." Exactly. He would get ashamed of his natural idioms and pepper his speech and writing with strained and ill-fitting expressions.

In another book I found the word *to brachiate* among those to be studied. The definition was *to swing by your arms from the branches of a tree like a monkey.* Which reminded me of the wise old lady's rule to "keep away from fancy words because you never can tell what they mean."

# ℞ FOR READABILITY

*When a thought is too weak to sup-
port a simple expression, reject it.*

**VAUVENARGUES**

AND now let's get down to brass tacks.
Suppose you are facing some bread-and-butter writing job
—like the Employee Manual of the Wondrous Widget Company
—and you want to apply what I've told you so far in this book.

Here is what you do:

First, make sure you know who you are writing for. Have a
look at your prospective readers. Talk to them. Find out what
they know, what they don't know, and what they *want* to know.
Take your own private opinion poll on the questions and answers
they have in their minds. Use the results: write for your readers
and nobody else.

Now collect your material. Get all the information you need;
pay special attention to little things that will add color and
human interest. Look out for human touches like the fact that
old Christopher Crusty, the founder of the firm, was laid up with
poison ivy when the millionth Wondrous Widget rolled off the
assembly line.

Then, when you have all the stuff you need, stop for a while
and do something else. Catch up with your correspondence or
work on another assignment for a couple of days. Give your unconscious a chance.

When you are ready to start writing, you will probably have
at least one idea for an "angle" or a "plot." Maybe you can

build your manual around the life of Matthew Mumble, who just finished his fiftieth year as assistant bookkeeper; or you can describe the first day at work of Betty Brandnew, who has just been hired as a typist. Or maybe that sort of thing doesn't suit your purpose; but *some* kind of basic structure will. There must be a way for you to write something people are going to read— not just a heap of facts.

Once you have gotten that far, it will be easy to figure out what should come first and what last. Don't make that old mistake and start your Employee Manual with four pages on how the company got off to a slow start in 1853. Start with something interesting and promising; wind up with something the reader will remember.

As you write, make sure there's plenty of narrative and a good deal of dialogue. There should be live people in your booklet. When you talk about the company, say *we*; when you talk about the employee, say *you*. There's no excuse for the It-is-expected-that-Employees-of-the-Company-shall school of manual writing.

And now do something about your sentences and words. Short sentences are easy to write. Remember that *compound* sentences —those with *ands* and *buts*—are not so bad; go after the *complex* sentences. Look for the joints where the conjunctions are—*if, because, as,* and so on—and split your sentences up.

Short words are harder to manage. Again, it's not the long word that's the trouble, but the *complex* word. Look out for prefixes and suffixes—syllables like *pre, re,* or *de,* and *ality, ousness,* or *ization.* Words with these syllables are those to split or replace. Do it consistently and you'll be surprised at the results.

Probably it won't be easy for you to express yourself in short, simple words. You *say* them every day, but they don't come to you when you sit down to write. This is where you need help— devices, tricks, rules. Here are a few:

First of all, get yourself a dictionary of simple synonyms. I don't mean an ordinary book of synonyms, and I certainly don't

[ 155 ]

mean Roget's *Thesaurus*. (If you pick synonyms out of Roget, you will poison your style in no time.) What I mean is a dictionary where words are explained by the simplest possible definitions. Ordinary dictionaries don't do that; the one I recommend to you is the *Thorndike-Barnhart Dictionary* published by Doubleday & Company.

Let's say you want to use Thorndike-Barnhart to improve this sentence in your manual: "The Company encourages the continued education of staff members of all ranks to supplement the practical training and experience acquired during office hours."

Look up the key words in this sentence in Thorndike-Barnhart. You will find:

> *encourage* ............................ *urge*
> *continue* ............................. *keep up*
> *supplement* .......................... *add to*
> *acquire* .............................. *get*

Now use these simpler words with *we* and *you*: "We urge you to keep up your education and add to the practical training and experience you get during office hours."

This gives you a fair idea what Thorndike-Barnhart will do to improve your style.

But you don't even have to use Thorndike-Barnhart to find simple synonyms. I shall give you a sort of miniature Thorndike-Barnhart right here and now.

My simple-word finder comes in three parts—three lists of words. If you use these three lists conscientiously and fully, your style will soon lose its heaviness and begin to look like the girl in a diet advertisement *after*.

The first list consists of "empty words." These are particles—prepositions, conjunctions, adverbs, etc.—that belong to the structure of the language. When you remember, as I said before, that these words make up more than fifty percent of all the words you use, you will understand that it makes a tremendous difference whether they are simple or elaborate. Follow the rule that in general one "empty" word is better than two or three, and a short one is better than a long one. If you can get rid of the "empty" word altogether, so much the better, of course. Here is my list:

TOO HEAVY PREPOSITIONS AND CONJUNCTIONS:

*along the lines of:* like
*as to:* about (or leave out)
*for the purpose of:* for
*for the reason that:* since, because
*from the point of view of:* for
*inasmuch as:* since, because
*in favor of:* for, to
*in order to:* to
*in accordance with:* by, under
*in the case of:* if
*in the event that:* if
*in the nature of:* like
*in the neighborhood of:* about
*in terms of:* in, for (or leave out)
*on the basis of:* by
*on the grounds that:* since, because
*prior to:* before
*with a view to:* to
*with reference to:* about (or leave out)
*with regard to:* about (or leave out)
*with the result that:* so that

TOO HEAVY CONNECTIVES:

*accordingly:* so
*consequently:* so
*for this reason:* so
*furthermore:* then

*hence:* so
*in addition:* besides, also
*indeed:* in fact
*likewise:* and, also
*more specifically:* for instance, for example
*moreover:* now, next
*nevertheless:* but, however
*that is to say:* in other words
*thus:* so
*to be sure:* of course

And here are three more words that are almost always superfluous:

*concerned*
*involved*
*respectively*

(Example: "The teachers and students concerned should distribute and complete the forms involved, respectively.")

My second list consists of auxiliary verbs. This one works on the principle that the more natural and idiomatic English gets, the more it expresses ideas by auxiliary verbs. Take, for instance, this passage from an employee manual: "With a view to broadening the individual's training and increasing his knowledge of the Company's organization, operations and service, members of the staff are selected periodically for advanced training. These training programs are designed to give the individual an opportunity . . ." etc. What you would *say* is something like this: "We'd *like to help you add* to your training and *get to know* the company better . . . Our advanced training programs are *meant* to give you the opportunity . . ." etc. So you see that ordinarily you use a lot of such words as *like to, get to,* and *mean to.* Here is my list:

*aim to*
*be apt to*

*be bound to*
*be known to*
*be supposed to*
*care to*
*claim to*
*get to (got to)*
*happen to*
*hate to*
*have to*
*help* ——*ing*
*keep* ——*ing*
*like to*
*mean to*
*mind* ——*ing*
*plan to*
*seem to*
*stop* ——*ing*
*use(d) to*
*want to*

My third list is the longest. Maybe it needs a little explanation. It's a list of simple verbs that describe movements of the human body, with a list of adverbs that can be combined with them. Verb-adverb combinations are a specialty of the English language; it's what the language naturally uses when it needs a new expression for a new idea. Think of the war and of *breakthroughs, blackouts,* and *pinup girls.* Or think of sports and of *lineup, strikeout,* and *touchdown.* Or think of *tryout* and *stand-in, walk-on* and *closeup, checkoff* and *sitdown.*

Of course all kinds of verbs can be combined with all kinds of adverbs, but most important are a group of short Anglo-Saxon verbs that deal with movements of the human body. They are the most idiomatic words in the language; there is a theory that they are also the oldest—those all others stem from. Whether that's true or not, the fact remains that practically all abstract ideas can

[ 159 ]

be expressed by one of these verbs, either by itself or combined with an adverb. Translating high-sounding abstractions into such words as *set up* or *fall through* is a fascinating game.

My list contains fifty verbs and twenty adverbs. Not every verb can be combined with every adverb, of course; but what with different meanings in different contexts, the list covers about a thousand abstract ideas. So it really *is* a miniature Thorndike-Barnhart dictionary.

| VERBS: | | | ADVERBS: | |
| --- | --- | --- | --- | --- |
| *bear* | *go* | *slip* | *about* | *forth* |
| *blow* | *hang* | *split* | *across* | *in* |
| *break* | *hold* | *stand* | *ahead* | *off* |
| *bring* | *keep* | *stay* | *along* | *on* |
| *call* | *lay* | *stick* | *apart* | *out* |
| *carry* | *let* | *strike* | *around* | *over* |
| *cast* | *look* | *take* | *aside* | *through* |
| *catch* | *make* | *talk* | *away* | *together* |
| *come* | *pick* | *tear* | *back* | *under* |
| *cut* | *pull* | *throw* | *down* | *up* |
| *do* | *push* | *tie* | | |
| *draw* | *put* | *touch* | | |
| *drive* | *run* | *turn* | | |
| *drop* | *set* | *walk* | | |
| *fall* | *shake* | *wear* | | |
| *get* | *show* | *work* | | |
| *give* | *skip* | | | |

This list will not only make your words simpler but will force you to streamline your sentences too. You'll learn to rely on verbs rather than nouns and adjectives. Psychologists have used the ratio between adjectives and verbs for years to measure the forcefulness of writing; writing teachers have been preaching the gospel of the active verb ever since anybody can remember.

The main trouble with most current writing is that it consists of nothing but nouns and adjectives, glued together with prepositions or with *is, was, are,* and *were.* Here are a few random examples:

A historian: "His [Charles A. Beard's] attack on the consequences of intervention is not accompanied by any demonstration of the feasibility of isolation."

An economist: "A problem which has deadlocked top corporate and union officials with no prospect of satisfactory solution is the determination of the appropriate subjects for collective bargaining and the definition of spheres of authority which are of sole concern to management. Rulings of the National Labor Relations Board have not been helpful in drawing a line of demarcation between those matters which are bargainable and those which remain the sole function of management."

An English teacher: "Marcel Proust's vivid description of the long train of recollections invoked by the taste and smell of a little cake dipped in tea, in *Remembrance of Things Past,* is the ultimate expression of the tremendously important role played by associative processes arising from re-experiencing a sensory impression which was originally associated with a powerful emotion."

A biologist: "Modern taxonomy is the product of increasing awareness among biologists of the uniqueness of individuals, and the wide range of variation which may occur in any population of individuals. The taxonomist is, therefore, primarily concerned with the measurement of variation in series of individuals which stand as representatives of the species in which he is interested."

(This last example comes from the Kinsey report *Sexual Behavior in the Human Male*—which seems to prove that it wasn't exactly readability that made it a bestseller.)

Now let me do a little translating with my verb-adverb list: "He *takes a stand* against intervention and what *it brings about,* but he doesn't *show* how we could have *got along with* isolation."

[ 161 ]

"Management and labor have been trying to *set down* rules for what should be *worked out* by collective bargaining and what should *stay under* the authority of management alone. But they are deadlocked and it doesn't *look* as if a real solution is going to *turn up* soon. . . ." etc.

It so happens that these four passages also contain excellent examples on two other points. One is the question of the preposition at the end of the sentence. Take "the species in which he is interested." People don't talk that way. They say "the species he's interested in." Putting prepositions at the end of sentences is one of the things that will unfailingly turn stiff prose into idiomatic prose.

Perhaps you wonder why I haven't discussed this together with the other grammatical superstitions I talked about in Chapter 10. It certainly isn't because Shakespeare never put a preposition at the end. He did—hundreds of times—from "The thousand natural shocks That flesh is heir to" to "We are such stuff as dreams are made on."

Yet the preposition at the end really doesn't belong with doubtful or controversial usages. It is one of the glories of English prose. Originally it was attacked by grammarians for the silly reason that *prepositio,* in Latin, means something that "comes before"; and when people realized that Latin rules don't always work in English, they defended the old rule for the equally silly reason that a preposition gets too much emphasis at the end of a sentence. As if anyone would say "that flesh is heir *to*" or "as dreams are made *on*"! The truth is, of course, that the English language is capable of fusing a preposition and another word together whenever they are closely joined by the meaning of the sentence. The word *in,* in the sentence from the Kinsey report, may be grammatically part of the phrase *in which,* but for the speaker of the sentence it is part of the expression *interested-in.*

Which is why the President of the National Council of

Teachers of English recently called a preposition "a good word to end a sentence with" and why Winston Churchill, when such an "error" was pointed out to him, answered: "This is the type of arrant pedantry, up with which I shall not put."

And what would English prose be without sentences like *He was an executive who knew what he was talking about, He could thus be argued with, not muttered at* or *The average American has a fixed idea that liver and iron are substances he ought to be getting more of?*

The four passages on page 161 are also good examples for the difference between *that* and *which*. There are eight *whiches* in those sentences—all of them misused. In good, idiomatic English it should be *A problem that has deadlocked* and *spheres of authority that are* and *those matters that are* and *those that remain* and *a sensory impression that was* and *the wide range of variation that may* and *individuals that stand* and, of course, the *species he is interested in.* The rule is this: *which* should be used in a "non-restrictive" clause that could, without damage, be left out or put between parentheses; whenever you can't do that, the clause is "restrictive" and you should use *that.*

Now you will say that after spending a lot of time ridiculing grammatical rules I suddenly turn into a stickler for the *that*-and-*which* rule. But wait a minute. That's exactly the mistake the "progressive" grammarians are making. They see that *which* is used instead of *that* all over the place and so they proclaim that the rule should be thrown into the ashcan with all the other outmoded rules.

But the situation here is quite different. This isn't a case of a grass roots movement against a strict grammatical rule. It's exactly the other way round. The natural idiom is to use *that* for "restrictive" clauses; it always has been and still is. The use of *which* instead of *that* has been dragged into the language by the writers, the literati, the clerks. Jespersen, in his *Essentials of English Grammar,* says: "*Which* . . . has been gaining ground at the expense of *that,* chiefly in the last few centuries and in the more pretentious kinds of literature. One of the reasons for this preference was probably that [*which*] reminded classical scholars of the corresponding Latin pronoun. When Addison in the *Spectator* complains of the injury done recently to . . . *which* by the "Jacksprat" *that,* he turns all historical truth topsy-turvy, for *that* was really the favorite relative word in literature from the Middle Ages on; but in deference to his erroneous view of the historical development he corrected many a natural *that* into a less natural *which,* when he edited the *Spectator* in book-form."

When I read this, I naturally looked the matter up in Addison. Sure enough, Jespersen was right: the original version sounds more natural in every single case. Here is one example:

> A screech-owl at midnight has alarmed a family more than a band of robbers; nay, the voice of a cricket hath struck more terror than the roaring of a lion. There is nothing so inconsiderable *that* may not appear dreadful to an imagination *that* is filled with omens and prognostics.

That's the way it originally appeared in the *Spectator;* in the book edition Addison left it *imagination that is filled* but changed it to *nothing so inconsiderable, which may not appear dreadful.* He shouldn't have; the sentence was perfect as it stood.

Addison, however, was an exception. Usually writers, like the authors of the four examples I quoted, pepper their sentences with unnatural *whiches* right from the start. When they do find out about the distinction, it is often a real revelation to them and they turn into determined *which*-hunters and *that*-fans. Wilson Follett, for instance, who once ran a column on "The State of the Language" in the *Atlantic,* wrote that he was a *which*-writer until late in life, when he was "converted" and "saw the light." And H. W. Fowler tells us that Lord Morley, when he prepared a revised edition of his works, "was particularly keen on having the word *which,* wherever there was the possibility, exchanged for *that . . ."*

After reading all this, you will start *which*-hunting yourself, I hope. You will find it a pleasant and rewarding indoor sport.

## PS

The main point of this chapter—and of the last one—is how to simplify your vocabulary. This is the core of the book. After some thirty years, I know it's easier to teach people to collect facts, do interviews, put people in their writing and shorten their sentences, than it is to teach them to use simple words.

Like everyone else, you spend your life in a world filled with all kinds of bureaucratic, technical or legal gobbledygook. The only way to fight it is active, daily, unceasing resistance. You must learn to replace every *prior to* by *before,* every *subsequently* by *later,* every *we are endeavoring to ascertain* by *we're trying to find out.* It takes years until this becomes an invariable habit and you automatically translate jargon into English.

If the reporter quoted on page 142 had used jargon instead of English, he wouldn't have written "The United States has a doctor for every 700 people." Instead he'd have written "The per capita distribution of doctors among the total population of the United States reflects a ratio of one physician to 700 potential patients."

How would *you* have written it?

CHAPTER 14

# DEGREES OF PLAIN TALK

---

*Everything which is written is meant either to please or to instruct. This second object is difficult to effect without attending to the first.*

SIDNEY SMITH

---

POPULARIZATION is a mysterious business.

In November 1941, the *Journal of the American Medical Association* printed a paper by Drs. Rovenstine and Wertheim, in which the authors reported on a new kind of anesthesia called "therapeutic nerve block." This was obviously of interest to doctors, but nobody bothered to tell the general public about it. The nerve block was not then considered news.

Six years later, the popular magazines broke out into a rash of nerve-block articles. On October 25, 1947, the *New Yorker* began a three-part profile of Dr. Rovenstine; two days later, *Life* published a four-page picture-story of his work. Other magazines followed. Suddenly, the nerve block had become something everybody ought to know about.

I came across this mystery when I was looking for a good example of what popularization does to language and style. The nerve-block articles are perfect specimens. On its way from the *A.M.A. Journal* to *Life* and the *New Yorker,* the new method of anesthesia underwent a complete change of coloring, tone, and style. A study of the three articles is a complete course in readability by itself.

On the following pages are excerpts from the three articles. Nothing has been changed; but to show clearly the differences in sentence length, I put / between the sentences, and to show the differences in human interest, I capitalized the "personal words" (see Chapter 7) and italicized the "personal sentences" (see Chapter 8). (You will notice the difference in word length without my pointing it up.)

This is the beginning of "Therapeutic Nerve Block" by E. A. Rovenstine, M.D., and H. M. Wertheim, M.D. (*Journal of the American Medical Association,* vol. 117, no. 19, Nov. 8, 1941):

> "Therapeutic nerve block" is but one of the many ramifications of regional analgesia./ The history of the introduction and development of perineurial injections of analgesic and neurolytic agents for therapy coincides with that of similar types of injections to control the pain associated with surgical procedures./ The use of surgical analgesic nerve blocks has eclipsed by far similar procedures employed to cure or alleviate pain or symptoms resulting from disease or injury . . ./

The paper ends as follows:

> The most interesting and probably more promising and fruitful results from therapeutic nerve blocking are the technics for interrupting sympathetic pathways with analgesic or neurolytic solutions./ This recent practice has already gained wide application and produced many favorable reports./ A comparison of the value of the chemical destruction of sympathetic pathways or surgical section cannot be made accurately with present knowledge and experience, but there are indications that for many conditions the former are to be preferred./
> Interruption of the sympathetic pathways at the stellate ganglion is used to cure hyperhidrosis of the upper extremity./ It is useful to relieve sympathalgia of the face and causalgia./ It has been employed successfully to treat post-

traumatic spreading neuralgia, the pain of amputation stumps and vasomotor disturbances./ The treatment of angina pectoris after medical remedies have failed to relieve pain is now conceded to include alcohol injections of the upper thoracic sympathetic ganglions./ The same procedure has been effective in controlling or alleviating the distressing pain from an aneurysm of the arch or the descending aorta./

Interruption of the lumbar sympathetic pathways is indicated for conditions in the lower extremities similar to those enumerated for the upper extremities./ This therapeutic nerve block has been employed also to treat thrombophlebitis of the lower extremity./ The results from these injections have been dramatic and largely successful./ Not only is the pain relieved immediately but the whole process subsides promptly./ This remedy represents so much of an improvement over previous therapeutic efforts that it should be used whenever the condition develops./

In *Life* (October 27, 1947) the article about the nerve block carried the heading

## PAIN-CONTROL CLINIC

**New York doctors ease suffering by
blocking off nerves with drugs.**

Eight pictures were accompanied by the following text:

Except in the field of surgery, control of pain is still very much in the primitive stages./ Countless thousands of patients suffer the tortures of cancer, angina pectoris and other distressing diseases while THEIR physicians are helpless to relieve THEM./ A big step toward help for these sufferers is now being made with a treatment known as nerve-blocking./ This treatment, which consists of putting a "block" between the source of pain and the brain, is not a new therapy./ But its potentialities are just now being realized./ Using better drugs and a wider knowledge of the mechanics of pain gained during and since the war, Doctors E. A. ROVENSTINE and E. M. PAPPER of the New York University College of Medicine have been able to help two-thirds of the patients accepted for treatment in THEIR "pain clinic" at Bellevue Hospital./

The nerve-block treatment is comparatively simple and does not have serious aftereffects./ It merely involves the injection of an anesthetic drug along the path of the nerve carrying pain impulses from the diseased or injured tissue to the brain./ Although its action is similar to that of spinal anesthesia used in surgery, nerve block generally lasts much longer and is only occasionally used for operations./ The N.Y.U. doctors have found it effective in a wide range of diseases, including angina pectoris, sciatica, shingles, neuralgia and some forms of cancer./ Relief is not always permanent, but usually the injection can be repeated./ Some angina pectoris patients have had relief for periods ranging from six months to two years./ While recognizing that nerve block is no panacea, the doctors feel that results obtained in cases like that of MIKE OSTROICH (*next page*) will mean a much wider application in the near future./

The *New Yorker* (October 25, 1947) in its profile of Dr. Rovenstine describes the nerve block like this:*

. . . Recently, HE [Rovenstine] devoted a few minutes to relieving a free patient in Bellevue of a pain in an arm that had been cut off several years before./ The victim of this phantom pain said that the tendons ached and that HIS fingers were clenched so hard HE could feel HIS nails digging into HIS palm./DR. ROVENSTINE'S assistant, DR. E. M. PAPPER, reminded ROVENSTINE that a hundred

* From an article by Mark Murphy in the *New Yorker*. Copyright 1947 The New Yorker Magazine Inc.

and fifty years ago the cure would have been to dig up the MAN'S arm, if its burial place was known, and straighten out the hand./ ROVENSTINE smiled./ *"I tell YOU,"* HE said./ *"WE'll use a two-per-cent solution of procaine, and if it works, in a couple of weeks WE'll go on with an alcohol solution./ Procaine, YOU know, lasts a couple of weeks, alcohol six months or longer./ In most cases of this sort, I use the nerve block originated by LABAT around 1910 and improved on in New Orleans about ten years back, plus one or two improvisations of MY own."*/ (Nerve blocking is a method of anesthetizing a nerve that is transmitting pain.)/ ROVENSTINE does little anesthetizing HIMSELF these days, except when HE is demonstrating HIS methods at HIS lectures./ HE carries on only a small practice outside Bellevue./ If HE is called in on routine cases, HE asks extremely high fees./ HE proceeds on the principle that a person who wants HIM to handle a routine operation ought to pay well for HIM./ If HE is asked to apply HIS special- ized knowledge to an unusual case, HE doesn't care what the fee is./ Like a great many other doctors, HE feels that only millionaires and indigents get decent medical care./ PEOPLE of these two classes are the only ones who feel that THEY can call on the leading surgeons and ROVEN- STINE./

The MAN with the pain in the non-existent hand was an indigent, and ROVENSTINE was working before a large gallery of student anesthetists and visitors when HE exorcised the ghosts that were paining HIM./ Some of the spectators, though THEY felt awed, also felt inclined to giggle./ Even trained anesthetists sometimes get into this state during nerve-block demonstrations because of the tenseness such feats of magic induce in THEM./ The patient, thin, stark- naked, and an obvious product of poverty and cheap gin mills, was nervous and rather apologetic when HE was brought into the operating theatre./ HE lay face down on the operating table./ *ROVENSTINE has an easy manner with patients, and as HIS thick, stubby hands roamed over the MAN'S back, HE gently asked, "How YOU doing?"/ "MY hand, it is all closed together, DOC,"* the *MAN answered, startled and evidently a little proud of the attention HE was getting./ "YOU'll be O.K. soon," ROVENSTINE said, and turned to the audience./ "One of MY greatest contributions to medical science has been the use of the eyebrow pencil," HE said./* HE took one from the pocket of HIS white smock and made a series of marks on the patient's back, near the shoulder of the amputated arm, so that the spectators could see exactly where HE was going to work./ With a syringe and needle HE raised four small weals on the MAN's back and then shoved long needles into the weals./ The MAN shuddered but said HE felt no pain./ ROVENSTINE then attached a syringe to the first needle, injected the procaine solution, unfastened the syringe, attached it to the next needle, injected more of the solution, and so on./ The patient's face began to relax a little./ *"LORD, DOC," HE said. "MY hand is loosening up a bit already."/ "YOU'll be all right by tonight, I think," ROVENSTINE said./* HE was.

That the language of the three articles is different, everybody can see. But it's not so easy to tell *how* different. For that, let's look at a few figures:

|  | A.M.A. Journal | Life | New Yorker |
|---|---|---|---|
| Average sentence length in words | 20.5 | 22 | 18 |
| Average word length in syllables (per 100 words) | 194 | 165 | 145 |
| Percent "personal words" | 0 | 2 | 11 |
| Percent "personal sentences" | 0 | 0 | 41 |

What has happened is this: *Life* magazine naturally had to be more readable than the *A.M.A. Journal*. So it avoided words like *analgesic* and *thrombophlebitis* and otherwise presented the facts in more or less newspaper fashion. Effect: the words in *Life* are 15 percent shorter than those in the *A.M.A. Journal*. (The sentences would be shorter too if Drs. Rovenstine and Wertheim hadn't written exceptionally short sentences to begin with—for two doctors, that is.) But *Life* didn't bother to dramatize the facts and make them humanly interesting. (Probably the magazine relied on its pictures for that; I'll get to that question in Chapter 18.) The *New Yorker* began *its* popularization of the nerve block where *Life* left off: its sentences are a good bit shorter than those in *Life* (19 percent), and aside from that, there's a story, there's drama, there's something that's interesting to read. The nerve block has become an experience to the reader.

This gives us a good clue to the baffling question of what readability means. In most dictionaries, *readable* is defined as "easy *or* interesting to read." (It also has another meaning, *legible,* but we'll skip that here.) Actually, to most people, readability means ease of reading *plus* interest. They want to make as little effort as possible while they are reading, and they also want something "built in" that will automatically carry them forward like an escalator. Structure of words and sentences has to do with one side of readability, "personal words" and "personal sentences" with the other.

That's why, in this book, a piece of writing is given not one readability score but two: a "reading ease" score and a "human interest" score. Length of words and sentences are combined into one, "personal" words and sentences into the other. (If you want to learn how to figure a score, see pages 247 to 251.)

Working out the scores of our three articles on nerve blocking, we get this picture:

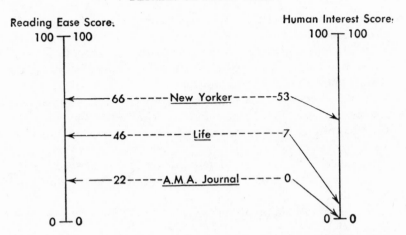

Reading Ease Score:
100 — 100

Human Interest Score:
100 — 100

66 ------ New Yorker ------ 53

46 -------- Life -------- 7

22 ----- A.M.A. Journal ----- 0

0 — 0          0 — 0

*Life* is much easier to read than the *A.M.A. Journal,* but gets hardly off the ground with human interest; the *New Yorker* is still easier than *Life* and, in addition, is as interesting to read as fiction.

All this doesn't mean, of course, that the writers for *Life* and the *New Yorker* consciously did something about their sentences and words. Naturally not. But if we want to find out something about any art or skill, we must analyze the work of leading performers, and then laboriously imitate their seemingly effortless performance. There's no guarantee that we'll ever become champions this way, but at least we can try.

PS

Many readers of this book told me that this is the chapter from which they learned most. It literally opened their eyes.

I suggest you study the three descriptions of the nerve block carefully. Read them sentence by sentence and word for word. Think about what the authors did and why they did it.

For example, Drs. Rovenstine and Wertheim wrote, "The results from these injections have been dramatic and largely successful." Why did they put it this way? Because in a scientific paper that's about as far as you can go in blowing your own horn.

Or why did *Life* magazine mention first the success of the nerve block in the relief from the pain of angina pectoris? Because the editors knew that readers would be more interested in the treatment of angina pectoris than in that of other, less widespread diseases. On the other hand, the *New Yorker* played up the relief from pain in an invisible amputated arm because it was the most dramatic.

In the *New Yorker* story note particularly the point where the patient says, "My hand, it is all closed together, Doc"—*the hand that isn't there.*

And think about the dramatic effect of the two-word last sentence "He was."

## CHAPTER 15

# RESULTS OF PLAIN TALK

---

*At a more advanced level, we have such tools as the equation or formula, which enable man to learn in a few hours fundamental and pervasive features of the behavior of things which he could otherwise learn only imperfectly with great labor or not at all.*

E. L. THORNDIKE, *Human Learning*

---

IF YOU want to widen your audience and reach readers with less education, you'll have to simplify your style. That much is clear. But what will happen to the readers you had to begin with? Will they resent simplification? Will they feel you are now talking down to them? Will they stop reading you in disgust?

Not at all. If you don't carry simplification too far into primer style, your old readers will not only stay with you but you'll get more of the same kind; and they'll *read you faster, enjoy it more, understand better,* and *remember longer.* Every single one of these statements can be proved by scientific evidence.

But first let's get back to the question of "educational level." The readability formula in this book, like any other, grew out of the idea of grading textbooks for children. There's no question that that's a worthwhile job: if you force children to study a book that is over their heads they will not only fall behind in their education but will have a miserable time in the bargain. So proper grading of texts may mean all the difference between real learning and merely being exposed to something "onpleasant"—to use Mr. Dooley's famous definition of education.

The difference between a graded text and a conventional one

is often clearly visible to the naked eye. Take the following parallel passages from two high-school history texts:

*Graded Text:*

In the year 1807 when the forces of Napoleon advanced on Lisbon, the Portuguese king had to choose between capture by the French or flight to Brazil. He took the latter course, and his great fleet of vessels carried many hundreds of the finest families of Portugal to Rio de Janeiro. They brought along all their worldly possessions, objects of art, books, and customs. Rio now became a much more cosmopolitan city. A few years later, in 1821, after Napoleon had been defeated, the Portuguese king was called back to his own country, but he left his son Pedro to rule in Brazil. Before leaving he is said to have told Pedro: "If the time comes when Brazil wants to be independent of Portugal, make yourself her ruler."

*Conventional Text:*

When Napoleon Bonaparte invaded England's ally Portugal in 1808, the prince regent, Joao, with the whole royal family and court, on the advice of the British minister at Lisbon, set sail for Brazil with a retinue of some 15,000 troops. Arriving at Rio de Janeiro, the prince was joyously acclaimed by the populace as Emperor of Brazil. But the years which followed saw the rapid waning of Joao's popularity. The arrogance of the Portuguese courtiers, the heavy taxes laid on the people, and especially the revolts in the Spanish Indies encouraged revolutionary uprisings in Brazil. Moreover, after the overthrow of Napoleon, the anarchy in Portugal called for the return of the regent, now King Joao I, to the throne. In April 1821, he sailed for home, leaving his young son Dom Pedro as regent, and taking with him most of the money in the treasury.

Obviously the graded text is easier reading than the conventional one. But how much easier? Apply the formula described in this book and you'll find that the graded passage has a "reading ease" score of 62, while the conventional passage scores only 45. Which means that the graded history was properly designed for the average high school student but the conventional text was not. Roughly, we can make these estimates on the basis of the table at the top of the next page.

In other words, a text with a "reading ease" score of 62 is 8th or 9th grade reading. The average high school student will find it easy; he will be able to learn something from it without being

| Description of Style | Average Sentence Length | Average No. of Syll. per 100 Wds. | Reading Ease Score | Estimated Reading Grade |
|---|---|---|---|---|
| Very Easy | 8 or less | 123 or less | 90 to 100 | 5th grade |
| Easy | 11 | 131 | 80 to 90 | 6th grade |
| Fairly Easy | 14 | 139 | 70 to 80 | 7th grade |
| Standard | 17 | 147 | 60 to 70 | 8th and 9th grade |
| Fairly Difficult | 21 | 155 | 50 to 60 | 10th to 12th grade (high school) |
| Difficult | 25 | 167 | 30 to 50 | 13th to 16th grade (college) |
| Very Difficult | 29 or more | 192 or more | 0 to 30 | college graduate |

bothered by sheer reading difficulty. A score of 45 means that the text is college-level reading: high school boys and girls will have to work their way through it, slowed down by 40-word sentences and stopped by words like *retinue* or *anarchy*.

What happens when we deal with adult readers? That's a more difficult question. People don't stay put educationally. Some who never got beyond eighth grade become self-made intellectual giants; others happily leave the world of books forever once they have got their college degree. But roughly the table above *can* be applied to adults and, even more roughly, it can, by way of census figures, be translated into percentages of the U.S. adult population. This is what we get:

| Description of Style | Average Sentence Length | Average No. of Syll. per 100 Wds. | Reading Ease Score | Estimated School Grades Completed | Estimated Percent of U.S. Adults |
|---|---|---|---|---|---|
| Very Easy | 8 or less | 123 or less | 90 to 100 | 4th grade | 93 |
| Easy | 11 | 131 | 80 to 90 | 5th grade | 91 |
| Fairly Easy | 14 | 139 | 70 to 80 | 6th grade | 88 |
| Standard | 17 | 147 | 60 to 70 | 7th or 8th grade | 83 |
| Fairly Difficult | 21 | 155 | 50 to 60 | some high school | 54 |
| Difficult | 25 | 167 | 30 to 50 | high school or some college | 33 |
| Very Difficult | 29 or more | 192 or more | 0 to 30 | college | 4.5 |

You'll notice that I changed the "reading grade" column into a "school grades completed" column, so that fifth-grade

[ 177 ]

reading is listed here as reading for someone who has *completed* fourth grade. I did this to follow the Census way of describing people's education; otherwise the tables are the same, of course. But does that mean that "standard" reading—readable for 83 percent of the American people—is the kind of reading they will always go for? Does it mean that "very difficult" reading is the kind most college graduates will curl up with on a rainy evening? It does not. The *typical* reader for each readability level will usually be found in the *next higher* educational bracket—and sometimes the gap will even be wider. *Time* magazine, which boasts of its readership among top executives, is written in breezy, high-school-level English; and Presidents and Supreme Court Justices have been known to devour extremely easy-to-read mystery stories.

The best proof of this principle is the writing you find in popular magazines. An editor has to know what his readers like; and that's what gets into his magazine. Since circulation and advertising departments usually know all about the typical reader's education, income, home ownership, car make and what-not, magazine writing offers a perfect check of typical reading levels. The rule seems to be that high-school-level readers prefer grade-school-level reading, college-level readers prefer high-school-level reading, and so on. Like this:

| Reading Ease Score | Typical Magazine |
|---|---|
| 90 to 100 | Comics |
| 80 to 90 | Pulp fiction |
| 70 to 80 | Slick fiction |
| 60 to 70 | Digests |
| 50 to 60 | Quality |
| 30 to 50 | Academic |
| 0 to 30 | Scientific |

Of course, you will say that most magazines are not staff-written but print contributed material. So how can they have an average "reading ease" score?

[ 178 ]

Well, the answer is that they do. You can analyze issue after issue of a given magazine: sentence length and syllable count will always be the same, within very narrow limits. There's no other possible explanation for this than the fact that every publication has its own editorial formula and—consciously or unconsciously—sticks to it. Try it for yourself—send a *New Yorker* story to *True Story* or a *Reader's Digest* piece to the *Atlantic*—and you'll see.

And what about differences in interest? Up to now, I have used only "reading ease" scores for grading; where does the "human interest" score come in? Can you grade by "human interest" too?

Yes, you can. But there's no reason on earth why you should do so in your own writing and deliberately aim for less human interest when you write for more educated readers. The "human interest" score simply gives you an estimate of the liveliness of your writing. The more human interest you get out of your subject—or put into it—the better.

However, if you do apply the human-interest yardstick to magazines, you get some interesting results:

| Description of Style | Percent of "personal words" | Percent of "pers. sent." | Human Interest Score | Typical Magazine |
|---|---|---|---|---|
| Dull | 2 or less | 0 | 0 to 10 | Scientific |
| Mildly Interesting | 4 | 5 | 10 to 20 | Trade |
| Interesting | 7 | 15 | 20 to 40 | Digests |
| Highly Interesting | 10 | 43 | 40 to 60 | New Yorker |
| Dramatic | 17 or more | 58 or more | 60 to 100 | Fiction |

As you see, the magazine lineup here is a little different from that on the other table. According to average "reading ease" scores, the *New Yorker* is harder to read than, say, the *Reader's Digest,* but according to "human interest" scores, it is more interesting. Which means that some *Reader's Digest* readers will find the *New Yorker* too sophisticated, while some *New Yorker* readers will find the *Reader's Digest* dull. In other words, the two measurements apply to different dimensions; if you want to be sure you're writing for your audience, you have to consider both.

In books on how to write short stories, beginners are always told to study first the magazines they want to write for. These formulas are a shortcut: they save part of the work of analyzing the magazine.

As I said a little while ago, if you do hit the right level, extra readability will usually pay a bonus. Highly readable stories and ads may attract almost twice as many readers as others; highly readable books may be read in almost half the time. On top of all this, your readers will understand and remember better what they have read. To be sure, there is much research still to be done on all this, but the basic facts have been proved. There is no doubt any longer that increased readability is worth the added effort.

In fact, now that you have gotten that far with this book, you will doubtless feel a lively rewriting itch whenever you encounter a piece of unreadable English—particularly legal English. A readability formula, you will find, is the ideal weapon in the age-old struggle of The Citizen *vs.* Small Type. Next time you get trapped by a tangle of wormlike sentences in agate type to which you signed your name, you will ask yourself why this stuff can't be rewritten so that anybody can read and understand it. You will discover that it can.

Let's take a life insurance policy, for instance. (Read your own and weep.) Here is a sample:

> If total disability occurs during the grace period for pay-ment of a premium, such premium shall not be waived, nor refunded if paid; provided that failure to pay such premium within the grace period therefor shall not of itself invalidate a claim hereunder for total disability commencing during such grace period if such premium with compound interest

at the rate of 5 per cent. per annum is paid at the time due proof of the claim is furnished to the Company.

The "reading ease" score of this is minus 12, the "human interest" score zero. Why not rewrite it like this?

> You have a 31-day grace period to pay a premium after it's due. Suppose you become totally disabled during the grace period before you've paid the premium. If so, we'll pay your insurance for total disability, but you'll have to pay us the overdue premium (with 5 percent interest) when you give us proof of your claim.

This has a "reading ease" score of 65 and a "human interest" score of 79. It's written so that a policyholder can get something out of it.

Or take a labor union contract. You think that union contracts are written in practical, down-to-earth language? Wrong. They are the most involved legal documents there are. Here is a mild example of their idiom:

> Such grievance shall be submitted to such impartial umpire in writing and he shall promptly afford to the Employee or Employees concerned, the Union and the Company, a reasonable opportunity to present evidence and to be heard in support of their respective positions with regard to such grievance.

The "reading ease" of this scores 10, the "human interest" 7. Let's rewrite it for the rank-and-file union member:

> The next step is a letter to the umpire. As soon as the umpire gets it, he must give everyone a chance to tell his side of the story and prove it.

"'Reading ease" 85; "human interest" 26; score in better labor relations—figure it out for yourself.

[ 181 ]

Or, finally, take the most important fine-print prose there is: the letter of the law. Have you ever read the exact words of a law? If you are a good citizen, you probably have, since every November you are asked to say yes or no to at least one new amendment. For instance, in November 1947, the citizens of the state of New York voted on the following proposed amendment:

The legislature may authorize by law the creation of a debt or debts of the state to provide for the payment of a bonus to each male and female member of the armed forces of the United States, still in the armed forces, or separated or discharged under honorable conditions, for service while on active duty with the armed forces at any time during the period from December seventh, nineteen hundred forty-one to and including September second, nineteen hundred forty-five, who was a resident of this state for a period of at least six months immediately prior to his or her enlistment, induction or call to active duty, provided he or she is a resident of this state at the time of making application for such bonus. The law authorizing the creation of the debt shall provide for payment of such bonus to the next of kin of each male and female member of the armed forces who, having been a resident of this state for a period or six months immediately prior to his or her enlistment, induction or call to active duty, died while on active duty at any time during the period from December seventh, nineteen hundred forty-one to and including September second, nineteen hundred forty-five; or who died while on active duty subsequent to September second, nineteen hundred forty-five, or after his or her separation or discharge under honorable conditions, while a resident of this state and prior to receiving payment of such bonus. An apportionment of the moneys on the basis of the periods and places of service of such members of the armed forces shall be provided by general laws. The

[ 182 ]

aggregate of the debts authorized by this section shall not exceed four hundred million dollars. The provisions of this article, not inconsistent with this section, relating to the issuance of bonds, for a debt or debts of the state and the maturity and payment thereof, shall apply to a debt or debts created pursuant to this section; except that the law authorizing the contracting of such debt or debts shall take effect without submission to the people pursuant to section eleven of this article.

Naturally, the citizens of New York were not expected to vote on this in its raw state, so to speak. No; the state of New York went to some length to print an abstract of the proposed amendment. And I mean length:

The purpose and effect of this proposed amendment is to provide for a veterans' bonus, for the payment of which the legislature is empowered to provide by law for the creation of a debt of the state in the maximum aggregate amount of four hundred million dollars by the sale of bonds by the state comptroller, the proceeds to be apportioned on the basis of periods and places of service and as so apportioned paid to every male and female member of the armed forces of the United States, still in the armed forces or separated or discharged under honorable conditions, who served on active duty at any time during the period from December seventh, nineteen hundred forty-one to and including September second, nineteen hundred forty-five, who was a resident of this state for a period of at least six months immediately prior to his or her enlistment, induction or call to active duty, and is such a resident at the time of making application for the bonus, and in the case of each member of the armed forces from this state who would have been qualified therefor but died either while on active duty during the designated period or subsequent thereto or after

[ 183 ]

separation or discharge under honorable conditions while a resident of this state and prior to receiving payment of the bonus, the sum payable shall be paid to his next of kin.

Well, that explains five 72-word sentences (on the average) in one 235-word sentence. Which is extremely funny until you think of the fact that every literate citizen of New York State was supposed to form an opinion on this proposal and base his vote on it. How could he? How could he without some real explanation like this one?

> This is about a veterans' bonus.
> We want to pay a bonus to New Yorkers who served in the armed forces during the war. This means all veterans who lived in New York State before the war and have come back to live here again. The next of kin of those who would have earned the bonus if they hadn't died in the war would get it too.
> The bonus would cost the state $400 million. You would have to pay for it in taxes.
> If you are for it, vote yes. If you are against it, vote no.

This rates "very easy"—its "reading ease" score is 93. The Census calls anyone "functionally literate" who has completed fourth grade. These are the people who are entitled to vote under the law of the state of New York; these are the people who have to have a "very easy" explanation before they can read with full understanding.

The state of New York—or any other state or the federal government—could easily pass a law requiring a tested fifth-grade explanation for every amendment to be voted on.

Maybe this is a radical idea. Or is it?

PS

Let me bring the figures of "estimated percent of U.S. adults" up to date. The figures on page 177 were based on 1948 U.S.

Census estimates. The latest available figures, for 1971, show that the percentage of those who have completed elementary school has gone up from 83 percent to 86.2 percent, those with some high school education from 54 to 73, high school graduates from 33 to 56, and college graduates from 4.5 to 11. This looks like tremendous progress in 23 years, but actually it hardly makes any difference if you want to make sure your writing is understood by your readers.

In the first place, a high school or college education isn't what it used to be in 1948: reading achievement levels have been dropping across the nation year after year after year. In the second place, as I explained, if you want to be sure you're reaching the readers you're writing for, you have to aim at an educational level one notch below the actual one. So, to reach a mass audience, you have to aim at the "standard" level and try to write in average sentences of 17 words with an average of 1.5 syllables. For high school graduates, you should write average sentences of 21 words with an average of 1.55 syllables.

As I said, it's not too difficult to get your average sentences down to about 21 words, but to go below that, you'll have to learn to write more lively English than you're probably writing now. And to reach an average word length of 1.5 or 1.55 syllables is a tough job. In cutting sentence length, you're swimming with the tide, but in cutting word length, as I explained, you're going against the current trend. These are times when almost everybody, every day, uses words like *demythologize, rebarbarized, nonentertaining, deaccessioning, misidentity, disenthusiasm,* or *institutionalized misogyny.* You'll have to resist the temptation of all those words starting with *de-, re-* or *non-* and ending in *-ize, -ance, -ment* or *-ation.*

People applying my formula have focused mainly on the "Reading Ease" part, cutting the length of sentences and words. My advice is to tackle the "Human Interest" part first, trying to bring in people and use quotes of what they *said.* This will auto-

[ 185 ]

matically bring down the word and sentence length and make it easier for you to reach a lower "Reading Ease" score.

Anyway, you'll get the most out of the readability formula only if you use it. Of course, it's a nuisance to count words and syllables and go through the routine of measuring your writing style. But unless you do it again and again, you won't know whether you're making any progress or how much.

## CHAPTER 16

# THOSE UNPREDICTABLE WORDS

---

*Everyone hears but what he understands.*

GOETHE

---

SOME time ago I had lunch at the Hotel Astor in New York. It was a good lunch; but what I remembered specially was the following item on the menu:

Demitasse (Pot)          20

I don't know whether this strikes you as funny. I thought it was. To me a demitasse means a little half-size cup of black coffee; to read "Demitasse (Pot)" makes me laugh. But the author of the Astor menu didn't mean to be humorous, of course. To him *demitasse* meant "black coffee." The way he put it on the menu was a reasonable way to tell customers what they would get for their money.

This little linguistic difference between the Hotel Astor and me is a good illustration of the fact that the same word doesn't mean the same thing to different people. Possibly you think this is the exception rather than the rule. Not at all. One of the basic facts about language is that *no word ever means exactly the same to two different people.*

Let me prove this. Take at random half a dozen given names: Bernice, Caroline, Ethel, Alexander, Max, Vernon. How do you feel about these names? Which do you like? Which don't you? To which are you indifferent? If you try to answer these questions, you will find that your feeling toward these names depends entirely on the people you know who bear each name—or possibly on characters with these names that you have met in fiction. Each name to you means a bundle of impressions connected with all the bearers of the name you have known. In other words, each name to you means the background of experience you have had with it during your life. And since no two persons live exactly the same life—not even Siamese twins—each name means something different to different people.

What goes for names goes for words in general. Take a word at random from the dictionary. Take the word *random*. To me it means *any old way, by chance,* plus a memory of the novel *Random Harvest* by James Hilton, plus the way that novel starts (". . . bombs fell at random . . ."), plus a suggestion of the publishing firm Random House, with the picture of a house that appears on its books . . . the face of one of the partners, Mr. Bennett Cerf, the raconteur . . . the impressive mansion of Random House on Madison Avenue in New York . . . the time I used to work in the next block for the Columbia Broadcasting System . . . and so on. Or take the word *dictionary*. To me it means a wordbook, the half-dozen of them I have around my house, particularly the Thorndike-Barnhart Dictionary which I use most, the months I spent years ago doing statistical research with that dictionary . . . how during that time I met my wife and we got engaged . . . etc., etc.

Obviously your background of experience with these two words—or any other word—can never exactly duplicate mine. The basic meaning of each word will usually be the same, of course—but the connotations, the overtones, the feel around the fringes cannot possibly be alike. You never can tell just what a seemingly innocuous word will conjure up in another person's mind.

And that really is the whole point I want to make in this chapter. Words are, by definition, unpredictable. In writing, you can predict more or less accurately what your general style and your language structure will do to your readers in general, but you can never predict what a given word will do to a given reader. That's a fascinating but exasperating fact anyone who writes has to face.

Take for example the following sentence with which H. L. Mencken ends a paper on such words as *Michigander* or *Idahoan:* "An inmate of the District of Columbia—it has no citizens— always calls himself a *Washingtonian,* for Washington is coterminous with the District." When I read this, I was delighted with Mr. Mencken's use of the word *inmate* in this context. During the last war I spent two years working for the federal government in Washington, and so I could fully appreciate Mr. Mencken's superb choice of the word. To anyone who hasn't had that experience, the word naturally wouldn't have quite so much meaning.

Or take the following passage, written by President Charles Seymour of Yale University in his annual report for 1946: "The past academic year has been one of reconversion from war to peace. Still committed to war schedules which could not be ended hastily, we have also been busied with preparations for the future." Probably no word in these two sentences means anything special to you. But read what the *New Yorker's* "Talk of the Town" had to say about it:

> "Busied" is the word we admire here . . . "We have been busy with preparations for the future" is the way the president of a bank, of a cement company, or of Princeton would probably have referred to similar activities, thus conjuring up a humdrum picture of tidy charts, brisk stenographers, dictaphones, and prefabricated houses for employees or undergraduates. President Seymour, with an extra, gentlemanly squiggle of his ivory quill pen, leads us into a world of urbane planning conferences in the windowless confines of the Russell Trust Association building and before the glowing grate of the Elizabethan Club—a world of long

clay pipes, portentous throat clearing, and a complete set
of the Loeb Classical Library for every returned bomber
pilot.

Or take the word *casual,* which may suggest a number of things
to you if you are a man, and a number of slightly different things
if you are a woman. But you have to think of the word in connection with women's wear and from a man's point of view to
arrive at the following definition from a famous Macy's ad "The
Man's Glossary of Unfamiliar Words & Phrases":

*"casual"*—You should live so.

Ordinarily, of course, we take these differences in connotation
for granted. Our language is, and always will be, an imperfect
tool of communication and we just have to make the best of it.
By and large, people do understand each other even if there
may be some amount of misunderstanding around the fringes of
practically every word they use.

But often different shades of meaning have different consequences. Whenever this happens the conflict immediately comes
to the surface: we start arguing about the meaning of words or
the appropriateness of names. Such arguments are never arguments about language, of course; they are clashes of interests
that happen to arise from words.

That all arguments about name changes are really fights for
opposing interests can be proved by the famous court case of
Mr. Kabotchnick who changed his name to Cabot, or by the
Congressional fight to rename dried skim milk "dried milk
solids," "defatted milk solids" or "non-fat milk solids," or by
the struggle to glamorize the humble horse mackerel into a
"California haddock." Obviously in all these cases the difference
between the two names meant a difference in dollars and cents.

The same is true of legal battles about the meaning of words.
It wouldn't make much difference whether you said that Western

Union "ships" telegrams, if the word *shipping* didn't appear in the Fair Labor Standards Act (against child labor), but since it does, the Supreme Court had to decide that Western Union *doesn't* "ship" and therefore can go on employing little boys on bicycles. In the same way, it didn't seem like much of a question whether newspapering is a "profession" or not, until the National Labor Relations Board had to rule that it was *not* and that therefore newsmen could join the CIO. And a District Court had to immerse itself in the question whether eggnog is a food or a beverage because alcoholic beverages are taxed but alcoholic foods are not.

And who would think that it could matter just what kind of weather people call a "heavy rain"? It *did* matter in a labor arbitration case between a group of Good Humor men and their employer. The union contract said, "Salesmen will not be sent out on their routes in a heavy rain," and one not-so-nice day in July the men stayed home. They said it poured. The company officials said they hardly noticed any rain and came to their offices without any rubbers or umbrellas. The arbitrator pondered, asked the Weather Bureau and was told the rain on that day was "moderate." Whereupon he threw up his hands and split the difference in pay.

All these disputes, mind you, are between people who use the same language. Naturally, when it comes to translation from one language to another, it becomes almost impossible to find words whose meaning matches exactly that of the original. In fact, it *is* impossible and even the most inspired masterpieces of translation are poor makeshifts. Behind each word in a language is the history of all the uses of the word in that language—and that history is always untranslatable.

It's the spirit of a language that defies translation. No translation, for instance, could do justice to the subtle differences between the French words *type, numéro,* and *individu,* as explained in Elliot Paul's *The Last Time I Saw Paris:* "A '*numéro*'

[ 191 ]

(number), in Mme. Berthelot's exquisite vocabulary, was one degree lower than a *'type'*, but less severe than *'individu'* or 'individual'. A *'type'* implies that the person to whom the word is applied is of little consequence. A *'numéro'* may be a chap who is dangerous and anti-social, or a droll fellow or Merry Andrew who can be counted on for harmless fun. But a woman with the regard Mme. Berthelot had for the spoken word would not apply the epithet *'individu'* to anyone less villainous than Landru."

And John Steinbeck tells about an interview in Russia: "To make sure that I was not misquoted by accident, I asked to have the translation of the Russian back into English. I was right, the answers I was supposed to have given did not very closely approximate what I had said. This was not done on purpose; it was not even the difficulty of trying to communicate from one language to another. It was more than language. It was translation from one kind of thinking to another. They were very pleasant and honest people, but we just could not communicate closely."

This is what leads to international misunderstandings whenever one nation gets hold of a word used by another. One of Adolf Hitler's pet words, for instance, was the German word *Lebensraum*. When English-speaking people first encountered it, they translated it into "living room" and thought it was funny. But it meant something like "life space" and turned out to be not funny at all.

As you can see, most of my examples—from *heavy rain* to *Lebensraum*—are abstractions of one kind or another. It's the abstract words in the language that are most apt to be interpreted in different ways. This applies to such common abstract nouns as those formed by adding *-ness* to an adjective as well as to what people now call *isms*. The word *hatlessness*, for instance, to me means "being without a hat" and nothing else. But recently someone, in a public speech, cried that "hatlessness has been rampant in the last five months." Clearly, *hatlessness* to that person was something menacing and dangerously radical. Needless to say, he was a millinery salesman.

Naturally, when it comes to words like *liberalism,* thinking up different definitions is practically a parlor game. In April 1948 the *New York Times Magazine* used the definitions by six Presidential candidates as an interesting Sunday feature; the six answers were as different as the six people who gave them.

Well, what can be done about all this? What can you in your writing do to make sure, as far as possible, that your words will mean the same to your readers as they mean to you?

It's impossible to touch on this question without mentioning a movement that has sprung up to deal with it: I mean the study of semantics. Followers of this movement have been trying to tell the American public for years that words are not things and that the true source of word meanings is not the dictionary but the people who use the language.

All this is fine; but unfortunately semanticists have gone much further and now define their aims in such terms as "the employment of scientific knowledge and the scientific method as an aid to sane living" or "a systematic attempt to formulate the general method of science in such a way that it might be applied not only in a few restricted areas of human experience, but *generally* in daily life."

Nevertheless, semanticists *have* proposed a few practical devices for clear writing—although they become quite coy and deprecating whenever they write about them. There are five of these devices: indexing, dating, the use of "etc.," the hyphen, and quotation marks. They work like this:

Indexing: Instead of writing about "Jews" or "Negroes" you write about "Jew$_1$" or "Negro$_2$" to show that you mean the individual and not the group.

Dating: You date words (e.g., "U.S.$_{1948}$") to show that you know that a thing in one year is different from the same thing in the next.

Using "etc.": This, I am sorry to say, is "to reinforce the

THE ART OF READABLE WRITING

attitude of non-allness"; it shows you haven't mentioned everything that might have been mentioned.

The hyphen: If you hyphenate words that are usually not linked together (like "space-time") you show that you know that the borderlines between words are not fixed. (This is where "non-Aristotelianism" comes in.)

Quotation marks: You use quotation marks whenever you want the reader to beware of a certain word.

These devices are quite ingenious and the semanticists use them with skill in their own periodical. But it's obvious that you can't use them in your own writing and pepper everything with index numbers, *etc.*, hyphens, and quotation marks. It looks too queer. Readers won't stand for it.

However, just for the fun of it, let's take a random sentence and see how the five devices would work. Here is a sentence by the newspaperman Robert J. Casey—one of those wild generalizations the semanticists are out to correct: "Newspapers are printed for people who can't read."

On the face of it, this is of course nonsense. But Mr. Casey meant to convey a definite idea—quite a shrewd one too—which can be expressed unmistakably by using the five semantic devices. Like this:

> Newspapers$_{\text{U.S.1940's}}$, *etc.*, are printed for people who can-cannot "read."

Which means, in ordinary language:

> Today American newspapers, magazines, and the like are designed for people who are *almost* unable to read with understanding.

Of course I don't mean to say that everything you write should be spelled out in this fashion. That would be the surest way to make your writing utterly unreadable. But you *can* adopt the basic principle of the five semantic devices, which is simply that the concrete is always clearer than the general and the abstract. Indexing—the Number One semantic device—is simply a reminder that you should always try to narrow your writing down to a single, concrete case.

All of which comes down to this: you cannot prevent a reader from reading meanings into your words that you didn't think of; but you can guide his interpretation of the more abstract words —which are the most dangerous—by using as many concrete cases, illustrations, and examples as possible. As a rule, you should never stay at the abstract level for long; as soon as you get there, turn around and plunge again into the down-to-earth world of people and things. This "up-and-down" writing is the only protection against misunderstanding. It is no guarantee; but it's the best method there is.

Practically all popular nonfiction writing today follows this up-and-down pattern. Here is one example: a passage from a *Saturday Evening Post* article by David G. Wittels on Dr. Samuel Renshaw's research in vision:

> Another factor involved in the miracle of seeing is expressed in what is known as the *Gestalt* theory, from the German word meaning "pattern" or "form."

(One sentence on the abstract level. And down he goes into a concrete example.)

> Renshaw drew heavily on this theory in developing his system for recognizing airplanes. For example, four equal lines going any which way may be confusing, but when these same four lines are joined to make a square, you have a thing with a special meaning of its own. The beholder sees a form which he immediately recognizes as a square, without needing to pause to examine, count and compare the lines.

(End of example. But he goes further down into an even more concrete example.)

[ 195 ]

A picture of Miss Betty Grable, fetchingly attired in next to nothing, has been used in a more interesting demonstration of the same principle. It was used by an instructor at a camp in Missouri, who was trying to teach the Renshaw Recognition System to a group of soldiers by showing them slides of airplanes. Without warning, he flashed the pin-up picture on the screen at one-hundredth of a second.

Instantly the men began whistling and uttering wolf cries. "What was that slide?" asked the instructor.

"Betty Grable!" they chorused happily.

"How did you know?" he demanded.

They saw he was serious. They thought it over. But the best they could do was: "Heck, we just knew."

"Okay," he said. "Why can't you learn to recognize airplanes the same way?"

(This ends the second illustration. Now back to the abstract level.)

The point is that we can recognize things from only a fleeting glimpse. The quickest and best way to recognize things is to look at them as wholes. That is the natural way of seeing, and up to about six years of age, children see that way. They usually do much better than their elders on the high-speed tachistoscope.

(Down we go into another example.)

One of Renshaw's graduate assistants, Robert L. Maurer, recently demonstrated this with his tiny blond daughter, Judy. She was three years and nine months old when he brought her into the laboratory, telling her only that she was "going to see some pictures." Though he holds world records for grasping and remembering strings of digits at high speeds, his baby beat him on recognizing pictures.

[ 196 ]

(And so on, in rhythmical "up-and-down" movement, explaining each concept concretely as it comes along.)

I said that this technique is used by all popular nonfiction writers. But it isn't new. It's probably as old as writing, or as teaching. Examples, illustrations, concrete imagery have been used for thousands of years by anyone who tried to convey ideas.

In the form of parables, this method is used constantly in the New Testament. Jesus told his disciples why: "Therefore I speak to them in parables: because they seeing see not; and hearing they hear not, neither do they understand."

## CHAPTER 17

# THOSE UNPREDICTABLE READERS

---

*Nobody tells a young writer that many of those
who read him are going to read him wrong.*

BERNARD DE VOTO

---

PUT this book down for a minute and think of what you do
when you read. How does it work? Your eyes look at printed
symbols on paper and your mind thinks the thoughts of the
person who wrote the words. How does this miracle happen?

It is a miracle, all right. I won't go into the long history of
the invention of writing and the alphabet; let's just look at you
with the letters on a page in front of you. Scientists know pretty
well what goes on in reading—up to a point; but when we have
learned all about fixations, regressions, spans of recognition, and
so on, the miracle is greater than ever.

If you think you just pick up the meanings of words one after
the other, you are wrong. Language is not as simple as that.
What you do is this: your eyes move along the printed lines in
rhythmic *jumps*. After each jump they rest for a short while,
focus on a word or two, and move on. From time to time, when
you unconsciously feel the need of checking back, your eyes move
*back*. And that's the pattern: rhythmic movements, brief fixations on a word or two depending on your span of recognition,
irregular regressions. All this at the rate of about 250 words a
minute if you are an average person reading average writing—
with your eyes taking about one-third of a second to do their
work between movements. And in this third of a second, they
take in, on the average, *more than one word*.

[ 198 ]

But that's not the whole story. Words don't mean anything by themselves or even in groups of two or three. Words get their meanings from the context—from the sentence they are in, or even the whole paragraphs. So after your eyes have seen the words, your mind assigns to these words a *provisional* meaning, "good only until further notice." Then, when your eyes have reached the end of the phrase, sentence, or paragraph, your mind *rethinks* the words in the light of what came after. Reading is really a miracle: your eyes pick up groups of words in split-second time and your mind keeps these words in delicate balance until it gets around to a point where they make sense.

Take the first sentence of this chapter, for instance. In slow motion, here is how you probably read it:

Put this

(No meaning yet)

book down

(You didn't put the book down at this point, did you? You waited with your decision until you had read a little more.)

for a minute

(You still didn't.)

and think

(?)

of what

(?)

you do

(?)

when you

(?)

read.

[ 199 ]

(Now at last you were reasonably sure of what each word meant in this sentence. But you didn't put the book down at this point either. You waited until you knew how serious I was with my suggestion.)

And that's the way we read: we race along, making quick guesses at the meanings of little bunches of words, and quick corrections of these first guesses afterwards. To anyone who knows the process, it's a wonder we ever read anything right.

What all this means to a writer is obvious. A writer must know how people read, what are the main sources of reading errors, and what can be done to possibly forestall them.

The commonest reading error, of course, is mistaking one word for another. As I said, our eyes take in a word or more in one-third of a second. That means that we don't have time to read words letter by letter; we look at the general shape of a group of letters and take them in *as a whole*. This is why good proofreaders are so rare: in ordinary reading we don't notice such things as typographical errors but take them in our stride.

For example, take the following passage from a story about prize fights by John O'Hara, which I read recently:

"See what I mean, Arthur? He knows when the fix was in. And of course ring stragedy. Does he know ring stragedy! . . ."

It so happens that *stragedy* was the only word in that story that was deliberately misspelled to indicate the character's level of speech. When I read it the first time, I *thought* I was reading the correct spelling *strategy*. (Maybe you did too.) Only when I came to the second *stragedy* did I catch on to Mr. O'Hara's excellent transcription of spoken English.

Or take the following from a book review:

Man has a brief memory for the gadgets he contrives to give him comfort and convenience in the world. He easily forgets, too, the means by which he labors to loose his spirit from the flesh . . .

[ 200 ]

When I had read up to this point, I realized that I had read first *to lose his spirit;* then, after having read *from the flesh,* I looked back, and, for the first time, saw the second *o* in *loose.* At first sight, I had taken it for granted that the sentence dealt with the common kind of spirit that is being *lost* and not with the rare kind that is being *loosed.*

Or, to take a rather outrageous example, consider what happened to me once when I tried to read Toynbee's *Study of History* late at night after a tiring day. I held the book in my lap, vainly struggling against intense drowsiness, when suddenly I was pulled up wide awake by a word that simply didn't belong in Toynbee. The word was *horseradish.*

This couldn't be. I reread the passage and this is what I read:

> Perhaps we can discern this even in the reactions of the Christianized Celts of Britain under Roman rule. We know very little about them, but we know that they produced, in Pelagius, a heresiarch who made a stir throughout the Christian world of his day.

So that was it. My eyes had encountered *heresiarch,* a word I had never seen before, and had conveyed to my mind the only word I knew that could possibly produce a similar general impression: *horseradish.* My mind had been willing to put up with something ludicrous rather than believe the evidence before my eyes that such a word as *heresiarch* existed.

Moral of all this: don't use unfamiliar spellings or strange words. People's eyes will refuse to read them.

Another source of trouble is little words. Since we usually read two or more words at one glance, it's the little words—like *of, in, if, that*—that we read out of the corners of our eyes, so to speak. In fact, we ordinarily don't read them at all but simply assume they are where they belong. This is the principle of much rapid-reading teaching—where people are trained to skip over particles —and it's also the basis of that money-saving language, *cablese.*

If you have never seen cablese, here is a nice example:

OTTAWA MACKENZIEKING TUESDAY EQUALLED WALPOLE RE-
CORD FOR LENGTH SERVICE AS PRIMINISTER BRITISH COMMON-
WEALTH COUNTRY

RESOUNDING DESK THUMPING FROM ALL CORNERS CHAMBER
GREETED PRIMINISTER AS HE TOOK SEAT SMILING BROADLY

SINCE ELECTION 29/12 1921 MACKENZIEKING BEEN CANADAS
NATIONAL LEADER 7629 DAYS

SIR ROBERT WALPOLE PRIMINISTER BRITAIN SAME NUMBER
FROM 3/4 1721 TO 11/2 1742

MEMBERS ALL PARTIES JOINED SPEECHES TRIBUTE

The words left out here—*of, of a, of the, the, his, his, has, for,
was, of, the, of, in, of*—are exactly those we are apt to skip over
in reading ordinary writing. We know we don't need to read
them to get the meaning.

But that's where the trouble starts. Quite often the little words
*are* important and by skipping them we are apt to misread the
sentence. Here are a few trivial examples from my own reading:

> The fact that the more sensitive and subtle writing is, the
> more difficult it is to analyze, is significant of the intricacy of
> the art of the narrative.

(When I came to *is significant,* I had to start the sentence all over
again. What I had first read was this: "In fact, the more sensitive
and subtle writing is, the more difficult it is to analyze . . .")

> Another man told me that shortly after the United States
> entered the war, he wanted a garbage can of a certain size,
> but because of priorities he was unable to locate what he
> wanted.

(I don't know at what point I realized here that I had skipped
the fifth word, *that.*)

> When that kind of talk got to Washington, it, of course,
> sounded like ridiculous—even dangerous—nonsense.

(The first time I read this, I simply didn't see the *it*.)

Or take the following excerpt from a bill of lading:

> If this bill of lading is issued on the order of the shipper, or his agent, in exchange or in place of another bill of lading, the shipper's signature to the former bill of lading as to the statement of value or otherwise, or election of common law or bill of lading, shall be considered a part of this bill of lading as fully as if the same were written or made in or in connection with this bill of lading.

This excerpt was given to 250 college students as part of a psychological test in reading comprehension. To make sure they knew the vocabulary, two words were specially explained to them: *shipper* ("one who ships or sends goods") and *bill of lading* ("an account of goods shipped by any one, signed by the agent of the transportation line, thus forming a receipt for the goods"). Then they were asked the following question:

> A bill of lading has been copied from a signed original because the shipper's copy is worn and torn and he wants a fresh copy. Must the shipper sign this new copy?

The right answer is no. But one out of five students gave the wrong answer. Why? Part of the reason, it seems to me, is that you have to focus sharply on the little words if you want to get the right meaning out of all that legalistic jargon. Probably most students would have given the right answer had the little words been emphasized this way:

> If *this* bill of lading is issued . . . in place of *another* . . . , the shipper's signature to the *former* bill of lading . . . shall be considered a part of *this* bill of lading . . . *as if* . . . written . . . in . . . *this* bill of lading.

There are two things you can do to avoid this kind of reading mistake: either make the particles less important by rewriting your sentences or, if you feel you have to stick to your sentence structure, underline (italicize) the particles. (If you don't like underlining, make them long enough to catch the eye: write *however* instead of *but,* and *but only if* instead of *if.*)

The classic paper on mistakes in reading was written by Professor E. L. Thorndike more than 30 years ago, in 1917. He analyzed children's mistakes in reading and discovered an important principle: words and word groups may have so much meaning for a reader that they blot out the meaning of other words around them. Thorndike called this the "overpotency" of words. For example, one of his test passages dealt with school attendance in the town of Franklin. But some of the children couldn't resist the strong connotations of the word *Franklin* and said the passage dealt with *Benjamin* Franklin.

Another of the test passages read as follows:

> John had two brothers who were both tall. Their names were Will and Fred. John's sister, who was short, was named Mary. John liked Fred better than either of the others. All of these children except Will had red hair. He had brown hair.

When the children were asked "Who had red hair?" *one-fifth* of those in grades 6, 7, and 8, and *two-fifths* of those in grades 3, 4, and 5, gave the wrong answer. The word-combination *Will had red hair* was too strong for them.

I have no doubt that this important principle applies to adult readers as well as to children. In fact, I have two pieces of evidence from my own reading. Here they are, for what they are worth:

In *Time's* Music Department I read this:

> To most U.S. music listeners, Milton Katims is not a familiar name, but it soon may be. No one else his age (38) has managed to link his career with the top names in two musical fields: Toscanini and the Budapest String Quartet.

This week for the first time he conducted Toscanini's NBC Symphony Orchestra in the first of two Sunday broadcasts.

He has fashioned his career as carefully as Amati fashioned violins. As a violist, he bows to few besides William Primrose. His recording with the Budapest String Quartet of the Mozart *C Major Quintet* was chosen, by five U.S. music critics in the *Review of Recorded Music,* as the outstanding chamber-music album of 1946.

(Reading this, I first thought that Mr. Katims had been a *violinist.* The Amati violins had blotted out the comparatively rare word *violist.*)

In the *Saturday Review of Literature* I came upon this:

Dr. Barr resigned as president of St. John's College in December 1946 to start a new college in Stockbridge, Mass., but was forced to abandon the project because of construction costs. He originated the radio program "Invitation to Learning," and has been on CBS's adult educational board since 1928. Fired by Clarence Streit's "Union Now," he . . .

(At this point I had the impression that the *Union Now* organization had dismissed Dr. Barr. No wonder: the writer of the paragraph, with his overpotent words *resigned* and *abandoned,* had given me the impression of a record of failure. So naturally, I gave the word *fired* the meaning that fitted in. But I was wrong!)

Fired by Clarence Streit's "Union Now," he became a director of the movement and served about a year as contributing editor to Freedom and Union.

There is no sure-fire remedy for this sort of thing, but it will help your writing if you watch out for pairs of "contagious" or "allergic" words—like *violins* and *violist,* or *resigned* and *fired.* Incidentally, there are two words in the English language that are constantly misused and misunderstood because of such a situation: *presently* (which is "allergic" to *present*) and *scan* (which is "allergic" to *skim*). *Presently* means *soon* (except in archaic English) and *to scan* means *to read carefully*. The dictionaries are beginning to yield to the universal mistake and to list *presently* (in current use) as *now,* and *to scan* as *to glance at.* Which is as it should be, of course.

A very common source of misreading, as everybody knows, is the use of the negative. This is so generally recognized that almost all languages provide for an emphatic double negative to make sure of understanding. In English, however, the double negative is frowned upon as illiterate, with the effect that practically every negative statement is open to error and misreading.

Part of the reason is that *not* is a short word—one of those we don't focus on or don't read at all. The Army and Navy have the sensible rule to use NOT REPEAT NOT in all telegrams. And a good idea it is too.

Another reason is that the double negative comes naturally— sometimes even to educated people. Witness the following two sentences from the usually grammatical *New York Times*:

> This is only one of the pictures which *never* would have been made *unless* the enterprising, tireless and often audacious [Clarence S.] Jackson had *not* made them.

And:

> The house [the Duke and Duchess of Windsor rented on Long Island] is approached by way of a narrow, inconspicuous driveway that runs parallel with the rear entrance to the Cedar Creek Club and would *not* be noticed *only* by persons looking for it.

Or this from a court decision:

> In respect to the other quantity discounts, it does *not* appear that the differentials resulting from the discounts are

*not* based upon or related to due cost allowances in the manu-
facture, sale and delivery of these products. *Neither* is there
testimony to the contrary.

What people don't realize is that every negative word will turn
a sentence upside down—not just *not, never* or *nothing,* but also
*unless, neither, refuse, decline, lack, failure, unable, belie,* and
hundreds of others. Read the following sentence from a recent
dispatch and understand it without rereading if you can:

NEW YORK, April 8 [1948]—A spokesman for Henry
A. Wallace denied today that Wallace had messaged the
Italian Foreign Ministry disavowing authorship of an article
front-paged in Rome last Friday by the Communist organ
Unita.

If you want still more evidence, this little news item is to the
point:

COLUMBUS, GA., April 15 [1948]—Embarrassed city
attorneys today discovered one of their legal fences contained
a *"not* hole."

The city had haled a contractor into court on charges of
failure to procure a license.

The contractor pointed out the law which said no license
was required if the construction job "exceeds a sum of $500."

The city hastily dropped the charges and corrected the
typographical error, making the law read that no license is
required if the project "does not exceed a sum of $500."

My point is *not* that these illogical negatives don't make sense.
On the contrary, the intended meanings were so clear that proofreaders and countless readers read them into the items without
noticing what was actually there in black and white.

Which brings me back to the underlying theme of this chapter:
readers are apt to read words that aren't there. Sometimes, as

I have shown, such mistakes can be predicted and avoided but often they cannot. There is nothing you can do about the kinds of mistakes Freud describes in his *Psychopathology of Everyday Life*:

> Both irritating and laughable is a lapse in reading to which I am frequently subject when I walk through the streets of a strange city during my vacation. I then read ANTIQUES on every shop sign that shows the slightest resemblance to the word; this displays the questing spirit of the collector.

Or:

> One woman who is very anxious to have children always reads *storks* instead of *stocks*.

Another case of misreading was reported by a psychologist who referred to Shakespeare's *Henry VIII* in one of his books. What appeared in print was a reference to "Shakespeare's *Edward VIII*" —in spite of the fact that the author, his wife, his collaborator, and a proofreader had each seen the false reference in first galley proofs, second galley proofs, and page proofs. The explanation for this astonishing case of multiple misreading is simple: all this happened in the fall of 1936, when the front pages and people's minds were full of King Edward VIII.

Finally, here is a possibly Freudian case that concerns a negative. William Empson tells it in his book *Seven Types of Ambiguity*:

> Misreadings of poetry, as every reader must have found, often give examples of the plausibility of the opposite term. I had at one time a great admiration for that line of Rupert Brooke's about
>
> > The keen
> > Impassioned beauty of a great machine,
>
> a daring but successful image, it seemed to me, for that contrast between the appearance of effort and the appearance of

certainty, between forces greater than human and control divine in its foreknowledge, which is what excites one about engines; they have the calm of *beauty* without its complacence, the strength of *passion* without its disorder. So it was a shock to me when I looked at one of the quotations of the line one is always seeing about, and found that the *beauty* was *unpassioned,* because *machines,* as all good nature-poets know, have no hearts. I still think that a prosaic and intellectually shoddy adjective, but it is no doubt more intelligible than my emendation, and sketches the same group of feelings.

It seems clear to me that in this case the reader, William Empson, was a better poet than the writer, Rupert Brooke. But the trouble is that you can't count on that kind of creative misreading: for every William Empson, who will read *unpassioned machines* into *impassioned machines,* there are thousands like you and me, who will read a *heresiarch* into *horseradish.*

CHAPTER 18

# ARE WORDS NECESSARY?

---

*"I don't see," said the Caterpillar.*
LEWIS CARROLL, *Alice in Wonderland*

---

"EASY writing's vile hard reading," wrote Sheridan. The reverse is equally true: easy reading is difficult to write. In fact, it seems to be so difficult that most people would rather try anything else but write when they face a job of simple explanation. They escape from words into pictures, symbols, graphs, charts, diagrams—anything at all as long as it's "visual." They point to the movies, the comics, the picture magazines. Obviously, they say, the trend nowadays is away from reading. People would rather just look.

That may be so; but unfortunately the idea that you can explain things without explaining them *in words* is pure superstition. A favorite proverb of the picture-and-diagram lovers is "One picture is worth more than a thousand words." It simply isn't so. Try to teach people with a picture and you may find that you need a thousand words to tell them exactly what to look at and why.

If that surprises you, look at the evidence. There's the psychologist, for instance, who tried to find out whether children understood the charts and diagrams in the *Britannica Junior Encyclopedia*. It turned out they did not. Most of the devices used blithely by the encyclopedia writers were way over the heads of the children. They had been taught how to read, but nobody had ever bothered to tell them anything about how to look at flow

[ 210 ]

charts, statistical graphs, process diagrams, and the like. (Unfortunately, the experiment didn't show whether a normal child, reading an encyclopedia, will even stop and look at a diagram. I suspect he won't: the temptation to skip what is baffling is too great.)

Another psychologist tested grownups—soldiers and college students—on their understanding of graphs and charts. The results were even more startling. The vast majority were unable to see what the charts and graphs were supposed to show: they couldn't even grasp general facts or spot basic trends. Again, the reason is clear: people need training to learn from visual aids. Usually, they don't have that training. In fact, the less education they have, the less they are able to profit from these "helps to readers." Let me quote the experimenter's conclusions: "It is not often sufficiently recognized by those who advocate visual methods of presentation that the graph and the chart are no more immediately representational and no less symbolic of the information they are intended to convey than are verbal and mathematical statements. But whereas nearly everyone in the course of their upbringing acquires some facility in making verbal statements of ideas and meanings, only the specially educated learn to interpret general factual information from graphs and charts."

Naturally, that doesn't mean you should never illustrate visually what you have to say. Not at all: anything pictorial or graphic does help *as long as there is enough text to back it up*. I don't mean captions; I mean that the running text has to tell the reader what the illustration means, how he should look at it, and why. Tell the reader what to see. Remember that graph-and-chart reading is not one of the three R's.

Let me give you an example. Some time ago *Time* magazine told its readers about a *Harper's* article by C. Hartley Grattan, entitled "Factories Can't Employ Everybody." *Time* summarized the article in three paragraphs plus the following chart:

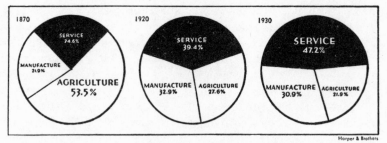

The caption under this chart read: EXPANDING SERVICE IN-
DUSTRIES NOW PROVIDE NEARLY HALF OF U.S. JOBS.

Now what did you get out of this chart? What do you think a
*Time* reader got from it (*if* he bothered to look at it way down
at the bottom of the page)? Certainly not more than what the
caption says: almost half of those now employed work in service
industries.

But Mr. Grattan in his original *Harper's* article meant to tell
much more with his three pie charts. And he did, by tying them
into his running text like this:

> Look first at this statistical pie, which shows the propor-
> tions of Americans engaged in various main occupations in
> 1870:

> You will see that more than half of all Americans who
> were classified as working in 1870 were in agriculture (with
> which we have included forestry and fishing); that a little

over a fifth were in manufacturing (with which we have included mechanical occupations and mining); and that a little less than a quarter were in the service industries.

By 1920 a vast change had taken place. The agricultural slice of the 1920 pie had shriveled; both the manufacturing slice and the service slice had swollen. Here is the 1920 pie:

Now look at the 1930 pie, and you will note a curious fact. Not only has the agricultural part of the pie undergone further shrinkage; *the manufacturing part has also shrunk a little, relatively,* while the service industries' slice has grown still more:

Why this change? The best answer has been given by two British economists, Allan G. B. Fisher and Colin Clark. They have shown that a comparatively primitive economy has a large proportion of its people engaged in farming; that as it develops, more and more people move over into manufacturing; but that in a really advanced economy, the proportion of people engaged in the services gains at the expense of *both farming and manufacturing.*

You see? Mr. Grattan used his charts to make a special point but was wise enough to explain the explanatory charts with 227 words of text. He was obviously afraid that even the educated readers of *Harper's Magazine* wouldn't get his point from the charts alone (although it's all there in black and white). There's hardly any doubt that he was right.

A second drawback in using visual aids is this. People not only don't know what to look for, their eyes also have a way of being caught by the wrong things. Take a dozen people and let them look at a picture in *Life*. Chances are each one of them will focus on a different set of details. Two chapters ago I wrote of "those unpredictable words." Pictures are even more unpredictable; you never can tell what a person will see in them.

It's an old story that pictures can be interpreted in different ways. Illustrations like this one

are old standbys in psychology texts. (You can "see" the cubes from above or from below.) There are even a number of widely used tests based on the fact that no two people will see the same things in inkblots or simple pictures. It's literally true that you can't tell what a given illustration will mean to a given reader.

Of course, even the most imaginative reader won't be able to do much with such simple charts as those used by Mr. Grattan.

But as soon as you add a bit of decoration, you are apt to get into trouble. There is even some danger in the so-called pictorial statistics with their rows of little men or coins or bags or boats: chances are your symbols for "one million unemployed" will remind at least one reader of his late uncle who was a millionaire.

Let me try to make my point by a little experiment. On the next page you'll find some census statistics as illustrated by Mr. Ray Bethers and printed in *This Week* magazine—except that I have left out the captions under the pictures and one line of explanatory text below.

Now look at this series of pictures and ask yourself what it suggests to you. Does it tell you what it is supposed to tell you— how the ratio between city and country population has changed? Does it tell you anything more? What else do the little pictures suggest?

When you have answered these questions, go on to page 217 and look at Mr. Bethers' little picture story the way it actually appeared. As you see, the point is that the country population has dropped from 95 percent to 43 percent, and the city population has risen from 5 percent to 57 percent. And there is that very important last line: "Cities and Towns are defined as having 2500 population or more." You couldn't possibly have guessed all that by just looking at the pictures; in fact, you probably were misled by the six-story apartment building under TODAY which made you think of a big metropolitan city rather than a small town. (At least that's what *I* thought at first.)

Mind you, I don't mean to disparage Mr. Bethers' pleasant and instructive piece of work. On the contrary, I think it shows well that the better and more imaginative the art work, the less it will be able to take the place of verbal explanation. If you want to give your reader something to look at, well and good; but if you have to tell him something, tell him.

In other words, nothing is self-explanatory—it's up to you to explain it. And you'll have to do it *in words*.

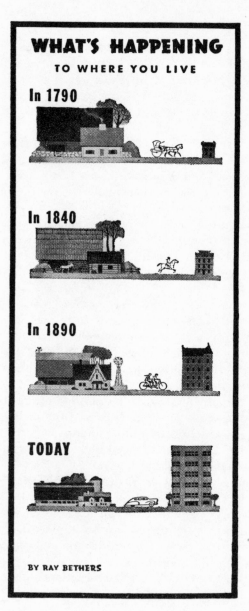

# WHAT'S HAPPENING

## TO WHERE YOU LIVE

In 1790

In 1840

In 1890

TODAY

BY RAY BETHERS

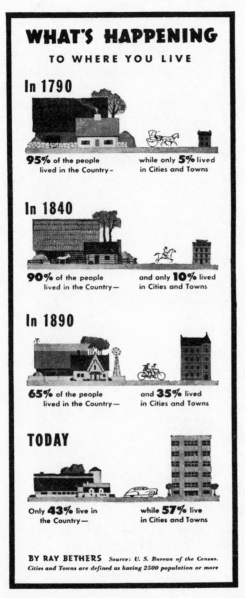

# WHAT'S HAPPENING

## TO WHERE YOU LIVE

### In 1790

**95%** of the people lived in the Country –

while only **5%** lived in Cities and Towns

### In 1840

**90%** of the people lived in the Country —

and only **10%** lived in Cities and Towns

### In 1890

**65%** of the people lived in the Country —

and **35%** lived in Cities and Towns

### TODAY

Only **43%** live in the Country —

while **57%** live in Cities and Towns

**BY RAY BETHERS** *Source: U. S. Bureau of the Census. Cities and Towns are defined as having 2500 population or more*

PS

By 1972 only 9 percent of all working Americans were in agriculture, 27 percent in manufacturing and 64 percent in service industries.

Only 26.5 percent lived in the countryside and 73.5 percent lived in urban areas and cities and towns over 2,500 population.

## CHAPTER 19

# HOW TO OPERATE A BLUE PENCIL

*In composing, as a general rule, run a pen through every other word you have written; you have no idea what vigor it will give your style.*
SIDNEY SMITH

I DON'T know whether efficiency experts ever made time and motion studies of the work done by copy editors in a publishing house. If they did, they must have found that editors spend 90 percent of their time crossing out words in manuscripts and shifting around those that are left. Look over any editor's shoulder for a while and you'll see that I am right.

It's hard to remember this when you are your own editor, revising something you have written yourself. Let's face it: those words you liked so well when you wrote them will probably have to be cut in half and completely rearranged.

Go to a library to get practical advice on writing and you'll find that nothing has been recommended so often and so warmly as cutting. Two thousand years ago Pliny the Younger wrote: "I apologize for this long letter; I didn't have enough time to shorten it." (This has also been attributed to a dozen other great writers.) Dr. Samuel Johnson's only rule for writing was: "Read over your compositions, and when you meet with a passage which you think is particularly fine, strike it out." This was echoed by the late Sir Arthur Quiller-Couch: "If you require a practical rule of me, I will present you with this: Whenever you feel an impulse to perpetrate a piece of exceptionally fine writing, obey it—whole-heartedly—and delete it before sending your manuscript to press. *Murder your darlings.*"

[ 219 ]

In other words, whenever you write, you are tempted to use expressions of which you are fond and proud. Usually it will be just these words and phrases that will stop the reader or throw him off. While you are writing you can't spot them; you are too strongly attached to what has just sprung from your mind. But in the cold light of the morning after you are able to look at them with a detached reader's eye.

The need for transposing may be harder to see. Somehow, at first writing, we don't always hit on the best arrangement of words for emphasis. The rule is simple enough: the place for emphasis is at the end. But while we write, we have a tendency to overlook the reader's need for sentence rhythm and buildup.

Take, for example, these two sentences from an Associated Press story about a government study of the effect of syphilis. Some four hundred Tuskegee Negroes had been given no treatment and someone had complained about it to the Center for Disease Control in Atlanta.

> Dr. William J. Brown, then in charge of the venereal-disease branch at the center, explained in a letter that the decision not to treat the participants had been made on the basis of their age.
>
> Because massive penicillin therapy, the treatment for syphilis, can cause serious side effects and because it was believed that the syphilitic condition of the survivors of the Tuskegee Study was dormant, there would be no treatment, Dr. Brown said in a letter.

The first of these two sentences ends with the word *age*. This puts the emphasis exactly where it belongs, since Dr. Brown's explanation for what had happened was the participants' age.

But the second sentence, which simply adds more detail to the first one, ends weakly and irrelevantly with the word *letter*. You have to go back 12 words to find the key word that *should* have ended it—the word *dormant*. Let's rewrite the sentence the way it should have been written (and leave out some unnecessary words):

> There'd be no treatment, he said, because massive penicillin therapy, the treatment for syphilis, can cause serious side effects and the condition of the survivors was believed to be dormant.

In contrast, let me show you a paragraph in which the emphasis is just right. It's from the *New Yorker*—a bit of reporting by one of its stars, James Thurber:*

> In the intolerable heat of last August, one Ezra Adams, of Clinton, Iowa, strode across his living room and smashed his radio with his fists, in the fond hope of silencing forever the plaintive and unendurable chatter of one of his wife's favorite afternoon programs. He was fined ten dollars for disturbing the peace, and Mrs. Adams later filed suit for divorce. I have no way of knowing how many similarly oppressed husbands may have clapped him on the back or sent him greetings and cigars, but I do know that his gesture was as futile as it was colorful. He had taken a puny sock at a tormentor of great strength, a deeply rooted American institution of towering proportions. Radio daytime serials, known to the irreverent as soap opera, dishpan drama, washboard weepers, and cliffhangers, have for years withstood an array of far more imposing attackers, headed by Dr. Louis I. Berg, a New York psychiatrist and soap opera's Enemy No. 1.

This is worth rereading for its perfectly balanced rhythm—from the languid beginning "In the intolerable heat of last August, one Ezra Adams, of Clinton, Iowa, strode across his living room" to the whiplash ending "soap opera's Enemy No. 1." Each sentence leads the reader up to something, with just the

* By permission. Copyright 1948 James Thurber. Originally published in *The New Yorker*.

right number of words to give him the right impression. (There is nothing wrong with a sentence average of 33 words if you are as readable as Thurber.)

As I said, you will have done most of your revision job when you have cut your original copy to pieces and turned the sentences upside down. The rest of your morning-after work is hardly more than odds and ends.

There is punctuation, for one thing. Since you will shorten your sentences, you'll make many commas into periods. Other commas you'll take out since the better sentence rhythm will make them unnecessary. You will tie some of your short sentences together by using semicolons instead of periods between them—or colons, if the first sentence serves as a curtain-raiser to the second. You will improve the paragraphing—usually by breaking longer paragraphs into two or three smaller ones. Your shorter sentences will force you into shorter paragraphs; there is a natural relation between the two.

You will use more devices for emphasis. You will underline (italicize) words and phrases to be stressed, and put parentheses around those you want to deemphasize. You will help the rhythm of your sentences by using a dash here and there—like this.

In short, you will try at this point to see your words as the reader will see them. If your writing is to be printed, this will mean you have to visualize it in type. You'll need to know these basic rules about readable typography:

(1) Any type size under 10 point is hard to read.

> This is 10 point type.
> This is 8 point type.
> This is 6 point type.

This book is printed in 10 point type.

(2) Anything printed in an unfamiliar type face is hard to read.

**(Imagine a whole book printed in this advertising display type.)**

(3) If there is no leading (white space) between the lines, lines longer than 40 characters and spaces are hard to read. The printers' rule of thumb is "one-and-a-half alphabets" (39 characters or spaces) per line. (This book is printed with about 62 characters per line, but has 2 points leading between the lines.)

(4) Headings printed in capitals only are hard to read. It is easier to read headings in capitals and lower-case letters, particularly if printed in bold face.

All this, of course, belongs to the garden variety of editing and revision. As I said, it's the kind of editing any ordinary person could or should do the morning after he has committed a piece of writing.

Things are different when it comes to tricky business like digesting or abstracting. Such editorial handicraft is beyond the call of duty of the ordinary person; but it's worthwhile to know something about the basic principles.

The first thing to understand is that abridgments are of two kinds: the *Chemical Abstracts* kind and the *Reader's Digest* kind. One boils things down for the hurried information-seeker, the other puts it in convenient shape for the reader who is faced with an empty little chink of leisure time. The difference, of course, lies in the principle of selection: in one case you look for the inner core of facts, in the other for the tastiest bits of reading matter.

Since most writing consists of a structure of facts and ideas covered with digressions, comments, and illustrations, this means that the same piece of writing may be shortened in two directions, so to speak, with entirely different results. The same scientific article may be digested one way for scientists and another way for laymen. On the face of it, it may look impossible that both versions were derived from the same material, but each may be just right for its readers.

Nowadays, the *Reader's Digest* type of condensation is familiar to everybody; the other type is familiar to the scientist or professional worker, but usually unfamiliar to the general public. In recent years, however, one such abridgment has become a national bestseller: D. C. Somervell's one-volume edition of Arnold J. Toynbee's six-volume *Study of History*. It is a perfect specimen of its kind: while Toynbee's original work is a fascinating maze of digressions and historical illustrations, the abridgment resembles, as one reviewer wrote, "a tree in winter." It presents Toynbee's map of world history without taking the reader on any of the author's delightful trips.

While I was reading Somervell's one-volume Toynbee, the question occurred to me what a *Reader's Digest* editor would have done with the same material. So just for the fun of it, I took a random passage in the Somervell volume, looked up the corresponding half-dozen pages in the six-volume original and then worked out a reasonable facsimile of a *"Reader's Digest* condensation" *of the same pages.* Here is the result.

This is the passage I found in Somervell:*

> Perhaps simplification is not quite an accurate, or at least not altogether an adequate, term for describing these changes. Simplification is a negative word and connotes omission and elimination, whereas what has happened in each of these cases is not a diminution but an enhancement of practical efficiency or of aesthetic satisfaction or of intellectual grasp. The result is not a loss but a gain; and this gain is the outcome of a process of simplification because the process liberates forces that have been imprisoned in a more material medium and thereby sets them free to work in a more ethereal medium with a greater potency. It involves not merely a simplification of apparatus but a consequent transfer of energy, or shift of emphasis, from some lower sphere of being or of action to a higher.

* From *A Study of History* by Arnold J. Toynbee, abridged by D. C. Somervell. Copyright 1946 by Oxford University Press, New York.

Perhaps we shall be describing the process in a more illuminating way if we call it, not simplification but etherealiza-
tion.

And here is my own corresponding *"Reader's Digest* article."*

About the middle of the 19th century, in the days of the
Industrial Revolution, there was an English sailing ship
that used to make the voyage to China, year by year, with
the same English crew and finish by going up the Yangtse,
three days' sail upstream, with the same Chinese pilot.

One year the owners scrapped the old sailing-ship and
sent their men out in a new-fangled steamer. All the way
out the crew speculated about the impression the steamer
would make on the Chinese pilot. Their curiosity was
titillated. As they approached the point off the China coast
where the pilot always came on board they had a tense
feeling of expectancy.

At last the pilot stepped onto the steamer's deck, made
his customary salutation to the Captain, and walked to the
wheel. "Now he will have his surprise," thought the English
men, "when he finds the ship moving forward with not a sail
bent on the yards." But when the engines started, they were
astonished to see that not a muscle moved on his face. He
kept his place at the wheel without uttering a word.

"Well," the crew said, "his mind works slowly. He'll
ruminate all day and tell us his thoughts in the evening."
But the day passed, and the evening, and the night. The
pilot said nothing, kept his place at the wheel, and quietly
did his business as always. The second day and night passed
likewise, and the third and last day arrived—the day on
which he was to take his leave.

At this point the Englishmen forgot their resolution to

* Abridged from *A Study of History,* 3rd vol. Used by permission.

leave it to the pilot to break the silence first. They asked him what impression their ship had made on him. "This ship?" the Chinese said. "Why, once upon a time we used to make ships like this in China too. Gave them up some time ago, though. Must be about two thousand years since we used them last."

The Chinese had only contempt for a steamship, or any other piece of clockwork. His own people, he meant to say, had anticipated the Western "Barbarians" in exploiting physical nature but had learned many centuries ago that this material world was not the place where human beings should lay up their treasure. So they had shifted their interest and energy from industrialism to a different sphere.

What does this comparison prove? That Toynbee's original work should have been used as the basis for a different popular version? That Somervell's one-volume edition is unreadable? But if that's true, you will say, how did it manage to stay on the bestseller lists for such a long time? Doesn't my little experiment prove just the opposite from what it was supposed to prove?

Well, I wonder. Compared with the millions who read and enjoy the *Reader's Digest* and similar magazines, the thousands of readers of even a nonfiction bestseller are only a drop in the bucket. And how many among those who bought the Toynbee abridgment ever got beyond the first hundred pages?

## PS

The key to self-editing is the fact that reading is faster than writing. Therefore, when you're editing something you've written, look for words and sentences that can be speeded up. Here are five things you should do:

1. Cut out all unnecessary words and phrases. Don't repeat names and specific references that aren't needed or can be replaced by pronouns.

2. Use more contractions.

3. Cut out unnecessary *that*'s. Many sentences can be speeded up by leaving out the word *that,* as most people do in speaking. Here's an example with two unnecessary *that*'s:

> Amsterdam police officials said *that* they had no reason to believe *that* any sizable group of Palestinian terrorists was hiding in this city or elsewhere in the Netherlands.

Without the two *that*'s, this reads:

> Amsterdam police officials said they had no reason to believe any sizable group of Palestinian terrorists was hiding in this city or elsewhere in the Netherlands.

4. Leave out all commas you can spare. You've got a good deal of leeway in this and the clear trend today is toward fewer commas. Here's an example—a sentence with six commas:

> But, whatever early Mine Worker influences had shaped his social attitudes as a trade unionist, and however personally likable he was, Green was unable to give any substantial support to Randolph's struggle in the A.F.L., because, even as president, he had virtually no power.

With only one comma, this reads:

> But whatever early Mine Worker influences had shaped his social attitudes as a trade unionist and however personally likable he was, Green was unable to give any substantial support to Randolph's struggle in the A.F.L. because even as president he had virtually no power.

5. Leave out unnecessary hyphens. Write as one word, without a hyphen, most words with prefixes and suffixes and such words as *bestseller, teenager* and *elbowroom.*

[ 227 ]

The other day I found this sentence in the *New York Times*: "These arrests were *byproducts* of *antihijacking* procedures." Most probably you'd have put a hyphen in *byproducts* and *antihijacking*.

Don't be timid. Follow the current trend.

## CHAPTER 20

# THE PEDIGREE OF PLAIN TALK

*Generally, style becomes perfect as it becomes natural—this is, colloquial.*

A. R. ORAGE

EACH year in March I tell the Collector of Internal Revenue that my occupation is that of a "writer." The rest of the year I am not so sure, however. My dictionary says that a writer is "1. one who expresses ideas in writing, 2. one engaged in literary work." I have no doubt that I am the first type of writer, but the second definition raises some questions in my mind.

The trouble is that *writer*, like most other words in the English language, has several different meanings. "To write" may mean anything from just putting words on paper to the creation of a literary masterpiece for the ages. Even "professional writer" may mean anything from a cub reporter to a major poet. I'm not afraid that the ordinary, words-on-paper kind of writer will have many objections to this book. Anybody who does his writing as a routine part of his daily living is naturally interested in doing the job as effectively as he can. In this book I have tried to stick closely to the known facts about readability; if it's part of your business to reach people on paper, that's what you want to know.

But there will be readers of this book who are professionals—people who make a living by selling verbal figments of their imagination. To some of them, the application of science and statistics to writing will be disgusting and even painful; they will feel that this book is an insult to literature.

Of course I could answer that I am not really talking about

[ 229 ]

literature. I could say: what I am saying applies to writing as communication; if you are interested in writing as an art form, this is not the book for you.

But that answer would be too easy. There is a better answer that doesn't dodge the question. Let me put it down in so many words: the simple style—the style that meets scientific tests of readability—is *the* classic style of great literature.

To be sure, not all great word artists wrote simply. Some of them were not even particularly interested in being understood. They felt, as the German poet Rilke said somewhere, that it was the writer's business to "express the inexpressible." They tried to do this the best they could, regardless of the effort readers would have to make to understand them. Henry James wrote like that, and Marcel Proust, and Franz Kafka, and Gertrude Stein, and James Joyce. They obviously didn't try to make it easy for their readers, and yet many people agree they wrote great literature.

But these are the exceptions. The classic tradition is that a writer should use the language so that the reader doesn't even notice his words and the way they are used. Anybody who has ever thought about the problem of literary style has come to that conclusion. Naturally: if you start to analyze what style is, the only possible general rule is that the reader must be able to understand what the writer says; and the surest way to that is simplicity. For instance, there are three famous 19th-century English essays on style by Herbert Spencer, George Henry Lewes, and Frederic Harrison. Each puts simplicity first. Spencer speaks of "the principle of economy," Lewes of "the laws of economy and simplicity," and Harrison quotes as the only law of style a sentence by Madame de Sévigné: "Never forsake what is natural; you have molded yourself in that vein, and this produces a perfect style."

The history of English prose is, in fact, the history of the plain style and successive attempts to replace it by something else. All these attempts broke down in the end; the plain style is the only classic style that has survived. The pomposities and complexities of Dr. Samuel Johnson, Edward Gibbon, Edmund Burke, Walter Savage Landor, Thomas Carlyle, John Ruskin, and Walter Pater are now museum pieces; the simplicity of John Bunyan, Samuel Pepys, John Dryden, Daniel Defoe, Jonathan Swift, and Oliver Goldsmith is still a model of good writing. In America, this tradition is even stronger: the classics of this country are Franklin, Emerson, Thoreau, and Mark Twain.

This is the Swift of *Gulliver's Travels:*

What became of my companions in the boat, as well as of those who escaped on the rock, or were left in the vessel, I cannot tell, but conclude they were all lost. For my own part, I swam as fortune directed me, and was pushed forward by wind and tide. I often let my legs drop, and could feel no bottom. But when I was almost gone, and able to struggle no longer, I found myself within my depth; and by this time the storm was much abated. The declivity was so small that I walked near a mile before I got to the shore, which I conjectured was about eight o'clock in the evening. I then advanced forward near half a mile but could not discover any sign of houses or inhabitants; at least I was in so weak a condition, that I did not observe them. I was extremely tired, and with that and the heat of the weather, and about half a pint of brandy that I drank as I left the ship, I found myself much inclined to sleep. I lay down on the grass, which was very short and soft, where I slept sounder than ever I remember to have done in my life, and, as I reckoned, above nine hours, for when I awoke it was just daylight. I attempted to rise, but was not able to stir. For, as I happened to lie on my back, I found my arms and legs were strongly fastened on each side to the ground; and my hair, which was long and thick, tied down in the same manner.

[ 231 ]

This is Daniel Defoe:

It is impossible to express the change that appeared in the very countenances of the people that Thursday morning when the weekly bill came out. It might have been perceived in their countenances that a secret surprise and smile of joy sat on everybody's face. They shook one another by the hands in the streets, who would hardly go on the same side of the way with one another before. Where the streets were not too broad, they would open their windows and call from one house to another, and ask how they did, and if they had heard the good news that the plague was abated. Some would return, when they said good news, and ask, "What good news?" and when they answered that the plague was abated and the bills decreased almost 2000, they would cry out, "God be praised," and would weep aloud for joy, telling them they had heard nothing of it; and such was the joy of the people that it was, as it were, life to them from the grave. I could almost set down as many extravagant things done in the excess of their joy as of their grief; but that would be to lessen the value of it.

This is Thoreau:

The night in prison was novel and interesting enough. The prisoners in their shirt-sleeves were enjoying a chat and the evening air in the doorway, when I entered. But the jailer said, "Come, boys, it is time to lock up"; and so they dispersed, and I heard the sound of their steps returning into the hollow apartments. My room-mate was introduced to me by the jailer, as "a first-rate fellow and a clever man." When the door was locked, he showed me where to hang my hat, and how he managed matters there. The rooms were whitewashed once a month; and this one, at least, was the whitest, most simply furnished, and probably the neatest apartment in the town. He naturally wanted to know where

I came from, and what brought me there; and when I had told him, I asked him in turn how he came there, presuming him to be an honest man, of course; and, as the world goes, I believe he was. "Why," said he, "they accuse me of burning a barn; but I never did it."

And this is Mark Twain:

The next few months showed me strange things. On the same day that we held the conversation above narrated we met a great rise coming down the river. The whole vast face of the stream was black with drifting dead logs, broken boughs, and great trees that had caved in and been washed away. It required the nicest steering to pick one's way through this rushing raft, even in the daytime, when crossing from point to point; and at night the difficulty was mightily increased; every now and then a huge log, lying deep in the water, would suddenly appear right under our bows, coming head-on; no use to try to avoid it then; we could only stop the engines, and one wheel would walk over that log from one end to the other, keeping up a thundering racket and careening the boat in a way that was very uncomfortable to passengers. Now and then we would hit one of these sunken logs a rattling bang, dead in the center, with a full head of steam, and it would stun the boat as if she had hit a continent. Sometimes this log would lodge and stay right across our nose, and back the Mississippi up before it; we would have to do a little crawfishing, then, to get away from the obstruction. We often hit *white* logs in the dark, for we could not see them until we were right on them, but a black log is a pretty distinct object at night. A white snag is an ugly customer when the daylight is gone.

As I mentioned before, the "reading ease" formula of this book doesn't apply to older English prose because sentences are now much shorter than they used to be. But let's apply it to these examples anyway. Here is what we get:

| | |
|---|---|
| Swift | 81 (Easy) |
| Defoe | 71 (Fairly Easy) |
| Thoreau | 83 (Easy) |
| Mark Twain | 77 (Fairly Easy) |

In other words, these four examples of great literature can be read and understood by a modern American who has never gone beyond grade school. And—to answer the question you are going to ask next—the same is true of another piece of great prose:

| | |
|---|---|
| Lincoln's Gettysburg Address | 70 (Fairly Easy) |

These figures do not prove that short words and short sentences are the hallmark of all great literature. Nothing could prove that. But the fact is, most literary people seem to think so nowadays. I mentioned the 19th-century British essays on style; they were followed in the twentieth century by A. P. Herbert, Herbert Read, Ivor Brown, George Orwell, and Robert Graves and Alan Hodge. There is less interest in prose style in America than there is in England; but it's typical that in a review of Steinbeck's *The Pearl*, John Hersey counted words and syllables to show the beautiful simple style, or that Malcolm Cowley, in an analysis of American literary style, praised its simple monosyllabic words, its loose sentence structure, and its avoidance of abstract nouns.

It is not so easy to find someone who says in print he doesn't like difficult literary prose, but it does happen. In the midst of the current revival of Henry James, I came across this quotation from James in a book review by Harvey Breit in the *New York Times:*

Other lights, some of which glimmered, to my eyes, as with the promise of great future intensity—hanging themselves as directly over the question of manners as if they had been a row of lustres reflected in the polished floor of a ballroom. Here was the expensive as a power by itself, a power unguided, undirected, practically unapplied, really exerting itself in a void that could make it no response, that had nothing—poor, gentle, patient, rueful, but altogether helpless void!—to offer in return. The game was that of its doing, each party to the whole combination, what it could, but with the result of the common effort's falling too short.

About this passage Mr. Breit says frankly:

> I concede, and marvel at, the exactness of this passage; but I also confess to having read it a number of times and my experience at first reading was a double one—of simultaneous lucidity and obscurity. I was reminded of Frank Moore Colby's amiable essay, "In Darkest James." "And, indeed," Mr. Colby wrote, "it had been a long time since the public knew what James was up to behind that verbal hedge of his."

There ought to be more criticism like this. The ordinary citizen, with his customary reverence for everything that's printed and his awe of everything that's unintelligible, has no way of knowing when to bow his head and when to say "Nuts!" He can't rely on what he has learned in school since he has been told that Swift and Defoe and Thoreau and Mark Twain wrote good English, and that Edward Gibbon and Thomas Carlyle and James Fenimore Cooper and O. Henry *also* wrote good English. Never has he been told that the prose of some of the literary great, by today's standards, is wretched and that he should avoid imitation of that prose like the plague. In short, what he has been taught about English literature has muddled his judgment and furnished him a handy excuse for being unable to say anything simply.

Open at random one of the accepted literary masterpieces—say, Hardy's *Return of the Native*—you will find sentences like these:

> On the young man's part, the paleness of face which he had brought with him from Paris, and the incipient marks of time and thought, were less perceptible than when he returned, the healthful and energetic sturdiness which was his by nature having partially recovered its original proportions . . .

> The gloomy corner into which accident as much as indiscretion had brought this woman might have led even a moderate partisan to feel that she had cogent reasons for asking the Supreme Power by what right a being of such exquisite finish had been placed in circumstances calculated to make of her charms a curse rather than a blessing.

It's about time someone said out loud that prose like this is ridiculous. Our literary critics are beginning to say it; maybe some day even our schoolteachers will have the courage to say it.

Meanwhile, of course, it's hard for people like you and me to say what we think in the hushed atmosphere of the temples of literature. It's like criticizing modern art or music or poetry. We are told we are not *supposed* to understand it, and made to feel thoroughly ashamed of ourselves.

Maybe it will help you if I quote here two expert criticisms of modern poetry from the *Saturday Review of Literature*. The writers are poets themselves, but poets with sense. Says William Rose Benét: "In reading much modern poetry, one finally finds oneself in a country of incertitude approaching nightmare . . . Several rereadings fail to reveal what the whole thing is about . . . When a modern poet writes 'The speechful day in knowing languors goes,' and entitles his poem 'N. B., Symmetrians,' it drives

me a wee bit mad . . . Could we have just a little less nonsense?"
And Dudley Fitts quotes

> O the flock of sheep
> breaking their flesh open
> with bones sucked
> from the brothels!
> O the grave of bats
> *sailing through shops*
> with the violent hands!

and adds: "I should like to convince myself that this is more
than noise, but I cannot do so."

# CHAPTER 21

# IT'S YOUR OWN LANGUAGE

*The only danger that threatens the native speaker of a standard language is artificiality.*

LEONARD BLOOMFIELD

LANGUAGE is the most democratic institution in the world. Its basis is majority rule; its final authority is the people. If the people decide they don't want the subjunctive any more, out goes the subjunctive; if the people adopt OK as a word, in comes OK. In the realm of language everybody has the right to vote; and everybody does vote, every day of the year.

The way you talk and write makes a difference in the English language that is being talked and written today. There is no fixed set of rules: *you* are making the rules. To be sure, there are limits to what you can do with your language; but they are wide limits, and there is lots of elbowroom for everybody.

In one way or another, your language differs from that of anybody else. It's part of your own unique personality. It has traces of the family you grew up in, the place you came from, the people you associated with, the jobs you had, the schools you went to, the books you read, your hobbies, your sports, your philosophy, your religion, your politics, your prejudices, your memories, your ambitions, your dreams, and your love life. The way you form your sentences shows your outlook on life; the words you choose show your temperament and your aspirations.

No wonder psychologists have analyzed language as a key to personality; they have even tried to trace mental diseases in statistics of sentences and words. But don't let that scare you;

these studies are still far from being practicable for everyday purposes.

Meanwhile the fact remains that your language expresses your personality, like it or not. It's up to you to go beyond that and use language deliberately to suit your own fancy or make it a better instrument for your own purposes. Look at Dr. Dingman (whom I quoted on page 110) and the unique book he wrote on life insurance—all in his own way. Or take the man who thought up the Burma-Shave jingles. Or the people who contribute "Spiced Tongue" items to the *Reader's Digest*. There are families that have a language all their own; there are others whose members write to each other in verse. There are people who are good at puns, people who have a knack at coining new words, people with a gift for imitation of speech.

You, like everybody else, have some such language talent— your own way of making creative use of words. Nobody can stop you from putting it to work. Dress up your business letters, express your own self in your reports: if you don't overdo it, readers will be grateful. Remember, there is no law that says you have to write like everybody else.

You are fortunate because your language is English. English is a great language; among the world's languages it is perhaps the one that gives the individual the greatest freedom. It is poetic and practical at the same time; it is tremendously rich; it's a sort of all-purpose language. One hundred years ago, the German writer Jakob Grimm wrote of English: "In wealth, good sense, and thrifty order no other of the living languages may be put beside it." He was just one of the many foreigners who envy us our language; there is almost nothing you can't do with it.

You are doubly fortunate because your language is American English. English is wonderfully free; American is even freer. It has more scope and more vitality; and it has more of just the thing I am talking about here: elbowroom for the individual speaker and writer. We Americans, as Gertrude Stein wrote, have "changed our language by choosing words which we liked better than other words, by putting the words next to each other in a different way than the English way, by shoving the language around . . ."

With all this wonderful opportunity, why do we speak and write the way we do? Why aren't our books and letters and speeches full of racy, colloquial, rhythmical, personal language? Why do we have to be told by books like this that we are stiff and formal and pompous and unnatural? Where does it all come from?

The answer goes far beyond grammar and usage; it even goes beyond psychology. Language is a social affair; we use it according to the social situation we are in. Our rhetoric is keyed to our place in society—either the one we have or the one we'd like to have. Formal speech and unreadable writing are mostly the products of social conventions.

We write stilted English because we unconsciously assume that this is expected of us in the position we happen to fill or the organization we belong to. If we analyzed the situation we would find this isn't true; but we never do. We have formed a set of habits, and in most of our speaking and writing we simply piece together the ready-made bits of language that are handy wherever we happen to be. Most of the time we keep our personality out of our language; it takes less effort to use the language anybody else would use in the same place. The easiest thing is to conform. Why bother?

It's like men's clothes. A business suit on a hot summer day is a repulsive garment; it's the least functional thing anybody could possibly wear. But men do: they prefer a mild form of torture to going against social convention. They are rather hot *en masse* than comfortable as individuals.

Like sack suits, formal language isn't limited to English-speaking peoples. It is found throughout Western civilization. There is a bookish language in all countries that have books, and officialese in all countries that have officials. It was probably used in the Babylonia of Hammurabi and the Egypt of the Pharaohs. It is certainly used in all countries that have paper and ink and regulations and files and clerks. In a famous German book about "Some Follies of Language," published 60 years ago, the author, Dr. Gustav Wustmann, wrote of "writing-language, ink-German, or paper-style, as it is sometimes called—that strange way of expression, which is never spoken but only written, and which is a peculiarity of the German language only." He was quite wrong: it is a universal curse of modern man.

Typically, it is the language of minor clerks, secondary officials, cogs in some social machine. It is their means of sharing in the social standing of an organization, their psychological substitute for personal importance. The farther toward the bottom, the thicker their coat of assumed dignity.

The same is often true of society at large. Great formality seems to be the hallmark of the still-insecure, the not-quite-arrived, the semi-accepted. The social sciences have a more pompous language than the natural sciences, psychology has a more luxuriant lingo than medicine, public administration is more unreadable than law. Among our social groups, the most formalistic style is that of labor. As I said before, union contracts are among the most involved legal documents; and it is no accident that a labor leader, John L. Lewis, loves to express himself like this: "No action has been taken by this writer or the United Mine Workers of America, as such, which would fall within the purview of the oppressive statute under which you seek to function. Without indulging in analysis, it is a logical assumption that the cavilings of the bar and bench in their attempts to explicate this infamous enactment will consume a tedious time."

Those who are secure in their position at the top usually know they don't need such verbal trappings. They know they can forget about false dignity and use language that suits their personality and the purpose in hand. They leave conventional rhetoric to those below who will never reach the top, and express themselves with the force and dignity that is natural to them.

In one of Franklin D. Roosevelt's election campaigns, Frances Perkins prepared for him a speech on social security. One section she summed up by saying "We are trying to construct a more inclusive society." But when Roosevelt delivered the speech, what he said was "We are going to make a country in which no one is left out."

## PS

In March 1973 I got a letter from Mr. Tom Hansen (not his name), who'd just discovered this book. He wrote:

> Dear Dr. Flesch:
>
> I've studied writing in schools for 15 years and I never ran across any of your books. The last quarter of Journalism School I picked up one of your paperbacks after reading about the Readability Formula.
>
> For the first time, I read something that really made sense. I've read things like "Using Yoga to Improve Your Writing" and Strunk and White's little stylebook. I've heard the sportswriter's definition of writing as "sitting down at a typewriter until little drops of blood appear on your forehead."
>
> I *knew* that writing was fun; that it wasn't a difficult task. But all the pros told with glee how much they suffer in front of the typewriter. That doesn't indicate a high degree of mental health among professional writers.
>
> You write as if you saw it all for the first time. You don't rely on the experts; you rely on what *you* think is right. And I saw that I wasn't alone in the wilderness, that what I had felt all along wasn't crazy.
>
> Dr. Flesch, where have you been all my life?
>
> This is my last quarter at [Far West] University and my

last quarter with pedagogues. I'm going to work as a reporter, writer and journalism teacher. Praise the Lord that I have happened upon your works. I'm reading all of them.

Sincerely,

Tom Hansen

Naturally I was pleased to get such an ardent fan letter 25 years after writing this book. But then I began to wonder. Isn't it strange that Mr. Hansen, after 15 years of elementary school, high school and college, hadn't ever run across a reference to my readability formula? Or that my approach to writing, which is based wholly on scientific evidence, struck him as entirely new and contrary to the wisdom of the experts?

This book is still alive because English teachers and textbooks have consistently ignored scientific linguistics and persisted in their prescientific, outdated approach to composition. Perhaps in another 25 years they'll catch up with the times.

# APPENDIX

# HOW TO USE THE READABILITY FORMULA

To estimate the readability ("reading ease" and "human interest") of a piece of writing, go through the following steps:

*Step 1.   Pick your samples*

Unless you want to test a whole piece of writing, take samples. Take enough samples to make a fair test (say, three to five of an article and 25 to 30 of a book). Don't try to pick "good" or "typical" samples. Go by a strictly numerical scheme. For instance, take every third paragraph or every other page. (Ordinarily, the introductory paragraphs of a piece of writing are not typical of its style.) Each sample should start at the beginning of a paragraph.

*Step 2.   Count the number of words*

Count the words in your piece of writing. If you are using samples, take each sample and count each word in it up to 100. Count contractions and hyphenated words as one word. Count numbers and letters as words, too, if separated by spaces. For example, count each of the following as one word: *1948, $19,892, e.g., C.O.D., wouldn't, full-length.*

*Step 3.   Figure the average sentence length*

Figure the average sentence length in words for your piece of writing. If you are using samples, do this for all your samples *combined*. In a 100-word sample, find the sentence that ends nearest to the 100-word mark—that might be at the 94th word or the 109th word. Count the sentences up to that point and divide the number of words in those sentences in all your samples by the number of sentences in all your samples. In counting sentences, follow the units of thought rather than the punctuation: usually sentences are marked off by periods; but sometimes they are marked off by colons or semicolons—like these. (There are three sentences here between two periods.) But don't break up sentences that are joined by conjunctions like *and* or *but*.

## Step 4. Count the syllables

Count the syllables in your 100-word samples and divide the total number of syllables by the number of samples. If you are testing a whole piece of writing, divide the total number of syllables by the total number of words and multiply by 100. This will give you the number of syllables per 100 words. Count syllables the way you pronounce the word; e.g. *asked* has one syllable, *determined* three, and *pronunciation* five. Count the number of syllables in symbols and figures according to the way they are normally read aloud, e.g. two for $ ("dollars") and four for *1916* ("nineteen sixteen"). However, if a passage contains several or lengthy figures, your estimate will be more accurate if you don't include these figures in your syllable count; in a 100-word sample, be sure to add instead a corresponding number of words after the 100-word mark. If in doubt about syllabication rules, use any good dictionary. (To save time, count all syllables except the first in all words of more than one syllable; then add the total to the number of words tested. It is also helpful to "read silently aloud" while counting.)

## Step 5. Count the "personal words"

Count the "personal words" in your 100-word samples and divide the total number of "personal words" by the number of samples. If you are testing a whole piece of writing, divide the total number of "personal words" by the total number of words and multiply by 100. This will give you the number of "personal words" per 100 words.

"Personal words" are:

(a) All first-, second-, and third-person pronouns except the neuter pronouns *it, its, itself,* and *they, them, their, theirs, themselves* if referring to things rather than people.

(b) All words that have masculine or feminine natural gender, e.g. *John Jones, Mary, father, sister, iceman, actress.* Do not count common-gender words like *teacher, doctor, employee, assistant, spouse.* Count singular and plural forms.

(c) The group words *people* (with the plural verb) and *folks.*

*Step 6.  Count the "personal sentences"*

Count the "personal sentences" in your 100-word samples and divide the number of "personal sentences" in all your samples by the number of sentences in all your samples. If you are testing a whole piece of writing, divide the total number of "personal sentences" by the total number of sentences. In both cases multiply by 100. This will give you the number of "personal sentences" per 100 sentences.

"Personal sentences" are:

(a) Spoken sentences, marked by quotation marks or otherwise, often including speech tags like "he said," set off by colons or commas (e.g. *"I doubt it."—We told him: "You can take it or leave it."—"That's all very well," he replied, showing clearly that he didn't believe a word of what we said.*)

(b) Questions, commands, requests, and other sentences directly addressed to the reader (e.g. *Does this sound impossible?— Imagine what this means.—Do this three times.—You shouldn't overrate these results.—This is a point you must remember.—It means a lot to people like you and me.*). But don't count sentences that are only indirectly or vaguely addressed to the reader (e.g. *This is typical of our national character.—You never can tell.*).

(c) Exclamations (e.g. *It's unbelievable!*)

(d) Grammatically incomplete sentences whose full meaning has to be inferred from the context (e.g. *Doesn't know a word of English.—Handsome, though.—Well, he wasn't.—The minute you walked out.*)

If a sentence fits two or more of these definitions, count it only once.

*Step 7. Find your "reading ease" score*

Using the average sentence length in words (*Step 3*) and the number of syllables per 100 words (*Step 4*), find your "reading ease" score on the How Easy? chart printed on the end papers of this book.

You can also use this formula:

Multiply the average sentence length by 1.015 ........

Multiply the number of syllables per 100 words by .846 ........

Add ──────

Subtract this sum from   206.835

Your "reading ease" score is  ........

The "reading ease" score will put your piece of writing on a scale between 0 (practically unreadable) and 100 (easy for any literate person).

*Step 8. Find your "human interest" score*

Using the number of "personal words" per 100 words (*Step 5*) and the number of "personal sentences" per 100 sentences (*Step 6*), find your "human interest" score on the How Interesting? chart printed on the end papers of this book.

Or use this formula:

Multiply the number of "personal words" per 100 words by 3.635 ........

Multiply the number of "personal sentences" per 1000 sentences by .314 ........

The total is your "human interest" score  ........

The "human interest" score will put your piece of writing on a scale between 0 (no human interest) and 100 (full of human interest).

In applying the twin formulas, remember that the "reading ease" formula measures *length* (the longer the words and sentences, the harder to read) and the "human interest" formula measures *percentages* (the more "personal" words and sentences, the more human interest).

For further interpretation of your scores, use the tables on pp. 177-179.

# NOTES

### Chapter 1

"A whole is that which has a beginning, middle, and end." (Aristotle, *Poetics*, Chapter 7.)—For Aristotle's distinction of three kinds of speeches, see *The Rhetoric of Aristotle*, tr. by Lane Cooper (Appleton-Century, 1932), p. 17.—The scientific paper mentioned is "A Study of the Relative Effectiveness of Climax and Anti-Climax in an Argumentative Speech" by Harold Sponberg (*Speech Monographs*, 1946, v. 13, pp. 35-44).—The Chase National Bank booklet quoted is "A Substitute for You" by Don Herold (1943).—John Dos Passos' article "Britain's Dim Dictatorship" appeared in *Life*, Sept. 29, 1947.—Hal Boyle's AP feature "Wanted: One Negotiable Freckle" appeared in January 30, 1948, newspapers.

### Chapter 2

Public opinion poll results are quoted from newspaper and news-magazine reports and from the quarterly tabulations of the *Public Opinion Quarterly*.—For the story about Rep. Andrews, see *Time*, May 31, 1948.—Farmers' vocabulary: see "Readability for Farm Families" by Amy G. Cowing (*Land Policy Rev.*, spring 1947, v. 10, pp. 29-31).—Meaning of *adjective:* personal letter by Mr. Leo Handel, Director, Motion Picture Research Bureau, dated December 2, 1947.—The goat pelt story is quoted from an article by Laura Lane, Texas Extension Editor (U. S. Extension Service 85-45).—The recipe comparison is from a *McCall's* magazine ad, Oct. 1, 1947.—Aristotle: see his *Rhetoric*, tr. by Lane Cooper (Appleton-Century, 1932), pp. 131ff.—Sex differences: a good source is *Women and Men* by Amram Scheinfeld (Harcout, Brace), p. 143.—The nylon story is from *Wallace's Farmer*. The experiment was reported on in "How Plain Talk Increases Readership 45% to 66%," by Donald R. Murphy *Printer's Ink*, Sept. 19, 1947, pp. 35-37.—"Interstate Tax Barriers to Marketing" by Robert S. Holzman appeared in the *Journal of Marketing*, July 1947; the other version was taken from the Prentice-Hall *State and Local Tax Report Bulletin*, Sept. 2, 1947.—The comparison between the *New York Times* and the *New York Daily News* is from the *New Yorker* profile of Reuben Maury by John Bainbridge, May 31, 1947, p. 31.—James Reid Parker's review of Laura Z. Hobson's *Gentlemen's Agreement* appeared in the *Survey Graphic*, May 1947, pp. 312-313.—For two stimulating discussions of the problems mentioned in this chapter see "The Public Opinion Myth" by Ernest Borneman, *Harper's Magazine*, July 1947, pp. 30-40, and "Machine-Age Art" by Lyman Bryson, *Saturday Review of Literature*, May 10, 1947, pp. 9ff.

## CHAPTER 3

The quotation from Schopenhauer is from his essay *On Style;* that from Harold Nicolson from "How to Write a Book" (*Atlantic Monthly,* January 1946, pp. 111-112); that from George Polya from *How to Solve It; A New Aspect of Mathematical Method* (Princeton University Press, 1945), p. 159.— Graham Wallas' *Art of Thought* was published in New York by Harcourt, Brace & Co. in 1926.—Dr. Vannevar Bush's essay "As We May Think" appeared in the *Atlantic Monthly,* July 1945, pp. 101-108. Albert Deutsch's article on "Unnecessary Operations" appeared in the *Reader's Digest,* December 1947.—The *New York Times* quotation is from the issue of February 8, 1948. —The story of Young Gauss: see *Productive Thinking* by Max Wertheimer (Harper & Brothers, 1945), p. 89.—Bennett Cerf's anecdote appeared in the *Saturday Review of Literature,* December 13, 1947.—*Practical Farming in the South* was published, and cleverly advertised, by the University of North Carolina Press.

## CHAPTER 4

Mr. Alexander's work on the article about St. Louis is described in *Writing —From Idea to Printed Page* by Glenn Gundell (Doubleday & Co., 1949), p. 102.— For the *Gestalt*-psychology approach to thinking, see *Productive Thinking* by Max Wertheimer (Harper & Brothers, 1945); "On Problem-Solving" by Karl Duncker (*Psychological Monogr.,* 1945, v. 58, No. 5, Whole No. 270); also *Directed Thinking* by George Humphrey (Dodd, Mead, 1948) and literature cited there.—The quotation by Allan Nevins is from *Writers and Writing* by Robert Van Gelder (Scribner's, 1946).—*Tested Sentences That Sell* by Elmer Wheeler was published by Prentice-Hall in 1937.—"Duet on a Bus" by Douglas Moore appeared in the *Saturday Review of Literature,* Jan. 20, 1945.—"Doctors Along the Boardwalk" by Bernard DeVoto appeared in *Harper's Magazine,* Sept. 1947, p. 215.—Alva Johnston's profile of Beardsley Ruml: see the *New Yorker,* Feb. 10, 1945.—"The Two-Fisted Wisdom of Ching" by Beverly Smith: see *Reader's Digest,* April 1948, pp. 71-76.

## CHAPTER 5

The sources for this chapter include Wallas' *Art of Thought,* Wertheimer's *Productive Thinking,* and, particularly, *An Essay on the Psychology of Invention in the Mathematical Field* by Jacques Hadamard (Princeton University Press, 1945).—The quotation about Mr. Zolotow is from *Writing—From Idea to Printed Page* by Glenn Gundell (Doubleday & Co., 1949), p. 210.—The "witness" quotations are from the following sources: *Briefe aus Muzot* by Rainer Maria Rilke (Leipzig, Insel Verlag, 1932); *The Queen of the Sciences* by Eric T. Bell (Baltimore, Williams & Wilkins, 1931); *The Magic of Believing* by Claude M. Bristol (Prentice-Hall, 1948); *The Conquest of Happiness* by Bertrand Russell (Garden City, 1933); *The Engineer in Society* by John Mills (Van Nostrand, 1946); *Writers and Writing* by Robert Van Gelder (Scribner's, 1946); *A Technique for Producing Ideas* by James Webb Young (Chicago, Advertising Publications, 1940); the story about Otto Loewi is adapted from *The Way of an Investigator* by Walter B. Cannon (Norton, 1945).—Henri Poincaré: see his *Foundations of Science* (New York, Science Press, 1913).— W. E. Leonard: see *How Writers Write*, ed. by Nettie S. Tillett (Crowell, 1937). —E. B. White's Christmas piece appeared in the *New Yorker's* "Talk of the Town" Department on December 23, 1944.

## CHAPTER 6

Psychological research in this area is particularly meager. Three interesting studies are: "An Experimental Study of the Relative Effectiveness of Certain Forms of Emphasis in Public Speaking" by R. Ehrensberger (*Speech Monographs*, 1945, v. 12, pp. 94-111); the study by Sponberg mentioned in the notes to Chapter 1; and "The Role of the Order of Presentation in Learning" by George Katona (*Amer. Journal of Psychology*, 1942, v. 55, pp. 328-353).—See also *Organizing and Memorizing* by George Katona (Columbia University Press, 1939).—The old-model business letter is from *The Elements of English Composition; a Preparation for Rhetoric*, by Miss L. A. Chittenden (Chicago, S. C. Griggs & Co., 1890).—For the origin of the 5-W lead, see any history of American journalism.—*A Key to the Secret of Writing and Selling* by Jack Woodford (Garden City, 1940) originally was published in 1933 under the title *Trial and Error*.—Attitude of magazine editors toward open-end stories: see "Notes from Inside a Glasshouse" by John Schaffner (*Saturday Review of Literature*, Feb. 28, 1948).—Quote from John Beecroft: see "The Book Clubs" by Merle Miller (*Harper's Magazine*, May 1948, pp. 433-440).— The remarks about Huxley and Conrad are from *The Dynamics of Literature* by Nathan Comfort Star (Columbia University Press, 1945).

## CHAPTER 7

*Time's* anniversary issue appeared on March 8, 1948.—The *Saturday Evening Post* article quoted is "New Hope for the Anemic" by Steven M. Spencer (December 14, 1946). It was awarded the 1947 AAAS–George Westinghouse Science Writing Award.—*On Understanding Science; An Historical Approach*, by James B. Conant (Yale University Press, 1947).—The Toynbee quotation is from the abridged edition of his *Study of History* (Oxford University Press, 1947).—The quotation from George Gamow is from his book *One Two Three . . . Infinity; Facts & Speculations of Science* (Viking, 1947).—The item about neckties is from a booklet sent out by Webb Young, Trader, Santa Fé, N. M. —The advertisement about the Martin family is one of the Life Insurance Institute series.—James Marlow's story about international trade appeared on May 5, 1948. For the literature on readability measurement, see notes to Chapter 14.

## CHAPTER 8

The two quotations about dialogue are from *Making Type Work* by Benjamin Sherbow (Century, 1916) and *Some Observations on the Art of Narrative* by Phyllis Bentley (Macmillan, 1947).—The examples are taken from: *Teamwork to Save Soil and Increase Production* by T. A. Waring (U. S. Dept. of Agriculture, Soil Conservation Service, Misc. Public, No. 486, 1942); *Philosopher's Quest* by Irwin Edman Viking Press, 1947); *Lawyer's Weekly Report*, Jan. 26, 1948 (New York, Prentice-Hall).—"Let's Help Them Marry Young" by Howard Whitman (condensed from *Better Homes & Gardens*) appeared in the *Reader's Digest*, October 1947.—For material on readability measurement, see notes to Chapter 14.

## CHAPTER 9

President Truman's remarks to radio men appeared on November 14, 1947. —For General Eisenhower's interview, see the *New York Times*, June 16, 1945. —The quotation from Jimmy Cannon is from his column of September 19, 1947.—*Risk Appraisal* by Dr. Harry Dingman was published by the National Underwriter Co. of Cincinnati in 1946.

## CHAPTER 10

The best current discussion of English usage from the scientific point of view is *Teaching English Usage* by Robert C. Pooley (New York, Appleton-Century, 1946); it also has an excellent bibliography on the subject. For the Shakespeare quotations I drew mainly on *Facts About Current English Usage* by Albert H. Marckwardt and Fred G. Walcott (Appleton-Century, 1938) and *A Modern English Grammar on Historical Principles* by Otto Jespersen (Heidelberg, C. Winter, 1909-40. 5 vols.).—The opening quotation is from *Usage and Abusage; a Guide to Good English* by Eric Partridge (Harper & Brothers, 1942).—Sources of the Shakespeare quotations: Sonnet 94; *Henry V*, I, ii, 9; *Antony and Cleopatra*, III, iii, 14; *Macbeth*, V, viii, 34; *Henry VI*, Pt. 1, III, iii, 62; *Twelfth Night*, II, iii; *Cymbeline*, IV, ii, 253; *Hamlet*, V, ii, 184; *Midsummer Night's Dream*, I, i, 3; *Tempest*, V, i, 304; *Merchant of Venice*, II, vii, 10; *Pericles*, I, i, 163.

## CHAPTER 11

*Analytics of Literature; a Manual for the Objective Study of English Prose and Poetry* by L. A. Sherman was published by Ginn & Co., Boston, in 1893.— For the development of the English sentence, see also "The English Sentence in Literature and in College Freshman Composition" by R. G. Lowrey

(George Peabody College for Teachers, Nashville, Tenn., 1928; Contr. to Ed. No. 50).—The two quoted books on chess were published by David McKay Co. in Philadelphia.—The two quotations on legal prose are from "The Simplification of Government Regulations" by David F. Cavers (*Federal Bar Journal*, July 1947, v. 8, pp. 339-356) and *Law and Literature* by Benjamin F. Cardozo (Harcourt, Brace, 1931).—The Conrad passage is from *An Outpost of Progress;* the passage from *The Federalist* is from No. 19.—*New Yorker* vs. *Reader's Digest*: According to an unpublished study of mine, the standard deviation of sentence length in the *New Yorker* is 14.04 words, in the *Reader's Digest*, 8.96 words.—The quoted *Herald Tribune* editorial appeared on March 3, 1948.

<h2 style="text-align:center">CHAPTER 12</h2>

The best edition of John Horne Tooke's *Diversions of Purley* was published in London in 1829 and reprinted in 1860; for an account of his life, see *John Horne Tooke* by Minnie Clare Yarborough (Columbia University Press, 1926). —Pomposity has been attacked by many writers; the best and most hilarious book is *What a Word!* by A. P. Herbert (Doubleday, 1936).—The item about the Veterans Administration appeared in many papers on June 28, 1947.— The true facts about vocabulary are excellently summarized in *The American Language; Supplement Two* by H. L. Mencken (Knopf, 1948), pp. 348-352.

<h2 style="text-align:center">CHAPTER 13</h2>

Auxiliary verbs, verb-adverb combinations, and "body-movement" verbs: see *English Usage* by Arthur G. Kennedy (Appleton-Century, 1942); *The Modern English Verb-Adverb Combination* by Arthur G. Kennedy (Stanford Univ. Publ. in Language and Literature, v. 1, No. 1, 1920); *Words and Idioms* by Logan Pearsall Smith (Boston, Houghton Mifflin Co., 1925), pp. 249-265; *Three Introductory Lectures on the Science of Thought* by F. Max Mueller (Chicago, Open Court, 1887); *The Science of Thought* by F. Max Mueller (London, Longmans, Green & Co., 1887).—Adjectives and verbs: "The Adjective-Verb Quotient: a Contribution to the Psychology of Language" by D. P. Boder (*Psychol. Record*, 1940, v. 22, pp. 310-343); see also "One Stylistic Feature of the 1611 English Bible" by Charles C. Fries (*Fred Newton Scott Anniversary Papers*, University of Chicago Press, 1929, pp. 175-187) and *Essai sur la Structure Logique de la Phrase* par Albert Séchéhaye (Paris, Champion, 1926).—*Which*: see *Essentials of English Grammar* by Otto Jespersen (Holt, 1933), p. 359, and *Selections from the works of Joseph Addison*, ed. by Edward B. Reed (Holt, 1906), *passim* and footnotes.

<h2 style="text-align:center">CHAPTER 14</h2>

The scientific derivation of the formula presented here is given in my article "A New Readability Yardstick" (*Journal of Applied Psychology*, June

1948, v. 32, no. 3, pp. 222-233); for the scientific derivation of its predecessor (as given in my earlier book *The Art of Plain Talk* [Harper, 1946]), see my *Marks of Readable Style; a Study in Adult Education* (Teachers College, Columbia University, 1943, Contr. to Ed. No. 897); also my earlier article "Estimating the Comprehension Difficulty of Magazine Articles" (*Journal of General Psychology*, 1943, v. 28, pp. 63-80). Both formulas are based on the tested passages in *Standard Test Lessons in Reading* by William A. McCall and Lelah M. Crabbs (Teachers College, Columbia University, 1926). The correlation coefficient of the "reading ease" formula with comprehension is .70, of the "human interest" formula, .43; for validation studies, see notes to the next chapter. For a variety of uses of the formula or its predecessor, see *Books for Adult Beginners; Grades I to VII* by Pauline J. Fihe, Viola Wallace and Martha Schulz, rev. ed. (Chicago, American Library Association, 1946); "Reading Grade Placement of the First 23 Books Awarded the John Newbery Prize" by L. R. Miller (*Elementary School Journal*, 1946, pp. 394-399); "They Speak His Language" by Amy G. Cowing (*Journal of Home Economics*, 1945, v. 37, pp. 487-489); "Lots of Names—Short Sentences—Simple Words" by J. Alden (*Printer's Ink*, June 29, 1945, pp. 21-22); "Gunning Finds Papers Too Hard to Read," "Foreign News Written Over Heads of Readers," "Some Add Shortening to 5-W Lead Recipe" (*Editor & Publisher*, May 19, 1945, p. 12; December 28, 1946, p. 28; February 22, 1947, p. 24); "Financial Reports Can Be Written So People Can Understand Them" by James M. Lambie, Jr. (*Journal of Accountancy*, 1947, v. 84, p. 40); "Some Critical Factors of Newspaper Readability" by Melvin Lostutter (*Journalism Quarterly*, 1947, v. 24, no. 4); "Communication Between Management and Workers" by Donald G. Paterson and James J. Jenkins (*Journal of Applied Psychology*, 1948, v. 32, pp. 71-80); "Principles of Readability Applied to Reporting Research," by Ruth Strang (*Teachers College Record*, 1948, v. 49, no. 7, pp. 449-451); "Are Our 'American Scriptures' Readable?" by David M. White (*School and Society*, 1948, v. 68, no. 1758, pp. 154-155); "Can Mass Audiences Read Institutional Advertising?" by Philip Ward Burton and Charles Edmund Swanson (*Journalism Quarterly*, June 1948, v. 25, pp. 145-150, 146). See also my article "A Readability Formula in Practice" (*Elementary English*, 1948, v. 25, no. 6, pp. 344-351).

For the literature on readability, see the basic work *What Makes a Book Readable* by William S. Gray and Bernice E. Leary (University of Chicago Press, 1935); the bibliographies listed in my *Marks of Readable Style* and "A New Readability Yardstick"; and "Progress in the Study of Readability" by William S. Gray (*Elementary School Journal*, May 1947, v. 47, pp. 490-499).

The differences between the formula given in *The Art of Plain Talk* and the one given here are as follows:

(1) The sentence-length factor is unchanged. However, the earlier formula contained a computational error due to certain statistics taken from previous work by Dr. Irving Lorge; this error has now been corrected. (Dr. Lorge discovered his error independently; see his paper "The Lorge and Flesch Read-

ability Formulas: A Correction" [*School and Society*, Feb. 21, 1948, v. 67, pp. 141-142]; also "A Formula for Predicting Readability" by Edgar Dale and Jeanne S. Chall [*Educational Research Bulletin*, Jan. 21, 1948, v. 27, pp. 11-20].) The earlier formula, because of the error, gave too much weight to the sentence factor.

(2) The affix count has been replaced by a syllable count. This change was made purely for the sake of convenience, since the affix count had proved to be troublesome for many users. Statistically, the correlation between the two measures is .87; in other words, they are practically equivalent.

(3) The "personal words" have been redefined; otherwise, this factor has not been changed.

(4) The "personal sentences" factor is new.

(5) The new formula was set up so that the user arrives at two scores, one for "reading ease" and one for "human interest." In both scores the ordinary range falls between 0 and 100, so that 0 means "unreadable" and 100 means "100% readable." Of course, there is no such thing as a percentage of readability, but the average person understands best scores that are patterned after percentage figures. Actually, the "100" point in both scores means material that is understandable for people who have finished fourth grade and are therefore, in the language of the Census, "functionally literate."

The references for the "nerve-block" example are: "Therapeutic Nerve Block" by E. A. Rovenstine, M.D., and H. M. Wertheim, M.D. (*Journal of the American Medical Association*, Nov. 8, 1941, v. 117, pp. 1599-1603); "Pain Control Clinic, New York Doctors Ease Suffering by Blocking Off Nerves With Drugs" (*Life*, October 27, 1947, pp. 99-102); "Anesthesiologist. I. The Cold and Drowsy Humour" by Mark Murphy (*New Yorker*, October 25, 1947, pp. 36-45).

The average "reading ease" score of this book is 63, the average "human interest" score 39.

## CHAPTER 15

Validation studies of the readability formula offered in this book (and its predecessor, published in my *Art of Plain Talk*) include: "Test Proves Short Sentences and Words Get Best Readership" and "How Plain Talk Increases Readership 45% to 66 %" by Donald R. Murphy (*Printer's Ink*, 1947, v. 218, pp. 61-64 and v. 220, pp. 35-37); my article "How to Write Copy That Will Be Read" (*Advertising & Selling*, March 1947, pp. 113ff.); "Empirical Test Proves Clarity Adds Readers" by Bernard Feld, Jr. (*Editor & Publisher*, April 17, 1948); "How to Write and Be Understood" by Edgar Dale and Hilda Hager (Bur. of Educ. Res., Ohio State University, Columbus, O., 1947); "Psychological Writing, Easy and Hard" by S. S. Stevens and Geraldine Stone (*American Psychologist*, 1947, v. 2, pp. 130-235; Discussion, pp. 523-525); *Reading Visual Fatigue* by Leonard Carmichael and Walter F. Dearborn (Houghton Mifflin, 1947) in conjunction with my article "New Facts About Readability" (*College English*, Jan. 1949, v. 10, no. 4, pp. 225-226); "How Valid Is the Flesch Readability Formula?" by Alberta S. Glinsky (*American Psychologist*, 1948, v. 3, p. 261); "Predicting Listener Understanding and Interest in Newscasts" by Jeanne S. Chall and Harold E. Dial (*Educational Research Bulletin*, September 15, 1948, v. 27, no. 6, pp. 141-153, 168); "Readability and Readership: A Controlled Experiment" by Charles E. Swanson (*Journalism Quarterly*, Dec. 1948, v. 25, no. 4, pp. 339-343). These studies show high correlations between readability as measured by the formula, and readership, reading speed, comprehension, and retention.—The two quoted history texts are *Story of Nations* by Rogers, Adams, and Brown (Holt, 1945) and *World History* by Smith, Muzzey, and Lloyd (Ginn & Co., 1946).—The population estimates are based on the U.S. Census release Series P-20, No. 15, May 4, 1948, "Educational Attainment of the Civilian Population: April 1947." This explains the differences between the table on page 177 and that published in *The Art of Plain Talk*, p. 205, which was based on 1940 Census figures.—The magazine averages cited are based on a number of unpublished statistical studies.

<br>

CHAPTER 16

The quotation from H. L. Mencken is from "Names for Americans" (*American Speech*, December 1947, v. 22, pp. 241-256).—The little essay on *busied* is from the *New Yorker*, March 29, 1947.—For *Kabotchnick-Cabot, skim milk, horse mackerel*, and the Western Union case, see newspaper reports.—Good Humor arbitration case: *American Labor Arbitration Awards*, v. 2, ¶67,843.—Steinbeck interview in Russia: *New York Herald Tribune*, January 21, 1948.—Hatlessness: *New York Times*, Sept. 20, 1947.—For two good accounts of semantics, see *The Wonder of Words* by Isaac Goldberg (Appleton-Century, 1938) and *The Gift of Tongues* by Margaret Schlauch (The Viking Press). The two quoted definitions of general semantics are from *People in Quandaries* by Wendell Johnson (Harper & Brothers, 1946), p. 33, and "General Semantics and the Science of Man" by Charles I. Glicksberg (*Scientific Monthly*, May 1946, pp. 440-446).—Up-and-down pattern: see particularly *People in Quandaries* by W. Johnson (above), pp. 276ff.—The quoted *Saturday Evening Post* article is "You're Not as Smart as You Could Be" by David G. Wittels (April 17, 1948).—The Bible quotation is from Matthew 13:13.

<br>

CHAPTER 17

The extensive literature on the mechanics of reading is well summarized in "The Study of Eye Movements in Reading" by Miles A. Tinker (*Psychological Bulletin*, March 1946, v. 43, no. 2, pp. 93-120) and *Reading and Visual Fatigue* by Leonard Carmichael and Walter F. Dearborn (Houghton Mifflin, 1947). A still good, nonscientific account is *How to Read* by J. B. Kerfoot (Houghton Mifflin, 1916).—The bill-of-lading example is from "The Effect of Language

Style on Reading Performance" by Francis P. Robinson (*Journal of Educational Psychology* March 1947, v. 38, no. 3, pp. 149-156).—Thorndike's classic paper: "Reading as Reasoning: A Study of Mistakes in Paragraph Reading" (*Journal of Educational Psychology* June 1917, v. 8, pp. 323-332).—The quotation from Freud is from his *Psychopathology of Everyday Life* (in *The Basic Writings of Sigmund Freud*, Modern Library, 1938).—The "Edward VIII" example is reported in "Post-Mortem on a Printer's Error" by H. Lundholm (*Character & Personality*, 1944, v. 13, pp. 22-29).—"Impassioned beauty": see *Seven Types of Ambiguity* by William Empson (London, Chatto & Windus, 1947).

### CHAPTER 18

The psychological studies referred to are: "The Ability of Children to Read Cross-Sections," "The Ability of Children to Read a Process-Diagram," and "The Ability of Children to Read Conventionalized Diagrammatic Symbols" by Morton Malter (*Journal of Educational Psychology*, 1947, v. 38, pp. 157-166; 1947, v. 38, pp. 290-298; and 1948, v. 39, pp. 27-34) and "Learning from Graphical Material" by M. D. Vernon (*British Journal of Psychology*, 1946, v. 36, pp. 145-158).—"Factories Can't Employ Everybody!" by C. Hartley Grattan appeared in *Harper's Magazine*, Sept. 1944, pp. 301-303, and was summarized in *Time*, Sept. 18, 1944, p. 77.—The psychological tests referred to are the Rorschach test, Thematic Apperception Test, and others. The literature on these "projective techniques" is very large.—The graphic feature "What's Happening to Where You Live" by Ray Bethers appeared in *This Week*, April 4, 1948.

### CHAPTER 19

For advice on typography see *How to Make Type Readable* by Donald G. Paterson and Miles A. Tinker (Harper & Bros., 1940) and *ATA Advertising Production Handbook* by Don Herold (New York, Advertising Typographers Association of America, 1947). On punctuation, see "Punctuation" by E. L. Thorndike (*Teachers College Record*, 1948, v. 49, no. 8, pp. 531-537).—The two corresponding passages from Arnold J. Toynbee's *Study of History* (Oxford University Press) were taken from the abridged edition, p. 198, and (shortened) from the unabridged version, vol. 3, pp. 188-189.

### CHAPTER 20

The essays on style by Spencer, Lewes, and Harrison are reprinted in *Representative Essays on the Theory of Style*, ed. by William T. Brewster (Macmillan, 1928), as well as in numerous other collections.—For a good account of the history of English prose style, see *The Reader Over Your Shoulder; a Handbook for Writers of English Prose* by Robert Graves and

Alan Hodge (Macmillan, 1944); see also *Enemies of Promise* by Cyril Connolly, rev. ed. (Macmillan, 1948).—The Swift passage is from *Gulliver's Travels*, the Defoe passage from *A Journal of the Plague Year*, the Thoreau passage from *On the Duty of Civil Disobedience*, and the Mark Twain passage from *Life on the Mississippi*.—Twentieth-century writers on style: *What a Word!* by A. P. Herbert (Doubleday, 1936); *English Prose Style* by Herbert Read (Holt, 1937); *A Word in Your Ear* and *Just Another Word* by Ivor J. C. Brown (Dutton, 1945); "Politics and the English Language" by George Orwell (*New Republic*, June 17, 1946, pp. 872-874, and June 24, 1946, pp. 903-904); and *The Reader Over Your Shoulder* by Graves and Hodge (see above). See also Mencken's *American Language* and *Supplements*, and "The Counterfeiters" by Jacques Barzun (*Atlantic Monthly*, May 1946, v. 177, pp. 128-130). —John Hersey's review of *The Pearl* by John Steinbeck appeared in the *New York Herald Tribune*, November 24, 1947.—For "The Middle American Style: Davy Crockett to Ernest Hemingway" by Malcolm Cowley, see *New York Times Book Review*, July 15, 1945, p. 3.—The two quotes from the *Saturday Review of Literature* are from the issues of March 20, 1948 and March 22, 1947.

CHAPTER 21

A good survey of studies of the relations between language and personality is "Speech and Personality" by F. H. Sanford (*Psychological Bulletin*, December 1942, v. 39, pp. 811-845). See also the entries *Language and Psychology*, and *Psychology of Language* in *Encyclopedia of Psychology* by Philip L. Harriman (Philosophical Library, 1947).—The quotation from Gertrude Stein is from *Wars I Have Seen* (Random House, 1945). On the characteristic quality of American English, see also *And Keep Your Powder Dry* by Margaret Mead (Morrow, 1942), pp. 81-82.—Dr. Gustav Wustmann's famous little book *Allerhand Sprachdummheiten* was published in Leipzig in 1891.—John L. Lewis was quoted in the *New York Times*, April 1, 1948.—The Roosevelt quotation is from *The Roosevelt I Knew* by Frances Perkins (Viking, 1946), p. 113.

# INDEX

# How Interesting?

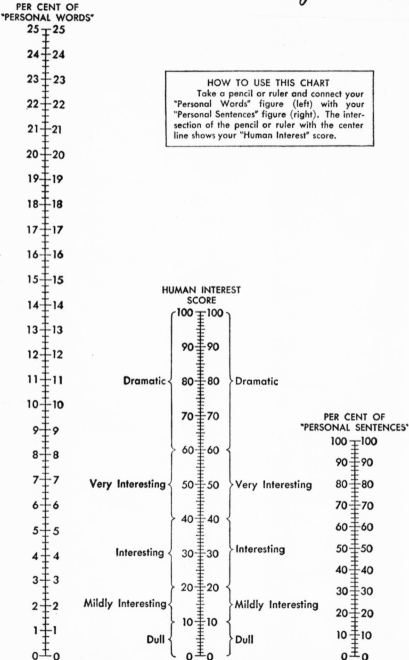

PER CENT OF "PERSONAL WORDS"

**HOW TO USE THIS CHART**
Take a pencil or ruler and connect your "Personal Words" figure (left) with your "Personal Sentences" figure (right). The intersection of the pencil or ruler with the center line shows your "Human Interest" score.

HUMAN INTEREST SCORE

Dramatic

Very Interesting

Interesting

Mildly Interesting

Dull

PER CENT OF "PERSONAL SENTENCES"